Gardener Scott's Guide to Raised Bed Gardening

Gardener Scott's Guide to Raised Bed Gardening

Scott A. Wilson

FIREFLY BOOKS

A Firefly Book

Published by Firefly Books Ltd. 2025
Copyright © 2025 Firefly Books Ltd.
Text copyright © 2025 Scott A. Wilson
Photographs © as listed below and on page 304

All rights reserved. No part of this publication may be reproduced, stored in a retrieval system, or transmitted in any form or by any means, electronic, mechanical, photocopying, recording or otherwise, without the prior written permission of the Publisher.

First printing

Library of Congress Control Number: 2024948058

Library and Archives Canada Cataloguing in Publication
Title: Gardener Scott's guide to raised bed gardening / Scott A. Wilson.
Other titles: Guide to raised bed gardening
Names: Wilson, Scott A., author.
Description: Includes index.
Identifiers: Canadiana 20240494520 | ISBN 9780228105367 (softcover)
Subjects: LCSH: Raised bed gardening. | LCSH: Beds (Gardens) | LCSH: Gardening.
Classification: LCC SB453 .W57 2025 | DDC 635—dc23

Published in the United States by
Firefly Books (U.S.) Inc.
P.O. Box 1338, Ellicott Station
Buffalo, New York 14205

Published in Canada by
Firefly Books Ltd.
50 Staples Avenue, Unit 1
Richmond Hill, Ontario L4B 0A7

Cover and interior design: Stacey Cho
Front cover photo: Scott A. Wilson
Back cover photos: Scott A. Wilson (top), Eli Appleby-Donald (bottom)

Printed in China | E

The purpose of this book is to inform readers about common methods for planning, building, and growing plants in raised beds. It is the reader's responsibility to source safe materials and evaluate their own abilities when it comes to using tools, lifting objects, performing gardening tasks, and so on. The Publisher and the Author are not liable for any damages or injuries caused by using the methods or suggestions described or shown in this book.

Dedication

To Kiri and Kael
My greatest accomplishments

And for Wyatt
Who left us too soon

Contents

Introduction 9

Chapter 1 **Why Raised Beds?** 15

Chapter 2 **Planning a Raised Bed Garden** 31

Chapter 3 **Building a Raised Bed** 61

Chapter 4 **The Importance of Healthy Soil** 105

Chapter 5 **Developing a Growing Plan** 147

Chapter 6 **Growing in Raised Beds** 189

Chapter 7 **Managing Problems in Raised Beds** 249

Chapter 8 **Preparing for the Next Growing Season** 273

Resources 291

Index 293

Acknowledgments 302

Photo Credits 304

Introduction

For many gardeners, the standard home garden is flat, with in-ground garden beds in large rectangles or squares carved out of the backyard and/or front yard landscape. Bare-earth paths divide rows of dark green plants crisscrossing the space. There might be a low fence that helps keep rabbits and family dogs away from the beds as the gardener squats or kneels to sow, weed, and care for their plants. The garden gate marks the divide between the outer world and the wonders within the garden.

That image is steadily being replaced by one of rectangular wooden beds rising alongside grass or wood chip paths. The symmetrical boxes are orderly and group plants into manageable blocks, contained and organized. Perfectly spaced and evenly sized, the vegetable garden becomes a grid of growing spaces no longer needing a picket fence and wooden gate. The same plants fill the beds, but now they are higher than the gardener's foot and closer to the gardener's eye.

Many new gardeners may think they are supposed to start with bland and boring when they first decide to garden in raised beds. The reality of raised bed gardening is much more than that, and this book will help you discover how raised beds can be used throughout the landscape with beauty and efficiency.

The benefits and advantages raised beds bring to basic gardening activities make them an ideal choice for gardeners. Older and more experienced gardeners are finding they make gardening easier, more comfortable, and more efficient. New gardeners are finding they are easier for planning, planting, and maintaining a garden.

I've been growing in raised beds for 25 years and I love them. When I began gardening more than 35 years ago, raised beds were not something gardeners generally considered as an option. Back then, an in-ground garden with its long parallel rows was the only method any of us knew. I'm not aware of popular raised bed gardening books from that long ago. Much of my raised bed

◀ **A happy, thriving raised bed garden.**

knowledge has come from decades of learning about them based on my own experience because there were no gardening mentors available to me with a background in growing in raised beds.

When I first sought to grow my own fresh vegetables, I set up the tidy rows, sowed seeds, and tended the plants. I anticipated bountiful harvests, but that didn't happen. It wasn't a successful garden. I didn't know that my inexperience, my poor Montana soil, and unusually harsh weather would pose problems for me, a novice gardener, but I did know I didn't want to give up.

I had better results after moving to California and setting up a small home garden in the heart of the remarkable San Joaquin Valley, one of the most productive agricultural regions in the world. The flat, rectangular garden patch along the fence in our suburban backyard could grow anything that was planted and produced abundantly. I put the Montana experience behind me and began to think that gardening could be easy.

Then a failed garden in Oklahoma followed, and my initial gardening efforts in Colorado were far from successful. I knew what went wrong, but I didn't know how to make it right. At no point did I think it was how I was gardening — in-ground beds versus raised beds.

In 2004, I became a certified Colorado Master Gardener and learned about the benefits of raised beds. Now, two decades later, most of my gardening is done in them. I've learned much more about raised bed gardening than was taught for Master Gardeners. My vegetable garden, fruit garden, pollinator garden, herb garden, and much of my landscape consist of raised beds of many varied types. Even my greenhouse includes a raised bed.

In 2014, I was hired as the Master Gardener for the massive Galileo Garden Project. Starting with no beds and no prepared growing space at a local school, I used a corps of volunteers to build a series of gardens that included 105 raised beds. This project helped teach gardening to students and produced more than 2,000 pounds of healthy produce for the school each year. That experience, managing the production of plants in raised beds, shaped much of how I grow in my home garden.

This book will highlight those and other benefits of raised bed gardening and how it can become easy, even when challenged by pests, poor soil, harsh weather, and all the other factors that negatively impact gardeners. My lifetime of experience and long gardening journey have led me to become a raised bed advocate and educator.

Walking through the Galileo Garden Project, which I started in 2014. This was a formative experience for me and helped shape how I grow plants at home.

We will begin with the basics of raised beds and move to the important planning considerations to get the most out of this fantastic gardening method. For DIYers, you'll find examples of many different raised bed types that you can build yourself. You'll learn how to select plants and how to grow them.

Each chapter provides the information you need to build a strong foundation in raised bed gardening. Throughout the book, you'll find key points highlighted, examples of my preferred gardening methods, and money-saving tips. The chapters are filled with beautiful photos of what you can achieve with raised beds. You'll see pictures of beds of all types in many different places.

If you haven't grown in raised beds before, you may find them intriguing and want to give them a try. If you've been resistant to raised bed gardening, you may find reasons to transform a garden section with a new bed or two. If you are a regular raised bed gardener, you will find new and creative ways to garden better with the raised beds you already have and will desire to add more.

I'm convinced that raised beds help make gardens more successful. While that is the common goal of many gardeners, I feel the gardening journey is why we like to spend time in our gardens, regardless of failure or success. I garden in raised beds because of their many benefits and how much they add to my journey. Above all, they help me enjoy gardening.

◆ My home garden early in the growing season.

Chapter 1

Why Raised Beds?

There is more than one way to grow a garden. I've grown plants in the ground, in bags and buckets, in pots and towers, in ponds, in greenhouses, in grow tents, and in hydroponic cubes. I've had small gardens with only a few vegetable plants edging the lawn. I've had expansive gardens with thousands of plants that provided more than a ton of food each year for a public school. I've grown plants in a greenhouse, with cucumber and tomato plants that reached 15 feet tall.

Currently, I have a series of gardens, from a pollinator garden and an herb garden to a mini orchard and xeriscape garden. Many of my landscape gardens are in-ground beds, but my vegetable garden is almost exclusively raised beds, and scattered throughout my yard are containers for plants. I use many different methods to match my plants, my space, and my experience. Every garden is unique, and every gardener is presented with unique gardening situations, but I firmly believe that raised beds can almost always make gardening easier and more productive.

What Is a Raised Bed?

When you look for a definition of raised beds, you'll often find a reference to a box, container, or enclosed space that holds soil. I want a definition that dispels some of the confusion and misunderstanding around raised beds, so my definition is simply this: A raised garden bed is any garden space that is intentionally elevated above the surrounding area for the purpose of growing plants.

Size doesn't matter. A raised bed can be a few square feet in size, or it can cover a large area. It can be in the shape of a diamond, hexagon, star, circle, or cross. Also, the type of construction is not a factor. Wooden beds may be ubiquitous, but steel beds are gaining popularity. Stacked stone and mortared rock beds can be powerful visual elements in the landscape. A child's plastic swimming pool becomes a raised bed when filled with soil. Concrete blocks and pavers can define the sides of raised beds. I use logs to create some of my raised beds.

Soil raised above ground level with no sides or border can also be a raised bed. It's important to note that raised beds with no sides or borders are different from the furrows that rise when the ground is plowed into rows. The makeup of furrowed soil is consistent in and between the rows. What makes raised beds unique is that the space is created as a raised bed to grow plants, and the soil within the bed will differ from the soil in paths between them. Usually, it is much more fertile.

A Bit of Raised Bed History

When I began gardening nearly four decades ago, it wasn't that I avoided raised beds, I just wasn't aware of raised bed gardening. Raised bed gardening was virtually unknown until the 1960s. English horticulturist Alan Chadwick is credited by many with introducing raised bed gardening to North America with his gardens at the University of California, Santa Cruz. It was there, in 1967, that Chadwick turned a hillside with poor soil into a highly productive garden. With a focus on improving soil, raised beds were key to growing plants close together for better yield. He pioneered raised bed gardening, along with organic and biodynamic gardening. In 1980, *Mother Earth News* highlighted his work and that of John Jeavons.

In his 1974 book *How to Grow More Vegetables*, Jeavons used Chadwick's method, along with ideas from Stephen Kaffka, a senior apprentice at the university's garden. Chadwick and Jeavons influenced generations of gardeners to come. The intensive gardening method produced more food in smaller spaces and was ideal for home gardeners. The emphasis on organic methods paved the way for gardeners seeking freedom from synthetic chemicals.

As prevalent as they are now, for many gardeners raised bed gardening is still a new method that runs counter to how they learned to garden at the side of a parent or a neighbor. It isn't until they see a video or visit a garden that uses raised beds that they appreciate what this "new" option has to offer.

Common Raised Bed Types

Wooden raised bed.

Brick raised bed.

Metal raised bed.

Mound raised bed.

Stone raised bed.

Concrete block raised bed.

Container Gardening

The relative permanence of raised beds and in-ground beds defines a garden landscape. Container gardening, in contrast, is more mobile and portable. A pot can be placed anywhere in the landscape and then moved as needed, even hourly, to follow the movement of the sun. It is that mobility that makes this type of gardening unique.

Container gardening offers a great alternative for gardeners with limited space or sun availability. Tomato plants can be grown in 5-gallon buckets on a deck or patio. I grow potatoes in fabric grow bags in areas outside my raised beds as a simple way to expand my garden space. I grow flowers, herbs, and salad crops in a GreenStalk vertical garden just outside my kitchen door for ease of harvest.

The smaller size of most containers requires less soil, so gardeners often change the soil in their containers with each season, matching the mix and the nutrients with the annual plants they grow. For perennial plants in containers, regular fertilizer and

These are some of the GreenStalk vertical planters I use in my garden.

top dressing with compost and mulch help revive the soil and replace depleted nutrients.

Growing plants in pots may be the most common container gardening practice, but buckets, grow bags, grow towers, and any portable container can be used as well. The endless choice of sizes and colors for pots and other containers makes them an easy design component to add to the landscape. Separate garden areas don't need to be set aside for container growing. This ease of design and placement makes container gardens a nice complement to both in-ground and raised beds.

Pots make for an easy, portable garden.

18

The Benefits of Raised Beds

I'm clearly a fan of raised bed gardening, but raised beds by themselves do not solve all of a garden's problems. Although I've found using raised bed gardening methods is the best solution for the issues my garden presents, they may not be best for every gardener in every gardening situation. There are many factors that affect how well our plants grow and how successful a harvest can be, but raised beds can be a major one.

To get the benefits of raised beds, there is effort involved. Garden planning is needed for positive results. Good plant selection and plant care are still necessary, and the gardener needs to like the way they garden. One of my core philosophies is that "a good garden grows where a good gardener goes." The basic concept is that it really doesn't matter how you garden, but that you are taking the time to visit your garden and tend to plants and learn all you can to benefit the plants in your garden.

Raised beds are not the best answer for every gardener, but they might be for most gardeners. The following information explains why I think raised beds are a great option when planning a garden. I recognize that a benefit for one gardener may prove to be a disadvantage to another. The balance between the pros and cons of raised bed gardening rests within each gardener and that gardener's unique perspective.

Easier garden planning and planting: With square and rectangular raised beds, garden planning is a breeze. These types of beds become simple mathematical grids for developing a planting plan. Many methods plot plants on a grid and recommend how many plants to put in and how far apart to place them. I can plan my entire growing season with a pencil and grid paper or on my computer with basic spreadsheet software. There are also many garden-planning apps, and they all use a basic grid system. When planting, I sometimes hammer small nails into the top of a wooden bed, run twine around them to form squares above the soil, and make a grid for precise planting that matches my gardening grid plan.

Better accessibility: For gardeners with mobility or physical limitations, raised beds can be built to provide better access to the garden. Height, width, and depth are variable, and beds can be designed to match the gardener's needs. They can be made to the perfect height for people with limited mobility. Tall

Raised beds, like these tall ones, are accessible to wheelchair users.

beds can have sturdy supports for standing or leaning. I build some of my beds high and strong, so I can easily sit on the side and tend to plants with minimal bending over. Some of my beds are lower, so my young granddaughters can easily reach the plants when helping in the garden.

Access from all sides of a raised bed also makes every part of a plant available for harvesting with minimal effort and plant disruption. I like being able to harvest most of my plants in raised beds without bending over. I can stand next to the raised bed to harvest fruit or sit on the edge of the bed and comfortably dig up root vegetables. For the tallest plants, I can stand on the sides of my wooden beds, if needed.

More control over the soil: This is the primary reason I use raised bed gardening for my vegetables. Gardeners can easily customize soil to match their plants' needs in the confined space of a raised bed. If you're starting with poor native soil, it can take years to improve an in-ground bed with amendments. A raised bed can be filled with good, rich soil from the start, and the quality of the native soil is not a limitation. You can choose organic ingredients and blend your own rich soil as you fill the bed. It doesn't matter if your native soil is clay or sand when you can have better soil in your raised beds.

Raised beds can also reduce soil compaction (since you have little reason to walk on a raised bed) and erosion from snow and rain (since the vertical sides will help the bed retain soil).

Better disease and pest control: When disease finds its way to your plants, it can quickly spread throughout the garden. By keeping beds separate, with paths in between, disease might infect one bed but can be isolated from another. Quarantining the problem bed and using appropriate disease control and crop rotation can help eradicate a soilborne disease. If the control involves replacing or treating the soil, the treatment is limited to a single bed and not the whole garden.

The individual nature of raised beds also allows for focused pest control. Floating row covers are a common method for keeping insects away from plants and can be sized and anchored easily in raised beds. Insect traps can be

Fine mesh like this, mounted on hoops in the raised bed, keeps insect pests out.

effortlessly mounted. New soil brought in for a raised bed may be less likely to harbor native insect pest eggs and larvae due to the process of loading and unloading it. Pests that live in soil as part of their life cycle can be easily confined to a single bed and, with the help of crop rotation, can be disrupted from spreading in the garden.

There are garden pests beyond hungry insects. Snails and slugs are often better controlled in raised beds. The symmetrical base of a rectangular raised bed makes it easy to place a wire barrier underneath to keep gophers, voles, hedgehogs, and other burrowing animals from reaching your plants. A high-sided bed can help keep out rabbits.

Better harvests: With good soil, reduced disease and pest concerns, and easier maintenance overall, plants can grow better and produce more abundant harvests in a raised bed. In 1989, a three-year experiment at the Dawes Arboretum at Ohio State University showed that raised beds can produce more than double the vegetables per square foot compared to traditional in-ground beds. New raised bed gardeners are often surprised by bigger plants and better harvests.

Can be built anywhere: You can put a raised bed just about anywhere on your property. They can be placed on a patio, a rooftop, or any landscape with concrete, rocks, or gravel. Renters can have a garden using raised beds in an unused corner without disturbing or digging up the landscape. The beds can be oriented in any direction to match limited sunlight or physical obstructions. Essentially, any spot with ideal sunlight can work for a raised bed.

Raised beds can be an ideal solution for gardens with a slope. Space is dug into the hill to create a level spot for a raised bed, with the uphill side partially buried and the downhill side fully exposed. When gardening on a severe slope, raised beds can be installed as a terrace, with the sides stabilizing the soil in the bed and preventing it from flowing to the bottom of the hill.

Raised beds also allow for gardens over contaminated soil. The contamination may be salt, chemicals, or anything that prevents plants from growing. A raised bed with a solid bottom separates the soil and plants in the bed from whatever contamination is underneath. Similarly, plants won't grow well in areas with excessive tree roots. A solid-bottomed raised bed will keep the tree roots from growing into the bed, providing the opportunity for more growing space.

With raised beds, even patio space can be used to grow plants.

Added aesthetic appeal to the garden: Raised beds can add a distinctive design element to your yard. They can vary by construction material and size with aesthetic appeal in mind. Stone and rock raised beds can be visually stunning. Metal beds in different colors and unique shapes offer great opportunities in garden design. Wooden beds can be stained or painted. Every gardener can find a raised bed to match their artistic vision.

Personally, I find that symmetrical rows of basic wooden boxes look good, especially when filled with plants. Long, parallel paths between the beds can provide a clean appearance,

Steep slopes can become gardens.

Evenly spaced rows of raised beds can keep things looking neat.

particularly when the paths are mulched with wood chips or covered by mown grass. Raised beds with vertical sides keep the soil inside from spilling into pathways, and the ease of pruning plants in raised beds can keep plants from interfering with simple movement through the garden. The level soil in raised beds is often more appealing to gardeners than lumpy, uneven rows of an in-ground bed.

Raised beds can be placed with the permanence of common landscape features. I like places to sit in my garden, and sturdy rock or wooden raised beds make good benches. I use tall raised beds to separate different sections of my garden instead of building fences. Raised beds can surround and highlight landscape water features, greenhouses, and play areas. A long narrow bed can define and edge a garden path. I even use raised beds to anchor tall garden arches for vining plants.

Great for beginners and kids: With a bit of guidance, simple planning, good soil, and focused maintenance, growing plants in a raised bed is almost foolproof for beginner gardeners. There are no guarantees, but success for most beginners

Kids can work well in raised beds, as I witnessed when working on the Galileo Garden Project.

is often more likely than with an in-ground garden. Tilling, fertilizing, excessive weeding, and other common garden chores required with in-ground beds aren't necessary with a first-time raised bed. It can be as easy as building a bed, filling it, planting in it, growing healthy plants, and enjoying the harvest.

Because a raised bed can be set up and filled with good soil in minimal time, a garden can be created in as little as a day. As you'll learn, I recommend taking time to observe weather patterns and sun intensity when starting a garden, but for gardeners itching to get growing, quickly starting with a raised bed or two is a viable option while taking time for thorough observation. My current garden started that way: I was growing in two beds within two months of moving into my house as I took time to determine my final garden design with multiple beds.

The self-contained and enclosed aspects of raised beds also make it easier to focus children when gardening. Beds can be made kid-friendly by building them shorter and narrower, allowing for easy access for little ones. At the school garden, I was amazed at how quickly the students could identify which plants they had started themselves. Basic lessons on sowing, weeding, watering, and harvesting are more comfortable (but equally exciting) with a raised bed.

Some Cons of Raised Bed Gardening

Of course, raised bed gardening is not without its drawbacks. Many of these issues can be avoided with a good amount of know-how, planning, and resourcefulness, but I feel it's important to highlight some of the limitations here.

Higher costs: The construction costs of raised beds can limit some gardeners. If you have a patch of bare ground in your backyard, you can start growing in it. The cost is minimal, maybe nothing. If you want to grow in raised beds, in most cases there is a cost for the materials. Filling the bed with a good, amended soil has a cost, too. And if you don't have construction skills and you decide to hire someone to build the beds for you, it can be even more expensive. There are, however, some ways to trim costs, and I've included money-saving tips throughout the book, as well as instructions on how to construct several basic types of raised beds to get you started.

Longevity of the beds varies: Wooden raised beds don't last forever. They will break down and need replacing over time. Materials such as redwood, cedar, and pressure-treated wood increase the lifespan, but also add to the cost and will break down in time, too. Stone and concrete blocks last indefinitely but can be

Popular raised bed materials such as wood will break down in time, while other materials are longer lasting.

more expensive. Metal beds with coated steel offer affordable options, but even with a lifespan of up to 20 years, they pale when compared to the lifespan of a piece of ground that has been gardened for generations.

Can have a bigger carbon footprint: Most constructed raised beds use a lot of energy and resources. Manufacturing and transporting lumber and steel are two factors in making raised beds that use a good deal of fossil fuels. A University of Michigan study found that a raised bed used for just five years has approximately four times the environmental impact as a raised bed used for 20 years. Gardening responsibly with a long-term plan can promote sustainability, but it's important to acknowledge that there will be an impact.

Not great for large landscape plants: Trees and large perennial bushes and shrubs can be severely limited in raised beds. Their deep and expansive roots can be curtailed by bed sides that are too close. This is one of the biggest mistakes I see in landscapes, where a tree is planted in a stone or brick raised bed, and years later the roots of the now-bigger tree are misshapen and end up collapsing the bed walls. Gardeners should anticipate the size of the plant at maturity and match it to the best location.

Raised beds can't contain big trees, as the damage to this stone bed shows, and so they're unsuitable for larger landscape plants.

Weighing the benefits and disadvantages of raised beds, each gardener must decide which priorities in the garden will influence how they garden.

For gardeners unsure or on the fence, I recommend starting with one or two raised beds to see if it matches your style of gardening. Planning for the first bed, constructing it, filling it, and growing in it can provide the education and experience that make multiple beds easier to manage when a garden expands. Having an in-ground bed alongside a raised bed allows for comparison of practices and improved learning.

I loved raised bed gardening from the beginning, but I understand it can take time to appreciate it fully. Over the years, I learned to recognize and anticipate potential problems and how to use raised beds for an easier fix. Raised bed gardening is a process with many lessons to learn. In the following chapters, I'll explain all the steps to move from choosing to garden in a raised bed to having marked success with bountiful harvests.

➡ **Raised beds are not just for vegetable plants. They also work well for annuals and perennials of all kinds.**

Chapter 2

Planning a Raised Bed Garden

Patience is an important attribute that gardeners should develop, yet it can be difficult to cultivate. We see a new product for the garden, a new gardening method, or an interesting plant and we want to try it — right now. It is often better to wait. Garden planning can involve a lot of waiting. Beginning too soon before we have the most important things figured out seldom produces success.

Before even starting to build your raised beds and filling them with soil, there are a few things to consider, such as the placement and design of your beds. Observing your garden and then carefully thinking through how you'll use your raised beds and what they'll look like will help ensure the time and effort you put in will pay off — not only in the success of your plants, but also in your enjoyment of your garden.

As you read through this chapter, which is full of guidance and many photos of different raised beds, begin choosing which beds you think would look good in your garden. Highlight a design you like and use it to begin the process of adding raised beds to your garden.

◐ **Planning your raised bed garden before you start building your first bed will make your garden a pleasurable place to spend your time, like in this organized and well-planned growing space.**

Observing the Garden

Observing the garden site before any other planning step is important. I suggest gardeners spend a year of observation before the first beds and first plants are in place. Seeing what happens to the site over the course of an entire gardening season can be extremely educational. We want our beds to be in a spot with at least six hours of sun, so watch how the sun moves across the area at different times of the year and how shade affects the site. Anticipating that plants will be growing for many months, we should be looking at where the sun shines every month.

It is common for gardeners to start setting up a garden in early spring in an area with full sun. It may not be until the end of the season, after tall trees are covered with leaves, that they realize the site is in shade during important growing periods. Taking a snapshot view of sun and shade on a single day in the garden ignores all the other days that may be more important. Waiting a year and observing the sun's movement can help you choose the best location.

For impatient gardeners, starting small with a single bed and a few plants can help simulate a bigger, future garden while taking the time to observe. Animal movements may not be obvious without observation over a long period. Migration routes of birds and other animals can impact garden plants. I planted a couple of fruit trees before I completed a year-round assessment and discovered that a small herd of deer traveled through my area looking for food during winter. They were happy to eat the branches of my unprotected trees. I lost the trees but learned a lot about my environment before I planted more trees, ones that were protected from deer.

Household pets also develop habitual patterns that can be identified and used for garden planning. Dogs usually take a direct route from favorite spots in the yard. If they run to bark at something behind the back fence, they'll typically follow the same path. Putting a bed on that route may slow them down, but they may just run through it. It's better to look for those patterns and move the planned location, erect a garden fence, or build higher beds if pets are perceived to be a problem.

A small test plot in the beginning can identify problems with water access. A sunny spot seems ideal until the gardener realizes that it takes multiple hoses

Too much shade affects how plants grow.

to stretch from the faucet on the house to that location. If it takes extra effort to drag a hose to the single bed, imagine how much more effort it will be with multiple beds in place. One season of testing irrigation options can influence better site considerations.

Water runoff may not be a garden problem most of the year until the melting of snow in spring or the rains of April turn a favorite site into a muddy mess. I know too many gardeners who've set up a garden at a new house in late summer or early fall and then much to their distress discovered it was under water during the critical times in spring, when they wanted to sow seeds and get plants growing. A closer observation of their landscape contours to see how water flows could have saved much frustration.

Walking to the garden before the garden exists is a good habit and part of the observation process. Determining how long it takes to get from the house or shed to the garden gives an idea of how much labor will be involved in garden upkeep. For a vegetable garden, it's usually a good idea to place it close to the house, to reduce how much distance you need to walk to the garden. Testing how much you walk to different garden spots at different times of the year can influence the best placement.

In addition, some areas of a yard are windier, some are drier, some are rockier, and some are filled with weeds. These issues may not be obvious at first, but with time to observe, they become apparent. I spent many hours over many days walking through my garden long before the first bed was in place. Some days I just stood, watching, for long periods of time. Each day I spent in my future garden, I was closer to realizing the vision of what it would become. Patience made the final result satisfying and successful.

Our garden companions usually don't mean to cause damage when they're out in the yard with us.

I spent a good deal of time walking the bare garden space, envisioning my future garden.

Choosing a Raised Bed Design

When you choose raised beds for your garden, you have complete control over their design. Their depth, width, height, shape, and color can be customized in innumerable ways. And you're not limited to just one style in your garden. The construction material can match an overall garden design plan. The beds can be designed for functionality and production, or for comfort and aesthetics.

I suggest setting preconceptions of the ubiquitous wooden boxes aside and thinking of raised beds as an opportunity to enhance your gardening and complement everything else in your landscape.

Taking time to select the best bed choice helps ensure you match it with your preferred gardening process. It is nice when a bed is a welcome addition to your garden and will inspire and encourage you to garden more. Poor design planning may result in a bed that you don't like and want to replace. Unless you're set on basic wooden boxes, take time to observe, document, and analyze your garden environment, noting what you want and what you need. Explore different bed types and use your imagination to envision how you want your garden to look now and in the future. Look at images in books and online to get an idea of what's possible. You can turn to pages 52–56 for a gallery of raised bed inspiration that will help you think outside of the wooden box.

The first step in deciding what kind of bed to choose begins by answering basic questions about how and why you garden. Understanding who you are as a gardener makes beginning a new garden or transitioning to raised beds easier. Many gardeners decide

Think beyond wood for beautiful raised beds, like these attractive block beds that enhance my yard.

what they think their garden should look like before they know how they're going to garden. This is a backward approach. Instead, ask yourself some of these questions:

- **Why am I gardening?** Are you building a garden just to look at, or are you growing vegetables for family meals? Are you serious about learning how to garden or just looking for a fun hobby outside? Are you planting a garden for table cuttings, for herbal medicine, or even for sketching? Will your gardening be a solo activity, a family project, or part of a community garden?

- **How much space do I have?** How large will your garden be? Are you starting small, with an eye for a bigger garden in future years? Will your garden design allow for expansion? Will you have a collection of different garden spaces for vegetables, flowers, herbs, and fruit bushes as part of a larger landscape? Will your garden have sitting spots and garden art? Will it have paths for utility and maintenance or paths for enjoyment and comfort?

- **What's my budget?** Do you want to build a garden using recycled materials at a minimal cost? Do you want the look of a professional garden with the best possible materials? Are you able to construct raised beds with the skills and tools you have? Will you have volunteer helpers or can you afford to have someone build your garden for you? Can you afford just a single bed or do you want to begin with multiple beds?

- **What am I capable of building?** Before you choose a raised bed design, consider your experience and skills when it comes to executing the build. Ensure your experience level matches your plan. Is this something you can build yourself or should you hire someone? Do you have anyone who can assist you with the heavy lifting?

- **Do I have physical limitations to consider in the design?** Will the height of the bed impact how you grow plants? Can you kneel or squat when gardening? Do you use a wheelchair or a walker? Can you carry tools, supplies, and plant materials to and from the garden? Will gardening be a form of exercise?

Everyone can have the chance to garden when the space is designed with mobility needs in mind.

How and why we garden influence the type of raised beds we use. A raised bed used for food production with intensive planting will be different than a raised bed used for flower displays and garden art. Beds built for gardeners with mobility issues will be different than beds built for quick access. Beds made from recycled materials at a low cost will be different than manufactured steel beds.

With an initial understanding of the how and why factors of gardening, you can begin moving forward with the design of your raised beds. Your personal preferences should be prioritized to develop a design plan. Is appearance more important than functionality? Is cost more important than material? Is accessibility more important than how much you harvest? My raised garden beds reflect my preferred gardening methods, fit within my budget, and make my gardening chores as easy as possible. Because I garden in many different ways, I have different beds in different locations.

In the remainder of this section, we'll explore different sizes, materials, and other considerations — all of which will influence what your final raised bed will look like.

Raised Bed Dimensions

Determining the measurements of a bed can help in deciding exactly which bed to build. Knowing how you want to garden is an important step in deciding if you want a high bed or a low bed, a narrow bed or a wide bed, and a long bed or a short bed.

Height: Choosing the height of the bed is a good way to start your specific raised bed design. If you like the idea of sitting on the side of the bed to do gardening chores, then a tall bed may be the answer. To determine how tall, sit on your dining room chair and bend over, then lean side to side. Is it comfortable? Sit on your couch, the toilet, or an ottoman, and do the same thing. Once you find a height that you like, measure it and use that as a guide for the height of your raised bed.

Are you less concerned about sitting on the sides of your bed and more focused on what you'll be growing? Identify the plants you wish to grow and do a little research to find out how deep their roots grow. For example, salad crops

Gardening chores are easier when sitting, so you may want to consider the best sitting height when designing your bed.

Herb beds can be shorter.

such as lettuce, spinach, radishes, and arugula have relatively shallow roots and can do well in rich soil that is only 6 inches to 8 inches deep. Allowing for a little space between the top of the soil and the top of the bed, an appropriate raised bed for those crops would be 8 inches to 10 inches tall. Root crops such as long carrots and parsnips should have closer to 15 inches of soil, so the raised bed's walls should be at least 16 inches tall.

My wooden raised beds are close to 16 inches tall. That height is ideal for sitting and allows me to grow any vegetable that I desire. It's also short enough that I can kneel next to the bed, if needed. The soil depth is suitable for all the normal plants in a typical vegetable garden. Tomatoes, peppers, and corn will grow in those beds when filled with good soil. They can have surprisingly deep roots, and a tall bed supports them better.

I have shorter beds that I use for growing herbs. They don't need deep soil and those beds are only 8 inches high. My other short beds are closer to 12 inches tall. I use them for growing plants with my young granddaughters because they can garden more easily in a lower bed. Anticipate that shorter beds will require adults to kneel more and work on their hands and knees. For me, the short beds mean a lot more getting up and down for regular maintenance, so I choose plants for them that don't require much work.

Width: With the height determined, the width of the bed is the next thing to consider. The most common recommendation for raised bed width is 48 inches. With a 4-foot-wide bed, the assumption is that gardeners can access it from all sides and not have to reach more than 2 feet in to reach plants. That may be appropriate for most adult gardeners with long arms, but it isn't universal. As with the height consideration, take some time to sit or stand at a table and reach to the other side. Measure how far a comfortable reach is for you. Double that measurement to determine the maximum width of your raised bed, anticipating you'll work from both sides.

Creating a bed with a comfortable reach makes gardening easier.

For most gardeners, 24 inches will be the default width, but shorter gardeners may want narrower beds after determining their comfortable reach. Children and gardeners with mobility issues may want them narrower, too.

The location of the bed influences bed width. If you will have access to all sides of the bed, the total width should be no more than twice your comfortable reach. For example, if the bed will be placed against a fence or wall, and you only have access to one side, keep it only as wide as your comfortable reach.

Length: Determining the length of a raised bed is similar. A typical wooden raised bed is 8 feet long. A primary reason for that is because the length of the boards you can buy at home improvement stores is 8 feet. There is less cutting required to construct a bed when using precut lumber. Coincidentally, 8 feet is a comfortable distance for walking around the bed from one side to the other. Longer than that may take more effort when using tools or watering with a hose.

Long walls and long beds match well together.

Envision a bed that is 30 feet long. To get from the middle of one side to the middle of the other means walking 15 feet, then 4 feet along the end, and then another 15 feet back to your goal. That's not outrageous, but it might be excessive when you're preparing a bed, sowing seeds, and mulching. Every time you work in the bed, you can expect to work from both sides. Instead of an easy back-and-forth with an 8-foot bed, you're spending much of your time walking around a longer bed.

When not concerned with the back-and-forth activities, the bed length can be anything you want. Long beds can have dramatic visual appeal. It's common in raised bed gardens to place a bed against a wall or fence. A wall that is 30 feet long can adequately complement a 30-foot-long bed in front of it because the bed is only accessed from one side. A similar consideration is appropriate for raised beds on a slope. A common garden design on steep slopes is a central staircase or path with long beds cut into the slope and extending to the sides of the area.

The structure and materials of a raised bed may be limiting factors when choosing length. A wooden board that's 8 feet long can adequately hold the soil in a bed of the same length. For longer beds, the boards need to be connected to one another at intermittent joints. Each of those joints weakens the overall strength of the raised bed sides. Without lateral support, the joint can fail when the weight of soil pushes against it and the side bows out. My beds that are 25 feet long have extra support between the long sides at every 8 feet to reduce bowing concerns.

With specific bed dimensions in mind, and to visualize how a raised bed will fit in your garden, you can use cardboard or weed fabric to mimic the new beds. Take apart some cardboard boxes and place them flat in the location you're considering. You can do the same with rolls of weed fabric or plastic. Practice sitting, kneeling, and leaning around the cardboard. Walk around it holding tools or a hose. If the width and length allow for easy movement, and you find it comfortable, you've determined an appropriate dimension. If not, cut or fold the material to find the ideal size. Taking time to test for the perfect-size bed will pay dividends when you actually work in it.

Here, a hose outlines the planned raised bed and a piece of cardboard helps define it.

Raised Bed Materials

With the basic height, width, and length of your raised beds decided, the material you use to construct them will determine the actual measurements of the beds. For most gardeners, the exact size of a bed is not critical as long as it's close to the plan. A few inches narrower or wider seldom make much difference in gardening. A few inches of height difference, however, might be more noticeable to some gardeners.

Availability of materials (as well as your own skills and resources) plays a role in bed size. For example, the length of common wooden boards from a home improvement store is 8 feet long. Cut one board in half and you have two 4-foot boards. Use with another two 8-foot boards and you can easily assemble a bed that's 8 feet long and 4 feet wide. Many gardeners choose to garden in 4-foot by 8-foot beds because that's the size of the lumber they bought, and the building of the bed was easy.

> **Use What You Have or Can Get for Free**
>
> To work within a budget, it makes sense to use materials that you already have or can obtain easily. Wood from a dismantled deck, rocks from your yard, or free materials you find on the side of the road or online can all be used to make a raised bed. Of course, the final bed dimensions will be determined by the material you find, especially if you cannot cut it to size easily. And remember that a raised bed can be as simple as mounding amended soil above the surrounding ground. For a functional bed, that may be all you need.

The actual dimensions of the materials must also be considered. For my concrete raised bed, I used blocks that were 8 inches wide and 16 inches long. While I can cut wood to a precise length, I know that concrete blocks have no such flexibility. So my initial plan was made with the 8-inch by 16-inch measurement in mind, but as with most construction materials, the true measurements were different: 7¾ inches by 15¾ inches.

I had 14 blocks per side and was initially planning for a bed with an exterior measurement of about 18 feet 8 inches long. However, with that slight measurement variation per block, my concrete bed ended up about 18 feet 4 inches long. The width of the bed had similar variation. I planned for a bed that is

Some materials, such as concrete blocks, have defined dimensions, and your raised bed's final measurements will change based on those.

48 inches wide, but the actual measurement is 47 inches wide. I was okay with this, though.

This example helps highlight an important consideration when designing a raised bed: bed size versus planting space. I wanted the exterior measurement of my concrete bed to be close to 48 inches wide to match the width of the wooden beds next to it. However, the width of the concrete blocks limited my planting space in that raised bed to 17 feet long by 31½ inches wide. I accepted the reduced area of soil available for plants. This is a factor when planning other raised beds as well.

The issue of bed size versus planting space does come into play when you're trying to make beds of a specific size or if you need to fit bed accessories. For example, I use wire mesh beneath my raised beds to deter burrowing animals. It comes in rolls that are 48 inches wide, so the width of my beds is important when figuring out how I'm going to attach the wire mesh to the bottom. If the interior measurement is 45 inches wide, I can overlap 48-inch mesh over the bed

Livestock troughs are among the easiest raised beds to add to your garden.

With so many options in raised bed design, it's good to remember that basic wooden beds also work well.

sides and staple it in place. If the interior of the bed is 48 inches, the mesh fits perfectly side-to-side, but there is no easy way to attach it.

Planning and planting may also influence the desired width and length of the planting space. The Square Foot Gardening method breaks the raised bed into evenly spaced 12-inch squares. For easy math and consistent planting under this system, the interior measurement of a standard bed should be 4 feet wide and 8 feet long (or another measurement that's divisible by 12 inches). A bed that is 45 inches wide and 93 inches long can still be planted using such methods, but you must keep in mind that the seed spacing will be different between grid squares.

The exact size of a bed may not be as important to you as the material used or the look that you're going for. I've used metal animal troughs to make raised beds. Steel or plastic feeding troughs can be an easy option for raised bed gardening. They come in a variety of sizes, and constructing one is as easy as drilling a few drainage holes, placing it in the garden, and filling it with good soil. I opted for troughs that were about 2 feet wide and 4 feet long. The exact measurements weren't important, as I was looking for that general size for a particular spot in my garden and accepted that the troughs might be a few inches wider or narrower.

Each type of material brings its own set of benefits and drawbacks. Though you can make a raised bed out of a vast array of materials, in this section we will discuss a few of the more popular choices: wood, metal, concrete, and stone.

Wood: Wooden raised beds are often the first raised bed gardeners use because they require tools that most people already have and skills that are easy to learn. One reason that gardeners think of raised beds as elongated wooden boxes is that this bed type is so easy to construct and place in the garden. They are also among the least expensive beds to build.

Wooden beds don't need to be made of basic lumber. They may be constructed of redwood with a custom stain color, or cedar boards exposed to the elements and allowed to change from a beautiful red color to a weathered gray years later. Carved wooden sides or layered decorative inserts can be striking features in the garden. Fitted logs can look rustic and beautiful.

One key disadvantage of wooden beds is their longevity. Pine and other framing lumber may only last five years, while cedar may last as many as 10 years. Longevity will vary based on weather exposure, the water retention of the soil, climate and humidity, and the wood's thickness. The untreated fir beds in my Colorado garden are not rotting, but are beginning to show signs of cracking and damage after five years. My beds with pressure-treated wood, however, show few signs of damage.

Pressure-treated wood is a good option for longer-lasting beds. Misunderstood by many gardeners, modern-day pressure-treated wood uses copper-based chemicals and does not contain arsenic like it did decades ago. A multi-year study from Oregon State University tested whether the wood leached copper into garden soil and, if it did, whether vegetables would absorb it. The study results showed that the

Wooden raised beds can be attractive, with quality materials and nice stains.

Most of my vegetable garden beds are made from pressure-treated wood.

pressure-treated lumber did increase copper concentrations within 1 inch of the bed edge, but the increase was minor and within natural copper levels in soil. There was no increase in copper in the plants.

Metal: Metal raised beds are becoming more available and more affordable for many gardeners. Steel beds offer longevity that can't be matched by wooden beds. Modular steel bed kits can be ordered from a number of sources online. Invariably, the steel in the modular kits is coated and is less likely to corrode than untreated galvanized steel. The sides won't pull away from the ends when screwed together. My newest beds are treated steel from a kit.

Metal beds with a painted exterior come in a variety of colors. The modular panels can be configured into circular shapes in addition to squares and rectangles with rounded corners. I recently added a hexagonal steel bed to my pollinator garden. For gardeners with limited experience with DIY projects and few tools, modular kits have everything needed and are very easy to assemble.

For gardeners with more experience, galvanized steel panels can be made into long-lasting raised beds. The materials are available at home improvement centers and can be fashioned into beds that meet your custom design. Copper panels can be stunning, especially when the natural patina develops. It can degrade when exposed to soil and works best as an outer layer to a wooden or steel bed. Iron is rare in the garden, but I once saw a bed made from an old iron stove. It can be a unique visual highlight, but the iron will rust when exposed to outdoor conditions.

Metal beds excel in durability and versatility; however, they do have a few drawbacks. The initial expense for metal beds can be higher than for wooden beds. As well, the metal can affect the temperature of the soil surrounding the raised bed. I find the soil inside my metal beds is generally no warmer than the soil in my other raised beds, but the metal does reflect the sun and can heat the soil outside the bed. I've had plants suffer and die a few feet away

Steel bed kits offer many options in terms of size and shape.

This hexagonal steel bed kit was easy to build and looks attractive in the garden.

from my galvanized steel beds in summer because of their excessive reflective heat. Painting the metal can help reduce the problem, but isn't always a suitable option. Hardy shrubs and tall grass planted around the beds can help, but they may also be damaged by the heat. Untreated and unpainted galvanized steel will degrade in time, particularly when exposed to acidic soil, but these types of beds should still last longer than wood.

Concrete: Concrete is a versatile material for constructing raised beds. It can be poured into forms to make permanent walls of any height, thickness, and shape. Long, winding concrete beds are commonplace in botanical gardens and on university campuses. Many homeowners can develop basic skills to design and pour small concrete raised beds or hire professionals to create a beautiful growing

Concrete raised beds, like this poured concrete bed, epitomize permanence.

A Word of Safety

If you're choosing to grow vegetables, herbs, or fruit in a raised bed, be sure you know where the materials come from and whether they may contain toxic chemicals that could potentially leach into your soil. Toxic chemicals will likely kill or deform plants before they can be harvested; however, some plants can absorb harmful chemicals from the soil without showing injury. Arsenic is a chemical that most edible plants can absorb in small amounts, but usually not enough to affect your health. Of more concern is if your skin comes into contact with harmful chemicals in contaminated building materials, or if you ingest toxins because your edible harvests were not adequately washed.

area. Height, width, and length can be custom-sized when pouring concrete.

If you're looking for something simpler but just as durable, basic concrete construction blocks can be arranged and built up to create raised beds for vegetable and perennial gardens. They never break down and can be stacked to any level. When painted or stained, they can bring color to the garden. The square openings in the blocks are also great for extra plants, which you can use to grow a colorful border in the bed's walls.

The biggest barrier to building with concrete blocks is the labor involved in moving and placing the blocks. It should be noted that concrete construction blocks are sometimes called cinder blocks, but they are distinct from cinder blocks. Cinder blocks and some older bricks are likely made from fly ash, a residue resulting from the combustion of coal, and are therefore not safe for vegetable gardens.

Stone: Stacked stone and mortared rock beds make a bold statement in garden design. Not only are they strong and long-lived, but also they can be built as rectangles, circles, and free-flowing designs to fit any landscape. Like the metal beds, the colors of the stone and rock are endless and can be artistic. Flagstone slabs laid on end make beautiful beds. Retaining wall blocks are consistently sized and easy to stack into beds of variable heights.

Stone raised beds can be expensive and require a lot of planning, prep work, and possibly hired workers for building them. The labor needed to build with stones is more intensive than prefabricated concrete blocks. While they can become a stunning centerpiece of your garden, it's important to remember that, once built, they will become a permanent feature of your landscape.

The diversity in stone choice is endless, with countless shapes, sizes, and colors. This bed was built with large, colorful flagstones now accented with lichens.

The Surrounding Landscape

Another key consideration for your raised bed design is the surrounding landscape. Raised beds don't need to be stand-alone structures plopped in the landscape just to grow vegetables. They can become an integral part of the landscape. I love seeing an area filled with plants of all colors, shapes, and sizes, with the raised bed disappearing behind the scenes and becoming a background player. A well-designed bed can highlight the plants in addition to providing a place with good soil for them.

Raised beds can be designed to fit into a landscape with natural slopes and low hills. The beds can become terraces for holding back the earth and reducing soil movement and erosion. Retaining walls are often used to level ground and

Changes in elevation within a raised bed add much to the bed's visual appeal and enhance the landscape.

hold back soil, but retaining walls are flat and rarely add visual appeal. By lowering the wall and adding growing space behind it, a raised bed is created. A secondary wall at the back of the bed becomes a shorter retaining wall. Stacking raised beds of increasing height against a hill can achieve the same effect as a single retaining wall.

Raised beds can also be designed to sculpt a landscape. Many city parks and public gardens use mounded earth beds to separate garden areas. Raised mounds are covered with plants and are high enough to create natural walls between paths. Anchored by rock borders and covered with woody mulch to reduce erosion, they sculpt the land by adding slopes and high spots artificially. Only gardeners would recognize them as raised beds.

There are no limits when designing raised beds, and any combination of materials can be mixed. Wood and metal, wood and stone, metal and stone, stone and concrete, stone and brick, and wood and brick are common materials used side by side to construct beds. A balance of functionality and aesthetics is often achieved by mixing materials. The strength of one material can blend with the appeal of a different material.

Multiple levels make multiple beds on this slope.

This mounded bed at the Denver Botanic Gardens hides other gardens behind it.

Finding Inspiration

Unique raised bed designs are endless, and choosing an individual design may be a challenge because there are so many options. As I mentioned earlier, to make the decision easier, I suggest beginning with the "how" and "why" gardening questions. It's important that you determine your priorities of functionality and aesthetics. Your budget and construction abilities are also major factors.

I like to visit gardens — both public and private — to get ideas. A big botanical garden is filled with examples of many types of raised beds. The gardens of my friends and neighbors are filled with beds that are examples of how to grow in soil and conditions similar to mine. I take photos and notes of what I like and what I think might work in my garden. Another reason I have so many raised beds in so many styles is that, as I add new beds, I am copying or modifying an idea I got from somewhere else.

The following section is a gallery of inspiration to give you some ideas of unique raised bed designs that go beyond a basic wooden box. This, of course, is not to say there's anything wrong with building a simple type of raised bed. You don't have to reinvent something that is proven to work. A raised bed is still just a basic way to garden, and basic design and construction may be all that's needed. Some of the most functional beds are simply boxes filled with soil.

This unique bed design I spotted at the Denver Botanic Gardens makes me want to try something similar in my garden.

Herb spirals add an interesting three-dimensional aspect to raised bed design. A common part of permaculture gardening, they are often made of brick or stone and fit into a naturalized landscape. Herb spirals start as a circular bed, with the edge gradually rising and spiraling toward the center. In a compact space, a common design matches the height with the width, so a 4-foot-wide bed rises to 4 feet high. The swirl of rising stones covered with plants adds height and visual impact to the garden. You can find instructions to build your own herb spiral in Chapter 3, pages 94–97.

A similar vertical approach to raised beds is a pyramid of square wooden beds of decreasing size. The base bed is square and by itself would be satisfactory for planting, but a second, smaller square bed is placed on top of it, and on top of that one is another. Typically, the stacked beds are centered to appear as a pyramid with an equal planting area available outside the base of each bed. They can be offset as well, with one side of each bed being stacked to form a wall, creating the same vertical approach and allowing for the structure to be placed against a fence or in a corner.

Another common raised bed in permaculture circles is the keyhole garden bed. Inspired by an African method of gardening, a keyhole garden can be round or square. On one side of the bed is a cutout, a space that allows the gardener to walk into the bed, resembling a key in a lock. The primary purpose is to allow the gardener to step into the keyhole and access the entire bed from the middle. The African method includes a composting tube in the center of the bed, but it is not necessary for the basic design of a bed that can be worked from the inside rather than from the outside.

Old tires make for interesting beds. Stacked on top of one another and filled with soil, they can make a tall cylindrical bed, like the one shown here. Some nurseries and garden centers sell tires that are turned inside out, colored, and/or cut with triangles or curves at the top. This idea might be closer to container gardening in a big pot, but the tires tend to be relatively permanent when placed and can be treated as raised beds when tall.

Simple wooden raised beds can become an incredible visual statement when the beds are constructed with creative carpentry and stained or painted with vibrant colors. Some gardeners may want the visual components of their raised beds to outweigh the functional considerations. Set against the plain backdrop of gravel and ubiquitous green grass, these raised beds become the primary focal point in the landscape and are memorable for anyone who sees them.

Similarly, vertically raised wooden beds can become a beautiful design feature. This elevated raised bed not only is useful for growing plants but also accents everything around it. Careful color selection highlights the bed, the wall, the hanging baskets, and the potted plants as separate garden components that fit well together. Space under these vertical beds can be used for other garden pieces, such as these footrests, which match the wooden seats nearby (not shown).

55

Designing raised beds for nighttime appeal adds an interesting aspect to garden design. The simple addition of rope lights or solar lights allows gardeners to enjoy the garden after dark. When used in tiered beds like these, the bed sides reflect the light and become part of the garden illumination. Lights can highlight decorative beds, the plants inside, or both. Try different-colored bulbs for holiday or seasonal appeal.

In some settings the raised bed itself may become a work of art. These stacked stone beds at Denver Botanic Gardens look like sculptures set against concrete and native plants. Discerning gardeners will see the plants growing inside them while the public may focus more on the customized and unique design of these monolithic stone structures. Here the plants and the stone merge into a single stunning visual achievement.

Common Planning Mistakes

In a rush to get raised beds in place, gardeners often overlook some necessary steps for success. Preparation and planning for a raised bed garden include awareness of potential mistakes or omissions when beginning to garden. While the beds can be dismantled and moved, they become relatively permanent once they're in place and gardeners put them to regular use. It's better to get things right in the beginning when creating a raised bed garden than to redo things once an error is determined.

Choosing the wrong place for a bed: Putting the raised bed in the wrong spot is more common than you might imagine. Vegetable garden plants need sun, usually at least six hours each day. Focusing only on design and appearance, some gardeners end up placing beds in the wrong location. A bed placed in autumn after leaves have fallen from the trees may be in the sun then, but not in spring and summer, when the trees are full of leaves. Be aware of sun and shade in your garden and take the time to choose the best location for raised beds before building and filling them.

Placing beds near a water source is often overlooked. Plants need water, and not anticipating the daily watering activity can make gardening harder if long hoses have to be dragged between the beds. Setting up drip irrigation systems and irrigation timers can also be challenging when the water source is far away. Water pressure drops over distance, affecting how much time is needed for adequate watering. Ideally, beds are in full sun and near a faucet.

Not planning for how you'll move through the garden: Paths that are too narrow can create problems when multiple raised beds occupy a space. There should be enough room to drag hoses, push wheelbarrows and garden carts, and comfortably work between beds. In an effort to

The width of the paths between my raised beds gives me plenty of room to work.

grow as many plants as possible, mimicking in-ground gardens, gardeners often place raised beds too close together. Having to tiptoe or sidestep between beds is not efficient. The ends of my beds are at least 24 inches apart from one another, so I can walk and move comfortably. The sides of each bed are at least 36 inches apart from one another, so I can move equipment with no interference.

Bed placement needs to make sense and match a gardener's preferred gardening process. Garden design needs to take that into account. Of course, pay attention when you're in the garden because anything you place in a garden path can become a tripping hazard.

Not considering the best size: Building a raised bed the wrong size is one of the most common mistakes when starting. Typically, the mistake is to make the bed too big. A bed that is too wide makes it difficult for a gardener to reach the middle of the bed and tend to all the plants equally. I've seen gardeners climb into a raised bed to work because they had no other option.

A raised bed can also be too small and not adequately support all the plants the gardener wants to grow. Failing to anticipate the fully mature size of a plant and how it will fill a bed can lead to plant death or bed failure. Aggressive growth of one plant can smother and kill younger plants that cannot get sunlight and nutrients. Trees growing in small beds can destroy the bed when the roots get big enough to push against the sides of the bed.

As this tree grows, it could cause problems for the raised bed.

A raised bed that is too tall or too short can add physical effort as the gardener strains to make it work. I have built tall beds designed for gardeners who had trouble bending over and needed to stand. While ideal for them, the same beds were literally out of reach for young children who wanted to help. On the other hand, working in short beds that require kneeling and leaning can literally be a pain for gardeners with back problems.

Not customizing bed design for specific needs: Gardeners with mobility issues should consider customizing raised beds and not relying on standard designs or plans. A rectangular bed

Considering the right-sized bed will make gardening easier for everyone. For example, shorter beds will make the planting space accessible to younger gardeners.

makes sense for most gardeners when first beginning a raised bed, but a tall keyhole garden may make more sense for a gardener who needs support when standing and has difficulty moving. Standing in the center of a keyhole bed with access to three sides takes minimal effort and may be quite effective.

Choosing the wrong material for specific needs: Choosing the wrong material for a bed may pose problems when the material doesn't match how a gardener uses the bed. As mentioned before, planning to sit on a bed requires a design and build to support the weight of the gardener. Metal beds have longevity and aesthetic appeal, but most aren't suitable for sitting on unless a seat is constructed. Wood is usually not a suitable material for a bed meant for perennials with a very long life because the wood will degrade in time.

Now that you have a raised bed design in mind, it's time to make it a reality. The next chapter will give you basic raised bed plans, instructions, and tips to achieve just that.

Chapter 3

Building a Raised Bed

I like building things, particularly garden beds. I consider myself handy, I have many tools, and I have experience constructing many different types of raised beds over my many years of gardening. But I know not every gardener has the same skills or motivation as I do. While I encourage gardeners to try new things and experiment in the garden, when it comes to raised bed construction, starting with a basic design and construction method may be the best course of action, especially for new gardeners. For gardeners wanting a DIY approach, the first raised bed in a garden should be easy to build. A bad experience could deter you from raised bed gardening before it even has the chance to become your new favorite method.

My first raised bed was a simple box of wood that I was able to construct in about an hour. That basic design has been a part of my garden for many years, because it works. With more experience, in both building and gardening, I expanded my garden with taller beds made from heavier timbers, as well as stacked stones, concrete blocks, and a variety of other materials.

As I touched on in the previous chapter, when building raised beds for your garden, consider your expertise with tools and construction if you plan to do the work yourself. Especially with heavy materials, take breaks and don't overstrain your body. Having learned the hard way, it's better to wear a back brace and lift correctly than to make a trip to the emergency room for being lackadaisical with heavy lifting. There is also nothing wrong with asking for help and making it a project for two or three people. You might be surprised how much help becomes

⬅ Building my own beds is a source of great pleasure, from the planning to the execution to enjoying the result.

Basic boxes can make a beautiful garden full of thriving plants.

available if you just let friends and family know you need it. And it's okay to hire someone to build your beds if you don't think you can do it yourself.

Before you buy the first board for a new bed, develop a plan based on your expertise, abilities, and expected assistance. Determine how much the bed will cost by visiting a home improvement store and comparing different materials. (Be sure to add delivery fees to your estimate if you aren't able to transport the materials yourself.) Consider the spot where you'll construct the bed and have it prepared in advance. Do an inventory of your tools to determine if you have everything you need or if you need to purchase new ones. Different types of beds require different tools, so I will advise which ones you need for each building project in this chapter.

The Best Time to Build

Many gardeners think the gardening season begins in spring and any new gardening activities should start in spring as well. It is the start of the growing season, after all — the weather is warming, and you're ready to get outside. It makes sense to think that a new garden should be started at this time, with new beds built, filled with soil, and planted.

Spring bed building is fine, but I think a better time is in the autumn. For many people, fall offers more free time to work on their beds after the excitement and busy schedules of spring and summer are past. Ideally, gardeners have spent their first growing season observing and taking the time to plan the design of their raised beds. The more relaxed atmosphere of autumn is appropriate for the important task of building and filling beds. As you'll learn in Chapter 4, there are good reasons to fill your beds with soil in fall rather than spring — for the benefit of your plants and the soil microbes on which they depend.

Preparing the Bed Site

The location for a raised bed should be leveled beforehand to make installation easy. A level bed virtually eliminates soil erosion and makes water application more even. It is better for keeping mulch in place with reduced shifting. Irrigation lines run smoothly on level surfaces. Digging out excess or uneven soil underneath the bed before it's built can make the process easier.

Digging out extra soil from under a bed is a good idea if the soil is poor and vegetable plant roots are likely to extend below the bottom of the raised bed. The good, amended soil used to fill a bed will also fill the hole underneath. The soil that is dug out can be part of the native soil used to make a good soil blend (see Chapter 4 for more about blending soil). For tall beds, I rarely dig out any soil because the depth of the soil in the bed is enough for the roots of all the vegetable plants I plan to grow.

For raised beds on sloped ground, it is necessary to dig out the uphill soil to create a level base for the bed. The downhill side of the bed can rest on undug soil. To get an idea of where and how much to dig, drive stakes that match the corners of the bed placement. Run twine horizontally from the uphill stake where it touches the ground and level it to the downhill stake. Measuring how high the twine is on the lower stake tells you how much needs to be dug out. When the soil is dug out and the ground is level, the bed can be placed. The full

1. Run leveled twine horizontally between stakes. This twine is close to the ground at the high point of the slope.

2. Measure the twine at the low point of the slope. This tells you how much of the slope needs to be dug out for a level base.

3. Dig out the soil from the uphill so that the base of the bed is level.

4. Here is the level base for the bed. Some bed sides will be fully visible and other bed sides will appear to be buried in the slope.

lower side will be visible, while the top side will look like it is buried in the slope. (See sequence above.)

It usually isn't necessary to dig out grass before placing a bed. Most weeds can remain with the new bed placed directly on top. It is a common misconception that grass and weeds will grow through the bed. Plants need sun and air to grow, and the depth and weight of soil are usually enough to smother and kill plants growing under the bed. Most turf grass will not propagate when buried, but plants that spread with rhizomes can still grow when buried, so it is a good idea to dig out grasses such as Bermuda and Zoysia. Most weed seeds need to be near the soil surface to germinate and will rot if buried under 8 inches or more of soil.

If there is any concern about the possibility of plants growing up through the soil, you can place cardboard under the bed first. Like deep soil, cardboard will smother the plants. Cardboard or several sheets of newsprint can help for shallow beds that might not have enough soil to smother the plants underneath. Cardboard is devoid of nutrients and creates a barrier to air and water flow, but it will decompose over time and provide food for earthworms, as will the dead plants underneath.

Adding Barriers to the Raised Bed

There are instances when it's necessary to add a barrier to the bottom of a raised bed. Some reasons include trying to deter burrowing animals, avoiding tree roots invading your beds, or creating a garden over contaminated soil.

For gardens with burrowing animals, adding a metal wire barrier to the bottom of a raised bed is a good idea. A wire barrier is the easiest and most efficient way to keep animals out. I like to use hardware cloth under my beds. Hardware cloth is made by interlacing galvanized wire into a grid of small wire squares. Typically sold with ¼-inch or ½-inch openings, it is very effective at deterring moles, voles, gophers, and hedgehogs. It presents an obstacle to the burrowing animals, and they are unable to dig through it up into the raised bed. Rolls of hardware cloth come in different widths; the 48-inch width is ideal for typical raised garden beds.

Similarly, poultry netting or chicken wire can be used. The openings in chicken wire are bigger, typically 1-inch or 2-inch hexagonal holes. They may seem small, but they may be big enough for small burrowing animals such as baby moles or voles to fit through. Gopher wire has a similar design with ¾-inch openings. Chicken wire and gopher wire also come in widths that fully fit the bottom of raised beds. To keep animals from digging through any gaps, the wire should be attached to the bottom of

Hardware cloth has smaller openings, which is good for deterring small digging mammals.

Here, I have unrolled chicken wire to cover the base of this concrete block bed. I will eventually cut and fold the wire so that it lies directly on the ground, inside the bed.

the bed with staples or nails. As unlikely as it might seem, any gaps, however small, can be a way in for the smallest burrowing animals.

Though galvanized, the light gauge of the poultry wire means it will rust and corrode over time. The pH and moisture level of the soil affect its breakdown. Chicken wire tends to corrode faster and may have a lifespan of two to three years when buried. Hardware cloth can be bought with heavier gauge wire that will last longer. The cost of the options varies, and hardware cloth is usually more expensive than chicken wire, but the increased years of productive deterrence may make it worth the cost.

Tree roots can be a big problem if they invade the good soil of your raised beds, and a permanent, impermeable barrier such as metal or plastic may be necessary at the bottom of the bed. Digging a deep trench around garden beds and cutting invasive roots is effective for removing the initial threat of intrusion from trees and large bushes. Burying a vertical metal or plastic barrier wall in the trench about 2 feet deep will deter most tree roots. Removing the tree or bush with the intrusive roots can preclude the need for a barrier. It can be a difficult choice to cut down a tree, but it will eradicate the problem of roots invading the raised beds.

Wooden planks and plywood can be a long-term barrier for placing raised beds on contaminated soil or on top of troublesome weeds. It can take years before the wood decomposes, and that is often more than enough time to smother and kill problematic plants. For chemicals in soil that dissipate or break down over time, the wooden barrier should be able to isolate the raised bed soil long enough for the underlying soil to become safe for plant growth.

For areas with more severe contamination that won't dissipate in a few years, a more permanent metal base can work. Metal sheets or plates affixed to the bottom of raised beds can effectively separate good soil from bad. It may be an expensive option, but it can allow gardeners to build a garden in an area that's otherwise unusable. Metal sheets can be an effective barrier to tree roots and burrowing critters as well.

Barriers I Don't Recommend

I generally don't recommend landscape fabric, sometimes called weed fabric, as a barrier for most raised beds. Heavy-duty plastic landscape fabric can be used at the bottom of beds placed over contaminated soil. Thick weed block made from synthetic materials will last for years with little degradation. However, it is not as effective for areas with extensive tree roots, because roots will eventually find spaces between the fabric and infiltrate the good soil in the bed.

The fabric is made to be permeable, letting air and water flow through the soil, but it can limit the movement of soil organisms. I prefer an open-soil interface, so organisms can freely move through the soil. It is those many beneficial organisms that will work to improve the soil in the beds.

Gravel and rock are not effective as barriers that improve drainage. Numerous studies have shown that water does not move easily through different layers of soil. When moving from fine soil into gravel, the soil must be saturated before it flows through the gravel, effectively negating the idea of improving drainage. The rock can also become a barrier for the easy movement of soil organisms, and it may not deter burrowing animals for long.

Plastic sheeting is another product that may not be as effective as assumed. In the short-term, it will kill plants underneath, but not as effectively as weed fabric. It offers little deterrence to burrowing animals and, over time, will break down and contaminate the soil with plastic pieces. However, thick plastic or rubber can be used to create self-wicking beds and is suitable for that purpose.

The remainder of this chapter features eight detailed building projects using different materials and methods, and a section on common building mistakes to avoid. You'll see when we get to constructing the beds that I give you some pretty specific instructions and measurements. Please recognize that you are free to modify the beds to your own plans and use your own approaches when tackling the assembly. While some of you may have a lot of experience with construction, these projects are written for people with little to no building experience. For those with more experience, consider using premium materials and refined construction techniques to showcase your abilities.

Simple Wooden Raised Bed

Difficulty level: Easy
Final project dimensions: 4' × 8' × 10"
What you'll need:

- Three 2" × 10" × 8' wooden boards
- Tape measure
- Hammer and 3" galvanized nails
- Screwdriver and #8 or #10 3" exterior wood or deck screws (optional)
- Drill (optional)
- Four corner brackets (optional)
- Four 4" × 4" posts, cut to desired bed height (optional)

I prefer to use standard lumber that is available in most home improvement stores. It is relatively inexpensive, easy to work with, and comes in different widths to match my construction plan. Most of my wooden raised beds are made using 2-inch by 10-inch lumber, which is commonly sold in 8-foot and 10-foot lengths. I prefer the sturdiness of boards at least 1½ inches thick. Less robust lumber is more likely to fail sooner.

When filled with soil, that size bed gives my plant roots 8 inches or 9 inches of depth within the bed and additional room for the roots if there is suitable soil beneath the bed. That is enough for most garden plants.

1. The build begins with three wooden boards. Start by measuring one of the boards and mark the halfway point. This is the board that will be cut in two to make the ends. The two long boards become the sides of the new bed. I like to use a cordless circular saw at the location I'm constructing the bed. If you don't have a saw, most home improvement stores will cut the board in half for you if you ask.

2. Once the one board is cut, lay all the boards on the ground to form the basic shape of a rectangle.

3. With the boards lined up, nail or screw the corners together. Three-inch galvanized nails are suitable for securing the boards.

4. Gardeners with more experience opt to use screws as a primary connector during construction. Screws are less likely to pull out and they are my fastener of choice. One thing to note is that both nails and screws need to be long enough to adequately anchor into both boards. Standard boards such as the ones we're using here are closer to 1½ inches wide. A screw or nail that is 3 inches long has half its length into the second board, and that has always made my raised beds sturdy and long-lasting. As with nails, it's a good idea to choose exterior-rated or deck screws. They are made to remain durable when exposed to the

weather conditions that a garden bed will encounter. Interior screws can rust and corrode quickly when exposed to the elements. Because the nails or screws are near the end of the board, pre-drilling holes can reduce the chance of the wood splitting. Some exterior screws, particularly deck screws, are made to be self-tapping or self-drilling and do not require pre-drilling. Even when using those types of screws, I still choose to drill a pilot hole to avoid splitting the ends of the boards.

5. Continue connecting the boards at all corners, and in a very short time a finished raised bed is ready for the garden.

6. Wooden raised beds, such as this one or smaller, can be built with no additional support, but an angle bracket screwed into the corner can reduce the likelihood of the joint separating, especially if you're securing with nails only.

7. If you feel your beds need additional support, I suggest using corner posts for more strength. A corner post not only allows for a stronger corner for wider boards, but also allows you to stack beds for more height. I like to use 4-inch by 4-inch posts to anchor the corner, but scrap 2-by-4s or 2-by-2s can work well, too.

When using a corner post support, screws and nails can be driven directly into the post from both boards, so you can avoid nailing into the board ends. This reduces the chance that the board will split. With nails or screws from both the side and the end, it can double the stability and strengthen the corner joint.

For Taller Beds

With taller beds, there are two basic ways to construct them. (Note that you will need to purchase more lumber and 4-by-4 corner posts for these taller beds.) The first method is to build each layer as a stand-alone, single-level bed and then stack the beds.

1. Build two single-level beds with the boards nailed or screwed together at the ends.

2. Stack the beds, then place a 4-by-4 post in each corner that matches the total height, and anchor the beds to the corner posts with more nails or screws.

The second method involves building the layers by screwing individual boards to the corner support.

1. First, screw a long-side board to a corner post. Then attach a short-side board to the post. Continue on each corner with new posts and additional boards until you've built the base layer.

For building a high bed, a combination of the two methods can be used. This is what I normally do. I build the first layer as a stand-alone bed. I then attach corner posts cut for the final height I want and anchor the bed to the corner posts with nails or screws. With the base and corners in place, it's a simple process of adding a board on top of the base layer, attaching it to the post, and moving around the bed, adding more boards to complete a new layer.

2. For each level above the base, follow the same process by adding side and end boards to the corner posts.

After attaching corner posts to a stand-alone bed (as shown), I attach a second layer of boards to the posts.

Metal Raised Bed Kit

Difficulty level: Easy
Final project dimensions: Variable, depending on kit and configuration
What you'll need:
   A modular metal raised bed kit
   Screwdriver (optional)

The building process for metal raised beds is similar to basic wooden beds. Pieces are attached to one another to form a bed of the desired size and height. The modular system provides side pieces that can be attached to one another in numerous configurations. A single kit may allow for 10 or more different bed designs, depending on how many panels are used and how the panels are connected to each other. Kits are available to make beds in squares, rectangles, ovals, circles, and hexagons. I have built metal bed kits from Birdies, Forever Garden Beds, and Garden In Minutes.

1. As with the building process for a basic wooden bed, begin by laying all the pieces on your prepared site. The final design will determine how many pieces are used and how they attach to the corner supports.

2. The process is simple. Bolts, washers, and nuts supplied with the kit connect the panels through pre-drilled holes. It is virtually foolproof and can be done by nearly anyone. The necessary tools are usually included in the kit as well.

3. The first panel is attached to a corner support bracket. Then another panel is connected. The panels can be connected to one another to make a longer side or bolted to another corner piece. These modular beds can be built using the simple wrench tool included with the kit, but I like to use a screwdriver and wrench together. The initial connection should be tightened just enough to hold the pieces together.

4. In very little time, all the panels will be in place, and the final shape revealed. At this point, all the nuts and bolts can be tightened completely and fully secured. Modular steel beds offer not only one of the easiest construction methods, but also the opportunity to take the bed apart by reversing the process. For gardeners seeking a temporary raised bed, these may be a good choice. Renters and homeowners planning to move soon can set up a raised bed garden and then dismantle the pieces to set them up again at a new home.

Try a Steel or Plastic Culvert Bed
Steel or plastic culvert pipes make for easy raised beds. Cut the pipe to the desired height, and when laid on end it becomes a circular bed. Some sand and gravel companies can cut metal pipes up to 4 feet wide to any height. Plastic culverts can be cut to size with a jigsaw.

Pipe beds can be painted or left natural.

Galvanized Steel Raised Bed

Difficulty level: Intermediate
Final project dimensions: 8' × 32" × 26"
What you'll need:

    Three 26" × 8' panels of untreated corrugated galvanized steel
    Six 2" × 4" × 8' wooden boards
    Four 4" × 4" posts, cut to the desired bed height
    Metal snips, electric metal shears, or a drill with a metal shear attachment
    Screwdriver or drill
    Metal drill bit that matches the screw size
    Impact driver (optional)
    #9 or #12 1" roofing screws or self-drilling screws
    #8 or #10 3" exterior wood or deck screws
    Hand clamps or spring clamps (optional)
    Post hole digger (optional)
    Additional boards for reinforcing sides (optional)

This other option for a metal raised bed uses untreated galvanized steel panels and wood supports. These beds are built using a process very similar to the Simple Wooden Raised Bed construction on pages 68–73. Instead of wooden boards, you will attach steel panels to the 4-inch by 4-inch corner posts to create the sides. Additional 2-inch by 4-inch wooden supports are used as a framework for attaching the steel end and side pieces.

The most common material for these types of beds is corrugated galvanized steel roofing panels, which can be found at a home improvement store. The panels are 26 inches wide and sold in lengths of 8 feet or 12 feet. As with a basic wooden raised bed, three 8-foot-long panels can form the bed sides. One panel is cut into pieces that match the bed width. My beds are 32 inches wide, but you can cut the sheets in half to make two ends that are each 4 feet long.

The metal is quite thin — 32 gauge — and is relatively easy to cut, but special tools are needed. Metal snips or shears will do the job. Metal snips are scissor-like handheld tools for cutting metal. They are affordable, but can be tiring on the hand if cutting many panels. Electric metal shears make cutting much easier, but can be much more expensive. They plug in or use rechargeable batteries for a motor that moves the blades for cutting metal. I have a shear attachment for my cordless drill that cuts the metal like butter and is fatigue-free. For me, this was worth the expense.

The instructions here will give you a finished bed that is 8 feet long, 32 inches wide, and just over 2 feet tall. These steel panels are easy to make into longer raised beds, and I usually build mine longer than 8 feet (as you'll see in the photos). Build your bed to match the length you want. The 26-inch height is a little too tall for me, so to avoid lots of metal cutting in order to reduce the height, I usually dig trenches and bury the sides 6 inches deep for a final height of 20 inches. Doing this also adds stability.

Metal snips are affordable but can be tiring to use.

Electric metal shears are more expensive but make the job of cutting metal much easier.

1. To begin, cut four 4-inch by 4-inch wooden posts at least 26 inches long for the corners. This length matches the width of the panels. Because I bury the raised bed sides, I cut my posts to 36 inches, so they extend deeper than the metal panels when buried. A post hole digger is helpful to dig the holes for them. If you don't have a saw, you can ask an employee at the home improvement store to cut the posts to the size you want.

2. To cut the two shorter end pieces, lay the 4-by-4 posts on the ground and lay one metal panel on top of them to elevate the panel. You will need space below the panel for the shears to cut through the metal without obstruction. Measure the width and where you plan to cut at multiple points using a tape measure and permanent marker, and connect the measurements to make a line to use as a cutting guide.

3. Using manual or electric shears, carefully cut along the line. The curves of the corrugated sheet can make cutting difficult, so take your time. I recommend wearing gloves because the edges of the metal can be sharp.

4. Cut four 2-inch by 4-inch boards to 89 inches. These will be the top and bottom supports of the bed's long sides. Cut the remaining two 2-by-4 boards to get four 25-inch pieces for the bed ends. If you're making a bed that's 4 feet wide, you will need to cut the boards to 41 inches.

5. Attach the end of one of the 8-foot steel panels to a corner post using screws spaced 4 inches to 6 inches apart. For basic roofing screws, you will need to pre-drill a hole through the panel using a metal drill bit. If you are using self-drilling

screws and an impact driver, you can drill directly through the metal into the wooden post. Repeat with a second corner post on the opposite end of the panel.

6. If the bed sides are to be buried, the first side with end posts can be set in the trench before proceeding.

7. Place one of the 89-inch wooden boards between the posts along what will be the top edge of the bed and attach the steel panel to it with screws spaced 4 inches to 6 inches apart. If you have a helper, they can hold the board and panel while you drill and drive screws. If you're building the bed by yourself, clamps can hold the panel to the board while you screw it together.

8. Toenail exterior wood or deck screws (in other words, drive the screws at an approximately 30-degree angle) to attach the board to the corner posts.

9. Follow the same process to attach another 89-inch board along what will be the bottom edge of the bed. You should have a steel panel with wood supports on all four sides. Note that a 2-by-4 board is not really needed on the bottom if you plan to bury the panel because the soil will support the sides when the trench is filled in.

10. With the first long side complete, follow a similar process for attaching the two end panels. Dig trenches for the other three sides and the other two end posts, so the bed is constructed while resting in the trenches. Screw one end panel to a corner 4-by-4 post. Attach the other end of the panel to the corner post from the finished side. With the panel secured, hold or clamp a 25-inch 2-by-4 along the top, screw it to the metal panel, and toenail it to the corner posts. Add another 25-inch board to the bottom in the same way, if using. Repeat the steps to attach the other end piece on the other side.

11. With three sides complete, screw the fourth panel to the corner posts and attach an 89-inch wooden board on the top and one on the bottom. This makes a complete box ready to fill with soil.

12. If you choose to make longer beds, add additional 4-by-4 posts between the corner posts. If more than one metal panel makes up a side, overlap the panels when screwing them to the 4-by-4 posts.

80

Be Creative with the Construction

The wood can be on the inside or outside of the steel panels. Stained wood on the exterior can look attractive. These instructions are for securing the steel panels on the outside of the wooden pieces, but for a decorative bed with a wooden frame featured on the outside, the dimensions of the steel panels and wood supports would need to be modified.

Stained wood on the outside adds a striking, upgraded appearance.

When the bed is filled, the long sides may bow from the weight of the soil inside. For extra stability, place additional vertical supports at the midpoint of the long sides. This should be enough to hold the panel in place. Screw the panel to a 19-inch-long 2-by-4 spaced between the top and bottom wood supports and toenail it in.

For my long steel beds, I bury 40-inch-long 2-by-4s on the outside of the bed spaced 4 feet or 6 feet apart.

For my long steel beds, I bury 2-by-4s on the outside of the bed to prevent the steel from bowing from the weight of the soil.

Added wooden tops make sturdy seats.

The size and thickness of the wooden framework determine how strong the bed is and whether a gardener can sit on it. Using 2-by-4s makes a solid frame, and with the 4-by-4 corner posts, I can sit on the edge with no problems. Many gardeners will add boards on top of the sides to make wider seats, such as those for the beds pictured above.

Try a Trough

Steel raised beds typically have open bottoms with native soil below and amended soil within, but it's not a requirement. As mentioned previously, a solid barrier at the bottom allows for growing over ground that is contaminated or dense with tree roots. And building a steel raised bed with a solid bottom is surprisingly easy.

Metal animal troughs used for feeding and watering livestock are ideally suited to become raised beds. They are the same size and shape as other beds but don't require cutting, hammering, screwing, or changing the basic metal in any way. I do recommend adding drainage by drilling holes in the bottom. Most metal troughs have a hole in one side with a threaded plug as extra drainage.

Find the size you like at a ranch or farm supply store. If you like the look of bare galvanized steel, just place it in your garden, fill it with good soil, and it's ready to go. I opted for a couple of trough beds and chose to paint them with an exterior latex paint. The paint reduces the likelihood of exterior rust and adds color to the garden.

Galvanized steel troughs offer a rustic look.

Painted metal is a nice-looking option that reduces the likelihood of rust.

Concrete Block Raised Bed

Difficulty level: Easy

Final project dimensions: (exterior measurement) 8' × 4' × 8"

What you'll need:

    16 8" × 8" × 16" concrete blocks

    Four stakes

    Twine

    Line level

    Two to four bags of play sand or all-purpose sand

    Torpedo level

    Rubber mallet

    Long level (48 inches)

    Rebar (optional for taller beds)

    Mortar (optional for taller beds)

Concrete block beds have longevity that surpasses metal. The concrete won't rust like metal or decompose like wood, and the blocks won't require replacement. Hollow 8-inch by 8-inch by 16-inch concrete building blocks are easy to find at home improvement centers and hardware stores. With a stable, level, and strong base, they shouldn't shift and will stay in position indefinitely.

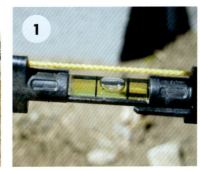

1. Measure the length and width of the bed on the ground to define the edges. Drive stakes just beyond where the corners of the long sides will be and string twine between two of the stakes 10 inches above the ground to define the first side. A line level ensures the twine is a good guide for placing the blocks.

2. Take time to dig out soil, plants, and roots where the blocks will go to create a relatively level base. If the ground is uneven, identify some high spots and low spots, then move the soil from the high spots to the low spots. Add a few inches of sand for a firm foundation to a level 8 inches below the twine.

3. The process of building the bed is fairly simple, and I would argue that the hardest part is just moving all the concrete blocks into position. The blocks are laid end to end to form the bed. Lay a block edge against the twine to keep each block in line and use the leveled twine as a guide to ensure the tops of the blocks are level. You may need to scrape away or add sand or soil to the ground underneath the block to ensure the block is as level as possible. I use a small torpedo level on each block to determine that it's level in all directions, and then I use a rubber mallet to pound it firmly in place (again, checking that it's level in all directions).

4. Carry on placing six blocks for the first side, continually checking that they're level and pounding the blocks with a mallet to secure them in place. The project uses six 16-inch blocks along one side to make a bed that has an exterior side measurement of 8 feet. The bed I'm creating in the photos is longer — the long side is 14 blocks and will measure 17.5 feet. Build your own bed to match the length you want.

5. At the corners, take advantage of the long and short sides of the blocks to get the desired width for your bed. This project uses the long sides of two concrete blocks on the end nestled between the short sides of the two concrete blocks that make up the sides of the bed. That means it has an exterior width of 4 feet. Because the blocks are 8 inches wide, the internal measurement is around 32 inches. You, of course, can fit the blocks to match the bed size you want.

6. Before placing the two end blocks, run more level twine between the corner stakes as a guide or use a 48-inch-long level. I have a long level that I lay side to side, to ensure each side is level with the other.

7. For the third side, once again string level twine. I use the twine to lay the blocks, but I also cut a board that matches the exact inner width of the bed (32 inches) and use that as a quick way to space the blocks apart. The long level is a backup to keep the sides level with each other. With the third side complete it is easy to add the final two end blocks.

8. While it's not necessary to level and space each block perfectly, they are more likely to stay in position if you take the time to do so. Inevitably, blocks that are just lined up without the extra preparation and care will shift when exposed to water, snow, and wind. My block beds have never shifted, even after years of exposure to Colorado winters, and I attribute that to the care and time I took placing each block.

9. To make taller concrete block beds, simply stack another layer of blocks. For increased stability, overlap the corners so the joints of the blocks are staggered. Driving long pieces of rebar through the open holes and into the ground below adds extra stability when the holes are filled with soil. In my opinion, if the base is stable and the blocks are level, it isn't necessary to use rebar or even mortar to secure the blocks together with just one or two levels of blocks on top of the base layer. Above that height, though, mortar and rebar will help. Construction adhesive is a suitable alternative. The weight of more soil in taller beds will add strain to blocks that are loosely stacked and not anchored, but even three levels can be built with minimal block shifting if the time is taken to build a strong foundation.

Try a Retaining Wall Block Bed

Home improvement stores and rock supply yards sell stackable retaining wall blocks. Also made from concrete, these blocks come in many different sizes and colors and can be easily converted to make decorative raised beds of any height.

Using the same basic procedure as the Concrete Block Raised Bed, begin with a firm and stable base. From there, lay out the first layer and then simply stack the blocks to the desired height. Many blocks have a lip on the back that overlaps the one below. The weight of the block holds it in place, and when the bed is filled with soil, they lock together and don't require mortar or other anchoring. Laying out a slight curve at the corners ensures the blocks anchor together and create a continuous wall of concrete.

Blocks, such as these red retaining wall blocks, can become a permanent decorative bed.

87

Cement Backer Board Raised Bed

Difficulty level: Easy

Final project dimensions: 5' × 5' × 18"

What you'll need:

    Two ½" × 3' × 5' cement backer board panels

    Metal straightedge

    Utility knife or carbide scoring tool

    Circular saw, jigsaw, or angle grinder with a carbide or diamond blade (optional)

    Goggles and respirator (if using a saw)

    Four 2" × 2" or 4" × 4" posts, cut to 18" height

    Cement board screws

    Drill

    Four metal angle brackets (optional)

A pair of cement backer board panels, ready to be cut in half.

Another option for a raised bed with great longevity and that uses construction methods like that of a wooden bed is a cement backer board raised bed. Also known as a cementitious backer unit (CBU), backer board is used in home construction as a foundation for tiles, flooring, and veneer stone. It is durable, strong, easy to work with, and can be fashioned into long-lasting raised beds.

A standard size for backer boards is 3 feet by 5 feet. They are available in thicknesses of ¼ inch, ½ inch, and ⅝ inch. For the garden, the ½-inch-thick panels work well. Each board can be cut into two 18-inch-high panels to make the sides of a raised bed. Two cement boards can be used to make a square bed with 5-foot-long sides.

1. There are a couple of options for cutting the cement board. You can use a metal straightedge and score the top of the board with a utility knife or carbide scoring tool along the line. Push hard with the knife and make multiple passes along the line. This weakens the cement, but won't cut all the way through.

2. Place a board underneath the center line you scored and grab onto the lower side for support. Starting at the end of the top side, push sharply against the board edge with your hand. Continue hitting the top edge with your palm as you move along the board. It should snap along the line. If there is fiberglass mesh holding the cut boards together, cut through it with a utility knife.

3. Alternatively, use a cutting tool to cut the board. A circular saw or jigsaw with a carbide blade can cut completely through the board. An angle grinder with a diamond cutting wheel is also good; make multiple passes along the line and don't try to cut all the way through at first. Wear goggles and a respirator because you can expect a lot of dust.

4. With the pieces cut, lay out the four panels that will form the sides of the square bed, along with four 2-inch by 2-inch or 4-inch by 4-inch corner supports.

5. Home improvement stores sell specialized cement board screws, and these are best to use. Corrosion resistant, they work well outdoors and don't require any pre-drilling. Drive the screw

through the backer board into the corner supports using a drill, overlapping the ends. Three screws will anchor each edge well. Metal angle brackets on each corner can be used for more support. If using brackets, screw through them into the cement board and into the corner posts. The brackets can be used by themselves, without the wood corner posts, but the joints won't be as strong.

Try a Poured Concrete Bed

Poured concrete beds are a great option for strong, permanent beds, but the cost can be high and beyond the skill level of most gardeners. Concrete beds a few inches wide and high are doable for gardeners with skills to build the form, add rebar, mix the concrete, and shovel it in place. Taller and wider raised beds can be constructed by concrete company crews to any size and shape. Painted or stained, concrete beds can add a nice visual element to gardens.

Poured concrete and stone work well together.

Concrete can be painted, adding color and interest to a garden.

Stone Bed

Difficulty level: Easy
Final project dimensions: Variable
What you'll need:
- Big stones or flat rocks
- Soil (see Chapter 4 for guidance on building good soil)
- Level
- Mortar (optional)

Stone or rock raised beds begin just like the concrete block beds — with a strong, level foundation. Prepare the base to the desired size and shape. Round or oval shapes work well for stone beds. If you can lift the stone safely, you can move it into position to create a bed of any shape. Big stones laid side by side are enough to make a low raised bed with no need for stacking stones. When filled with soil, the bed is complete.

For taller beds, stones need to be stacked. Stones with flat bottoms and tops work best. Flat rocks such as flagstone can be cut to size and easily stacked. Use a level when stacking and try to make each row as level as possible before stacking the next. Stacking round stones is a little like putting together a jigsaw puzzle. Each stone needs to be carefully selected to fit with the pieces next to it and under it. You can also use smaller stones, but it's advisable to secure them with mortar.

1. The walls of a stacked stone raised bed should be wider at the base to support multiple levels of stones. Start with the thickest and widest stones at the bottom, or place two stones side by side, to support the ones above.

2. For the strongest walls, ensure that no vertical joints extend from one layer to the one above it. So when two pieces butt up against each other, make sure the next layer above overlaps that joint. For a wide bed 2 feet or 3 feet high, the size and weight of the rocks should hold them in place, and the soil in the bed will help stabilize it from behind. Taller beds will benefit from mortar to hold the rocks together securely.

3. Filling the bed with soil after completing a layer will help stabilize it for the next layer. Watering the soil well will also help it flow into gaps between the stones. This makes the building process longer, but it is easier to stack on top of stones that don't wobble or shift.

Try a Brick Bed

Stacked brick beds can be a beautiful addition to the landscape. Low brick beds can be easily constructed by gardeners using the same basic methods of tall concrete block beds. No mortar is needed for beds with just a few levels of bricks. For visually striking beds, professional bricklayers can create beds of any height, shape, and size.

The classic look of red brick will lend a touch of drama to your landscape.

Herb Spiral

Difficulty level: Easy
Final project dimensions: 5' x 5' x 3'
What you'll need:

    Big stones, flat rocks, or bricks
    Soil (see Chapter 4 for guidance on building a good soil)
    Level
    Mortar (optional)

Another easy stone raised bed is an herb spiral. It relies on fitting the stones carefully and using the bed soil to hold everything together. The idea for an herb spiral is to create a center tower that throws shade on plants planted on different sides of the bed. The vertical walls can be as low or high as desired, depending on the light requirements of your plants.

1. After making a level foundation, begin the bed by laying out a layer of your biggest stones in a spiral shape approximately 4 feet to 5 feet in diameter. Tall spirals may benefit from a double layer of stones at the base.

2. Fill the spiral with soil to stabilize the stones. At the low point of the spiral (usually the outer end), begin stacking the second layer one or two joints from the end stone to create a stairstep spiral (remember, the sides will be more structurally stable if you overlap the joints).

3. Build new portions of the wall with increasing height as the stairstep spiral height gradually moves upward and toward the center of the spiral. With each new level of stones, fill the bed with soil to help anchor them. You can also use mortar if you want to secure smaller stones.

4. The goal is to have the highest point of the spiral at the center of the bed after stacking the stones below. If you're building your herb spiral without mortar or construction adhesive, use small stones to fill any gaps between the larger ones. Three feet to 4 feet high is a good goal height, but if you're carefully placing stones and interlocking the different sizes, the bed can be built much taller.

A brick herb spiral.

You can also try this project with bricks. The flat bricks are easy to stack, and the overlapping joints can be symmetrical. Stairstep each level to a final height of six or seven bricks high. The stability of the bricks allows you to build the spiral completely and then fill with soil. Wider brick spirals can be much taller.

Try Stacking and Backfilling a Log Bed

The stacking and backfilling method used for this herb spiral can also be used to make log beds. Small logs or big branches are stacked to construct the bed sides. A low bed may not need any stacking if the logs are big enough. For higher beds, build the sides like a log cabin. Cutting a notch close to the end allows the log to be stacked on the one below it. As the log sides are put in place, fill the bed with soil to stabilize the logs and help hold them in place. Nails and spikes can add additional support. As the bed is filled, smaller branches can fill gaps between the logs.

If logs are wide enough, they can create an interesting low bed.

Hybrid Wood-Concrete Bed with Planter Blocks

Difficulty level: Easy

Final project dimensions: Approximately 8' × 4' × 1'

What you'll need:

    Six 2" × 6" × 8' wooden boards

    Eight planter blocks

    Rebar (optional)

    Three 2" × 6" × 10' wooden boards (optional)

    Drill (optional)

    #8 or #10 3" exterior wood or deck screws (optional)

An easy bed option is a hybrid concrete and wood bed. Home improvement stores are now selling a type of concrete retaining wall block that is designed as a corner piece for holding wooden planks. Also called a planter block, it makes one of the easiest possible raised beds. The concrete corners have an opening centered on each side that is designed for sliding in a 2-inch by 6-inch wooden board. Four boards and four corner blocks would make for a low raised bed about 6 inches high.

1. Level the ground for the bed and place a planter block in each corner to make a 4-foot by 8-foot base. Cut two of the 8-foot wooden boards in half to make four 4-foot boards. The width of the concrete block will result in a bed with inner and outer side dimensions slightly more than 4 feet by 8 feet. Cut off 4 inches from the end of each board if you want a bed that is closer to 4 feet by 8 feet.

2. To assemble the bed, simply slide a board into the corner slot of each block to create a side. The planter blocks can be shifted as needed to get a tight fit. To get perfect 90-degree corners, measure the distance between opposite corners and move the blocks to get the same measurement for both diagonals.

3. Stack another layer of planter blocks on the corners to make a bed just under 12 inches high. The blocks are made with a central hole for inserting a piece of rebar vertically. Hammer the rebar through the top block and into and through the lower block to ensure the second layer is of the same dimensions as the first. For added stability, continue hammering the rebar into the ground to anchor the bed and strengthen the corner to reduce lateral movement.

4. Slide in four more boards to complete the second level of the bed. Taller beds can be built with additional layers and longer rebar pieces to stabilize the corners.

5. These beds are strong, and the rebar will stabilize them, but they might shift slightly when you're sitting on the sides. To make a stronger bed with a sitting top, you can place boards across the top from corner to corner. Cut one 10-foot-long 2-by-6 board into two pieces, each measuring 62 inches long. Cut the other two boards approximately 110 inches long. Make a 45-degree cut at the ends of each board so they fit together to make a miter joint

and create a rectangular cap on the blocks and sides. The boards will fully cover the end blocks. Screw the top boards to the side boards using 3-inch screws to anchor them.

The blocks make for a permanent corner brace and won't need replacing. In time, the wooden boards will need to be replaced as they break down. To make this bed last much longer, you could use composite deck boards instead of wood 2-by-6s. The composite boards are the same width and will fit the blocks to the same height, but they are thinner. While constructing the bed, the boards will be loose, but once the bed is filled with soil they will press to the outside and remain secure. The composite material won't break down like regular wood will.

There are no rules when building beds.

Get Creative!

The beauty of designing and building something yourself is that you're not bound to the conventional. With a little imagination and creativity, many building supplies and common items can be repurposed to become raised beds. The basic plan with four corners and four sides is enough to work from in designing and building a bed from repurposed materials. Using a combination of materials increases the options even further.

Common Building Mistakes

Experience can be a harsh teacher, and many of us act hastily and learn the hard way. What follows are examples of potential mistakes that can impact raised bed building for you to be aware of and, hopefully, avoid.

Investing too much money at the outset: Eager gardeners often spend too much money to start a raised bed garden. The best materials often equal a more expensive build. Cedar or redwood costs much more than pine or fir when making a wooden bed. Rather than starting slowly with one or two beds and then learning how to garden effectively in raised beds, materials for numerous beds for a big raised bed garden are purchased all at once. A big garden can be overwhelming — and costly. Few gardeners want to feel they've overspent in their hobby, and when they discover later that they could have done it more frugally, the whole experience may be tainted.

Using available materials can lessen the cost but is often overlooked. Use what you have to build a bed if it achieves your plan. If function and utility are the goals, then reclaimed lumber can be as good as purchased boards (as long as it's deemed safe to use, of course). Adding more beds as more free materials become available can be a very cost-effective way to build a garden. The beds may not match and may not be the prettiest, but some of the most productive gardens I've seen weren't made to win beauty contests. Many a happy gardener doesn't care about how their beds look while harvesting abundant crops.

Reclaimed wood can make productive beds.

Not installing a barrier (if needed): Not putting a barrier at the bottom of a raised bed to prevent burrowing animals is very common. I've made this mistake too often. Gophers, voles, groundhogs, hedgehogs, and rabbits may be attracted to the rich garden bed filled with soil organisms and tasty plants. Retrofitting the bed with a wire barrier requires much more effort than installing the barrier before filling the bed. Gardeners should learn if they have burrowing animals in their area and plan accordingly.

Not building a bed to properly fit a bottom barrier can be just as bad as having no barrier at all.

All edges of the barrier need to be firmly attached to the bed base. A gap just a few inches wide may seem inconsequential to the gardener, but gophers and other burrowing critters will find it. I speak from experience. By anticipating potential problems with nature seeking the rich soil and plants in your bed, you can lessen the negative impact.

Not building a sturdy-enough bed: Soil and the water it holds can weigh a lot. When designing and building raised beds, consider the stress that soil will put on the sides of the bed. Tall beds must be strong enough to support many cubic feet of soil pushing against the sides. When beds are not sturdy enough for the volume of soil, the sides can fail — bending or breaking. Corners will separate quickly without suitable supports.

Forgetting to maintain a raised bed: Gardeners often forget that beds need regular upkeep and preservation. Using a wood preserver can add years to the life of wooden beds. Not protecting the wood may lead to early replacement. For best results, sand rough wood that could cause splinters and uneven application. There are many options for wood oil and wood preservers available at home improvement stores. This is a process that should be considered a regular part of raised bed gardening.

In time, many bed components will deteriorate. Failure of bed supports and anchors can be reduced if they are caught early. Screws and nails will eventually corrode, and regular inspection can help identify a few that are failing before the entire bed corner pulls apart. Consider replacing parts before they corrode or rust. For example, paint bare metal before it has time to rust. Replace individual bed pieces when necessary to avoid replacing an entire bed. Do basic maintenance to help your beds last longer.

A gap of a few inches lessens the effectiveness of wire barriers in deterring burrowing animals.

Applications of linseed oil can add years to wood.

Chapter 4

The Importance of Healthy Soil

The value of using good garden soil cannot be overstated. For all types of gardening, healthy soil is the key to garden success. Before any plants are selected and even before beds are built, a good plan for building rich soil will help ensure a fantastic harvest. One of the primary reasons for choosing raised bed gardening is the opportunity to fill the bed from the beginning with a good soil. This advantage is paramount.

One of the first things I learned in my Master Gardener training is that more than 80 percent of plant problems can be caused by soil issues. Gardeners often assume that poor growth or bad harvests are because they failed in some way. You can do everything correctly, but if the soil is poor then poor results can be expected. Pest attacks and disease problems are often attributable to soil deficiencies and weak plants. By improving their soil, gardeners can improve their gardening results.

What Is Soil?

Many gardeners think "dirt" and "soil" are interchangeable terms for where plants grow. I think it's important to understand that dirt has little, if any, nutrients. It has no structure and cannot support plant growth. Dirt is what we sweep off the floor and what we wash from our clothes. Soil is what plants need.

◐ The health of the soil can mean the difference between a successful garden with a bountiful harvest and one with poor yields and weak plants.

Soil is alive, filled with billions of microbes in every handful. It supports other organisms such as earthworms, fungi, nematodes, and arthropods. It naturally consists of minerals and nutrients, and has an organic matter component. A good soil has good structure and the biology and chemistry to support plant growth. The Soil Science Society of America explains that soil is "a mixture of minerals, dead and living organisms (organic materials), air, and water."

While training to be a Master Gardener, I also learned that good soil is 45 percent mineral, 25 percent air, 25 percent water, and 5 percent organic matter. However, this commonly accepted recommended composition of good, healthy soil does not correlate directly to how gardeners use good soil because it is based on the soil mass, not the volume. A rough approximation of 5 percent organic matter is about 25 percent to 30 percent of organic matter within the soil by volume. The actual amount varies depending on the density of the mineral component.

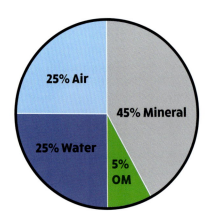

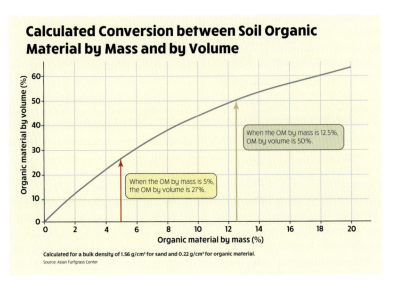

The key point is that soil is much more than dirt, with the organic matter a critical component. The nutrients that plants need come from the organic matter. With raised bed gardening, we take time to choose our beds, design them, and build them. We shouldn't shirk our gardening duties by filling the beds with dirt that can't support our plants. We should take the time to learn about soil and fill our beds with something rich and living that can provide everything our plants need. Choosing the right soil to fill raised beds should be as important a part of the garden planning process as any other.

This helps explain why so many experienced gardeners rate the ability to choose a good soil as the primary reason for gardening in raised beds. A bed filled with soil that is alive with bacteria, fungi, and other beneficial soil organisms will grow healthy plants.

The Challenges of Native Soil

Ideally, we would fill our beds with native soil, and that would have everything that plants need to grow well. Some regions have naturally rich soil and can do that, but most of us struggle with deficiencies in our native soil.

The mineral component in native soils is ample for almost all of us. The other aspects of healthy soil vary. Some of us have dry compacted soil with low air and low water levels, or sandy soil with high air and little water. Others have clay soil with low air and high water levels. The basics of the good soil components are the same, but the ratios are different for all gardeners.

It is important to note that organic matter and the accompanying nutrients are what are most lacking in most of our soils. At 5 percent of the total mass, it may not seem like much is needed, but when translated to 30 percent of the volume, we can visually recognize organic matter deficiencies. A professional soil analysis is the best way to determine precisely what the deficiencies are.

A basic analysis by a university or commercial laboratory can provide information that may include soil pH, soluble salts, texture, organic matter percentage, and levels of nutrients such as nitrates, phosphorus, and potassium. Additionally, precise levels of many other macro- and micronutrients may be an option for analysis.

The cost of a soil test is usually determined by how many different soil values are requested by the gardener. Tests for calcium, magnesium, sulfur, zinc, manganese, copper, and other elements usually cost more. Some local Extension offices offer free soil analysis through the Master Gardener desk. Home test kits can give a basic reference of pH, nitrogen, phosphorus, and potassium, but are not accurate enough for precise readings that will form the basis for corrective action.

Soil analysis is affordable for most gardeners. My state university offers basic tests beginning at U.S.$35, with many options for intensive testing at higher rates. Generally, testing does not need to be done every year. A professional analysis should be done when first setting up a garden to determine a starting point for your soil awareness — a baseline for identifying what nutrients are deficient.

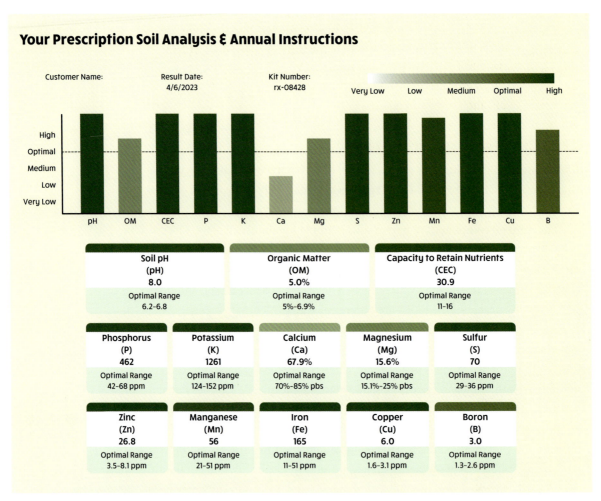

Getting a soil test before you start building your soil is a good idea. This is an example of what detailed soil test results will show you.

The Importance of Soil Organisms

There are six macronutrients that plants need for growth. Most gardeners know nitrogen (N), phosphorus (P), and potassium (K), but sulfur (S), magnesium (Mg), and calcium (Ca) are also necessary for healthy plants. Additionally, there are 21 micronutrients, including copper, iron, manganese, and arsenic, that plants need in lesser amounts. Soil naturally has some of these elemental nutrients, but soil organisms are necessary to convert them into chemical forms that plants can use.

As organic matter, such as dead plants and animals and waste, is decomposed by soil organisms, it breaks down into the core elemental nutrients mentioned earlier. Bacteria ingest nutrients and release them when they are either eaten by other organisms or die and decay in the soil. Fungi immobilize nutrients, keep them in the soil, and then die and make them available to other soil organisms. The interaction of these and other organisms in this soil enrichment process is commonly known as the soil food web.

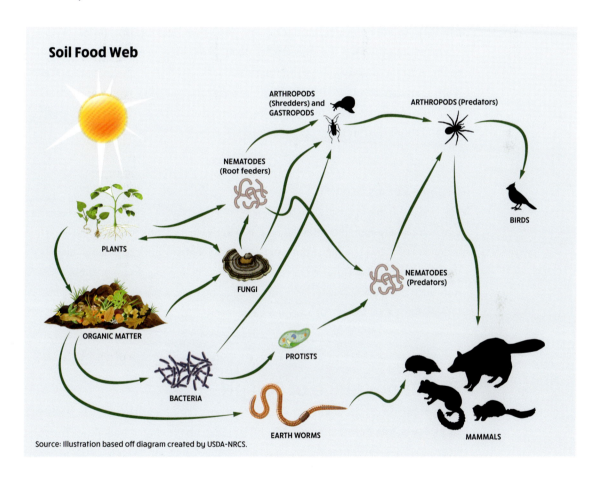

It is the life in soil that maintains nutrients in the soil. For example, soil organisms convert nitrogen into forms that plants can use, such as nitrates and ammonium. Some plants prefer one, and some plants prefer the other. Without soil organisms feeding on the organic material, there are fewer nutrients available for plant growth. When a synthetic fertilizer is applied to soil, some of the nutrients are absorbed by plants, but most of it drains out. But when soil life converts the nutrients, they are retained in the soil within the bodies of the organisms.

Too few gardeners recognize the importance of the science of soil and soil life in the garden. I highly recommend the book *Teaming with Microbes* by Jeff Lowenfels and Wayne Lewis. In it, they say that gardeners should be knowledgeable about how soils and soil food webs work because "then you can manage them so they work for you and your plants." When we recognize that we don't have to be alone in our gardening efforts, that nature and natural organisms play important roles, gardening and garden success become easier.

Providing the food that the soil life needs is a critical way we can manage them. Adding organic matter that might be deficient is an important step. When organic matter levels are low, there are fewer soil organisms and less nutrition available for plants. The inverse is true, as more organic matter provides more life and more nutrients.

> **Organic versus Organic**
>
> The type of organic material we're talking about here is different than the "organic" moniker that is applied to supermarket produce and food products. I refer to organic material that is derived from living matter. Commercial products that are labeled "organic" have been certified as organically grown or produced by certified organic growers. Kitchen scraps from such organically grown plants can certainly be used in the garden, but they are not required when we talk about adding organic material to our soil.

The Importance of Soil pH

Soil pH measures the acidity or alkalinity of soil. On a logarithmic scale, a soil pH of 7.0 is neutral. Below that, garden soil is acidic; above that, it's alkaline. You may hear seasoned gardeners refer to it as soil that is "sour" or "sweet." Most garden soils tend to have a pH between 6.0 and 7.0, and are generally considered neutral. Small changes in pH can have a big effect on plants. A soil with a pH of 6.0 is 10 times more acidic than 7.0, and a soil pH of 5.0 is 100 times more acidic than 7.0.

The soil pH affects soil health and nutrient availability to plants. Growth and yield tend to decrease with lower pH and will increase as it rises closer to neutral. Soil bacteria also tend to decline at a lower pH. Some diseases thrive when

pH Scale

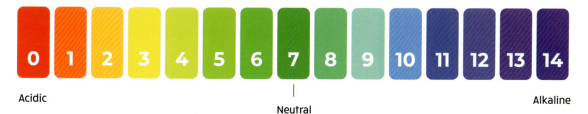

Acidic — Neutral — Alkaline

the pH is too low or too high. The ability of plants to absorb some important nutrients can cease when pH is too high. At 6.5 pH, all nutrients are available to plants. Most nutrients are present in good soil, and if there is a plant deficiency it may be due to the pH limiting the plant's ability to absorb them.

Neutral soil is important and a basic gardening goal because that is the range where most of our plants grow best. You can expect a vegetable garden with neutral soil to produce well. Of course, there are exceptions, with acid-loving plants such as blueberries and azaleas preferring a pH closer to 5.0. Lilacs and asparagus do fine in alkaline soil.

You can add ingredients to soil to adjust pH. Lime is the best amendment to raise pH, and elemental sulfur compounds are best for lowering pH. Home remedies such as vinegar, coffee, or pine needles may have a temporary effect, or no effect at all, and should not be used for a long-term pH change. Inexpensive home tests for pH can give a general idea of the acidity or alkalinity of soil, but shouldn't be relied upon as a guide for corrective action. A professional soil analysis, however, can give precise pH readings and will suggest exact remediation.

Many gardeners have soil that is slightly acidic or alkaline and see little impact on their plants, because the suitable range for plant growth is wide. If your soil rests on either side of neutral, amending with organic matter can bring it slightly closer to neutral. Ingredients such as compost can buffer soil pH and, over time, modify it.

Determining How Much Soil You Need for Your Raised Beds

It's important to begin the bed-filling process by determining the volume of the bed (or beds) to be filled. Guessing how much soil is needed invariably results in the gardener not buying or making enough soil to fill the space. When adding organic material to the soil, it's important to know how much is needed to meet the recommended 5 percent mass or 25 percent to 30 percent volume.

To determine the volume of the bed, you multiply the length by the width by the height of the bed:

Length × Width × Height = Volume

The typical raised garden bed in my garden is 8 feet long and 4 feet wide and has a soil height of 15 inches, or 1¼ feet. So, the volume of my garden bed is:

8' × 4' × 1.25' = 40 cubic feet

To fill my bed, I need 40 cubic feet of soil. It's important to note that you should aim to fill the bed completely, so the soil level reaches the top or very near the top of the bed. The soil level will sink once it's watered, so to maximize the growing space for your plants, you want to add as much soil as possible.

Low raised beds with only 9 inches of soil still require more soil than you would guess. Nine inches is ¾ foot. A 4-foot by 8-foot bed needs 24 cubic feet of soil (8' × 4' × 0.75' = 24 cubic feet). These calculations can be made for square and rectangular beds of all sizes.

The math is similar with round beds. First, find the area of the circular bed by starting with the radius (r) of the bed. The formula for the area of a circle is:

π × r² = Area

To find the volume of the bed, multiply the area by the height of the bed:

Area × Height = Volume

I have a round raised bed that is 4 feet in diameter and a height of 18 inches, or 1½ feet. Half of the diameter is the radius, so the radius of this bed is 2 feet. The volume of this round bed is:

(3.14 × 2²) × 1.5' = 18.8 cubic feet

To fill this bed, I need about 19 cubic feet of soil. Mounding or slightly overfilling a bed is okay in anticipation of the soil settling.

Knowing the cubic feet of soil needed per bed allows gardeners to compare prices and get what is needed. Bagged materials are often labeled with how many cubic feet are in the bag. Some bagged soil amendments may be labeled with how many dry quarts are contained; there are a little more than 25 dry quarts in a cubic foot.

Bulk materials are usually sold by the cubic yard, which is 27 cubic feet. You can determine how many cubic yards of soil you need to order by dividing your total cubic feet by 27. My bed, which can hold 40 cubic feet, will take about 1.5 cubic yards of soil to fill:

$$40 \div 27 = 1.48$$

In Canada, most bagged soils list the volume in liters, though they often list the cubic feet in a smaller font beside it. Nevertheless, here is a handy table to help you quickly convert both cubic meters and liters to cubic feet. To find the opposite conversion, use the opposite operation (divide instead of multiply and vice versa).

Unit	Cubic foot conversion	Calculation
Cubic meter	1 cubic meter = 35.135 cubic feet	Multiply the metric value by 35.135
Liter	1 liter = 0.035 cubic feet	Divide the metric value by 28.317

Using Bagged Soil

Buying bags labeled as "potting mix" or "garden soil" from a garden center is often the easiest approach. The idea is that you drive to the store, load up the bags, dump them in your bed, and be ready for planting. It sounds easy, and it is, but easy also means it can be the most expensive way to fill a raised bed because it is also one of the most misunderstood ways of filling a bed.

To start, gardeners almost always underestimate how many bags they need to fill their beds. Lucky for you, you now know how many cubic feet you need, and most bags are labeled with the number of cubic feet they contain. On a recent trip to the store, I found that most of the bags labeled as "garden soil" or "raised bed soil" varied between 0.75 cubic feet and 1.25 cubic feet of material per bag. It would seem, then, that for one of my typical wooden raised beds, which needs 40 cubic feet of soil, it would take approximately 32 to 54 of those bags to fill it.

Here's how that math works out. The total volume of my bed is 40 cubic feet. Divide that by the volume of the individual bags of soil. Let's assume each bag has 1.25 cubic feet of soil, so the calculation is as follows:

$$\text{Volume of bed} \div \text{Volume of bag} = \text{Number of bags}$$

$$40 \div 1.25 = 32$$

That means I need 32 bags to fill my raised bed. Buying that many individual bags would cost hundreds of dollars. On my recent trip to the garden center, I found that a name-brand 1.25-cubic-foot bag of garden soil cost U.S. $10.98. It would cost U.S. $351.36 to buy 32 bags to fill my bed with that product. Many people pay that much to buy the bags and fill their bed because they think a product labeled "garden soil" is what they need.

Not only is this approach expensive, but also it's not using the bags in the way they should be used. The bags sold as garden soil don't have any actual mineral-based soil in them. They are organic materials that are meant to be mixed with the gardener's native soil. If you read the directions on the bag, you're told to spread 2 inches to 3 inches of the bagged garden soil in the area for planting, then mix it into the top 6 inches to 8 inches of actual soil. By volume, the

Garden centers have many options for bagged soil.

The ingredients in bagged soil are organic matter.

bagged garden soil ends up being about a quarter or a third of the total volume of the soil where the plants will go. That corresponds to the recommended 25 percent to 30 percent organic matter by volume found in good soil.

Filling a raised bed with just bagged garden soil overuses the organic matter in it, wastes money, and isn't necessary. Instead, bagged soil should be used as an amendment to improve the native soil that is most likely lacking in organic matter. Using bagged soil without mixing it in native soil means the bed will be almost entirely organic matter with no mineral component.

You can save substantial amounts of money if the bagged products are used correctly. If I follow the recommended guidance of 25 percent to 30 percent organic matter by volume in a bed that holds 40 cubic feet of soil, that bed only requires about 10 cubic feet to 12 cubic feet of bagged garden soil. So, instead of needing 32 to 54 bags to fill a raised bed, depending on the volume of each bag, that number could be as few as eight bags. Assuming again that the volume of the bag is 1.25 cubic feet, this is how the math would work out:

25 percent to 30 percent of Volume of bed ÷ Volume of bag = Number of bags

10 ÷ 1.25 = 8

That lowers the cost to fill a bed from hundreds of dollars to a fraction of that.

Look Out for Damaged Bags

If you must buy bagged soil and amendments, look for torn or damaged bags. With a little searching of your garden center, you may find the hidden corner where they sell "ugly" bags at a big discount. If you don't see it, ask a manager because they may be hidden in the back.

You can also try buying bags of soil and other amendments during end-of-season sales. When garden centers are clearing inventory for holiday merchandise, buy the products that you may not need right away but will be useful in spring, though avoid buying what you won't use.

Using Bulk Soil

A slightly more cost-effective option is to buy garden soil in bulk from a landscaping supply store. These businesses offer rock, gravel, and soil in bulk. From huge mounds on their lots, a front-end loader can scoop up the soil a cubic yard at a time. As you may recall, a cubic yard is the equivalent of 27 cubic feet. For my raised bed of 40 cubic feet, it would take just under 1.5 cubic yards of bulk soil to fill it, or just a couple of scoops from the loader.

Bulk soil contains actual soil and not just organic material. Some of the bulk soil I get from my local sand and stone company is an equal blend of topsoil, composted cow manure, and aged humus. This works out to be roughly 33 percent mineral and 66 percent organic material (manure and humus) by volume. They sell a similar mix that is an equal blend of topsoil, manure, and compost, which works out to be 33 percent mineral and 66 percent organic material as well. They also sell a blend of three parts topsoil to one part compost (or 75 percent mineral and 25 percent organic material).

Bulk soil is a good option and can be more cost-effective if you are planning on using lots.

This third mix is suitable for filling a bed and planting right away. With 25 percent organic matter, it fits the definition of good soil with no extra effort. The blends with 66 percent organic matter are closer to bagged garden soil in how they should be used in the garden. Mixing it with native soil can bring the overall organic matter closer to 25 percent to 30 percent.

One cubic yard (27 cubic feet) of a bulk soil blend with 66 percent organic matter is 9 cubic feet of mineral content and 18 cubic feet of organic matter. Adding 13 cubic feet of native soil brings us up to the amount we need to fill a 40-cubic-foot bed. With the native soil, the ratio of mineral to organic material then becomes 22 cubic feet of mineral content to 18 cubic feet of organic matter. The amount of organic matter is 45 percent by volume — higher than the recommended 25 percent to 30 percent — but much closer than the original 66 percent. To achieve that ratio in any amount, add one part native soil to two parts bulk soil.

To get your soil closer to the target of 30 percent organic matter, mix a bulk blend with 66 percent organic material one-to-one with your native soil. Mixing 1 cubic yard (27 cubic feet) of native soil to 1 cubic yard of bulk soil gives us 36 cubic feet of mineral content and 18 cubic feet of organic material. That works out to be 33 percent organic matter, which is ideal for planting. By mixing with native garden soil, a bulk soil blend results in an even lower overall cost when compared to bags.

The biggest limitation to using bulk soil is getting it to your garden. I have a trailer and can drive it to the lot, get 1.5 cubic yards of a soil blend, drive it home, and use it in my beds. Depending on the blend, the total cost is about 30 percent to 50 percent less than using bags and mixing them by hand. Most landscape supply businesses can deliver soil to gardeners without a truck or trailer. However, there is a delivery fee, and it can be much more than the cost of 1 cubic yard or 2 cubic yards of soil. If it's going to be delivered, I suggest getting many cubic yards of soil for multiple beds to make it more cost-effective.

Get Bulk Soil with a Buddy

Going in with another gardener to split the cost of a bulk soil shipment will let you share the savings. Have a larger quantity delivered, and you both can use the pile as you need it.

Know the Ingredients

The choice of bagged or bulk soil will affect what you grow and when you can grow it. It's important to read the bag label or description from the landscape company to understand what the ingredients are. I know the ratios of my bulk soil blends because I researched them before buying. It's also important to know that in many areas, there are no regulations on what ingredients can be used in soil blends.

Buying topsoil is of particular concern. Look at a bag of topsoil from the garden center, and you'll probably see no ingredient list or a description of where it was sourced. And the more you talk to fellow gardeners, the more you'll hear horror stories of what they've found in bags of topsoil — from disposable diapers to rusted tin cans and broken bottles. Bulk topsoil is often what is scraped from construction sites before excavating the foundation. You can expect that it will be sifted to remove rocks, but there is no guarantee of its quality. I go into the landscape supply company's lot and physically inspect the material before buying.

Many of the bagged potting mixes and garden soil bags will include an ingredient list. Blends of peat moss, coconut coir, compost, and other organic material are what you can expect. Often "forest products" is in the list of ingredients. This is a loosely defined term for ground bark and wood. It may be a good material for absorbing and holding water, but it is not good for plant nutrition. The woody pieces need to decompose before any of their nutrients are available for plants. The pieces will vary in size and may be quite chunky, making decomposition a long-term proposition.

Many bagged compost mixes are similar. The material will vary with different stages of decomposition and probably won't be

fully decomposed. Some may appear to be nothing but wood chips. Mushroom compost can be of different types: it can be a rich, mostly broken-down product that is the byproduct of growing mushrooms, or it can be the raw wood pieces that are typically used in growing mushrooms. Reading the bag and inspecting the contents can be insightful for ensuring that what you are getting is what you really want.

The US Composting Council has a Seal of Testing Assurance (STA) Program that helps ensure proficiency and consistency with testing procedures and consistency within a network of compost producers and testing labs. You may see a bag labeled as "Certified Compost®" when it meets the specified STA standards. You can expect that a certified bag should provide a higher quality product than generic bags.

Meanwhile in Canada ...

The Bureau de normalisation du Québec (BNQ) developed the CAN/BNQ 0413-200 standard for compost manufacturers. This standard ensures any composts that bear this certification label are safe for human health, animals, plants, and the environment. The certification is accredited by the Standards Council of Canada.

Affordable Compost Sources

If you haven't started already, you should definitely make your own compost. You can easily recycle your kitchen scraps and yard waste into nutrient-rich compost that benefits soil organisms and your plants. Everything organic from your garden can go in the compost pile, and it will reward you with free compost that you know is high quality.

There are other free options: Many cities and municipalities offer free compost if you load it yourself. It can disappear fast once gardeners discover it, but it is replenished regularly. Talk to your local waste and recycling office about when new loads are available. Some local businesses or nonprofits accept yard waste and turn it into compost that is available in bulk at low cost or free. Community gardens and large nurseries may also offer compost.

As I touched on previously, bagged products labeled as "garden soil" will be filled with organic material and rarely include actual mineral-based soil. These growing media are referred to as soil-less mixes because they don't meet the definition of actual soil. They don't contain inorganic materials such as sand, clay, or silt — the key ingredients for good soil structure. The bags of potting mixes and garden soil often contain perlite or vermiculite to improve soil drainage, but because perlite and vermiculite are inorganic, they won't add much to the development of soil structure or provide nutritional value.

These mixes are also often sterile and devoid of beneficial soil organisms. Mixing the bags with native soil will introduce soil microbes and other soil life that are essential in breaking down the organic matter into usable nutrients for plants. Without the addition of the microbes, it can take more time for the organic materials in the bagged mixes to become effective for plants.

To overcome this deficiency, many bagged mixes have added fertilizers. They will be listed in the ingredients list. The fertilizers provide immediate plant nutrition while the bulky materials slowly decompose. Often they are slow-release fertilizers designed to last over a period of time as they dissolve. The fertilizers focus on adding nitrogen, phosphorus, and potassium (NPK) to the sterile mixes. This attention to NPK focuses on some of the primary macronutrients that plants need, but it does little to add the other macronutrients and micronutrients that benefit plant growth.

Many bulk soil providers sell similar products. My local provider sells one that consists of composted brewery waste, biosolids, and wood fiber. Intended as a soil amendment like the bagged products, it is exclusively organic materials with no soil added. My area of Colorado includes many brew pubs that make their own beer. I like seeing the waste products of brewing find their way into compost. One advantage of using products from a local business is that you can ask about the source material, and usually someone can tell you how they make the blend.

This becomes more important for gardeners who are concerned about the soil they grow their food in. The product that gets a lot of attention is biosolids. Biosolids is another name for composted sewer sludge. Yes, human waste is included in part of the process, along with other organic materials in wastewater. There are many state and local requirements to ensure pathogens are killed, and the material is suitable as a garden soil amendment for home gardens. Milorganite® is a popular brand of fertilizer made from biosolids and

Brewer's spent grain is a component of some soil amendment blends. This is a great use of beer-brewing waste products, and it might be something available to you if you have local breweries.

may be an ingredient in some commercial mixes. Biosolids are deemed safe for home applications.

Manure is a common amendment in home gardens. Plant-eating animals provide a waste material high in organic matter and nutrients. Bags of composted manure are available at garden centers, and composted manure is frequently mixed into bulk blends. It is most often poultry, cow, or steer manure. Exercise some caution when using manure products because salt levels can be high, and manures from commercial feedlots or farms may include antibiotics. I suggest trying to find a local source for manure, so you can ask the supplier about the product. Avoid using the excrement from meat-eating animals such as cats and dogs because of potential pathogens and health risks.

Soil Blends

Bagged or bulk ingredients are foundational materials for garden soil blends. The ratios may be given to you by a landscape company, or you can use your basic understanding of mixing native soil with organic matter to create a blend. When first starting with custom soil mixes, it can be helpful to know how other gardeners do it. Here are three soil blend recipes for you to study: Mel's Mix, the "Perfect Soil" Recipe, and Gardener Scott's Mix.

Mel's Mix

In 1976, Mel Bartholomew developed a process for gardening he called the Square Foot Gardening method. His 1981 book, *Square Foot Gardening*, revolutionized how many home gardeners plan and plant their garden beds. I used some of his recommendations from the second edition of his book *All New Square Foot Gardening* to help develop my gardening plans and to prepare some of my raised beds.

As Bartholomew was developing his method, he recognized that soil was key to gardening success. In his first book, he showed how he laid out a bed measuring 4 feet by 4 feet, dug out 6 inches of soil, and mixed it with 2 inches of peat moss, 2 inches of vermiculite, and 2 inches of compost. The resulting blend became 12 inches of rich soil for plants. The primary purpose of peat moss is to retain soil moisture. Vermiculite retains some water, but is primarily used to improve drainage. (Neither peat moss nor vermiculite provides nutrients to plants.) The compost provides the minerals and nutrients that benefit plants. Approximately one-third of the blend is organic matter from the compost and peat moss. This assumes that the native soil, like the soil in my garden, is deficient in organic matter and nutrients. A native soil with higher natural levels could help create a new soil blend much higher in organic matter.

In *All New Square Foot Gardening*, Bartholomew modified his approach to gardening by focusing on creating a raised bed with no digging. His suggested raised bed is built 6 inches high from common lumber available from home improvement stores. The beds are designed to provide a permanent grid for using the Square Foot Gardening method. Placed anywhere in the yard and without digging up the soil underneath, the beds are filled with what he calls "Mel's Mix."

Mel's Mix is an equal mix of peat moss, vermiculite, and blended compost. It is no longer mixed with native garden soil but is used as a growing medium for plants with just those three ingredients. Mel's Mix contains 66 percent organic matter. Bartholomew's reasoning, as he explains in the book, is that his mix is close to the same soil-less mixes that professional greenhouse growers use. He feels his is the perfect bed soil because it's lightweight, nutrient-rich, and holds moisture well.

Plant nutrition is supplied by the compost. Bartholomew stresses that the compost should be a blend of different composts, not just one type of bagged

Soil Composition: Mel's Mix

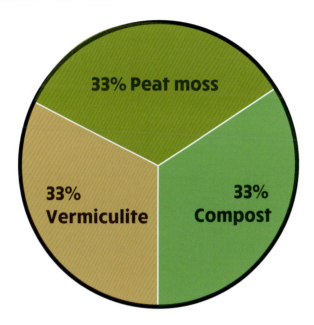

product. All composts are unique, depending on the organic material that was decomposed to make it, and blending composts helps supply varying amounts of nutrients from the different source materials. In a soil-less mix lacking soil minerals, there might be nutrient deficiencies that require the use of fertilizers.

The "Perfect Soil" Recipe

You may have seen the award-winning television series *Growing a Greener World*, distributed by American Public Television and airing on PBS stations. The show's host, Joe Lamp'l, also known as "Joe Gardener," comfortably explains his methods in a garden filled with beautiful raised beds. Lamp'l developed his own method for blending a soil mix to fill them.

Lamp'l refers to his blend as the "Perfect Soil" Recipe. Lamp'l allows for some personalization when making a soil mix without having to follow a specific recipe. His blend begins with 50 percent high-quality topsoil, then he adds 30 percent high-quality compost, and finishes with 20 percent additional materials from his preferred list: leaves, mineralized soil blend, worm castings, mushroom compost, ground bark, or composted cow or poultry manure. He recommends selecting 5 percent each of four products from that list. He encourages the use of mineralized soil as one ingredient choice, and if it is used, his mix can be as high as 45 percent organic matter.

Soil Composition: "Perfect Soil" Recipe

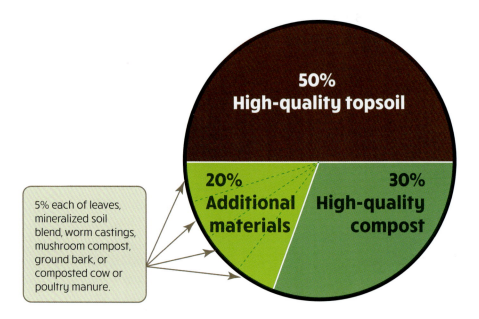

5% each of leaves, mineralized soil blend, worm castings, mushroom compost, ground bark, or composted cow or poultry manure.

I like Lamp'l's approach of focusing on soil health when filling a bed. Like me, he prefers to feed the soil and not the plants, because a healthy soil can provide all the nutrients plants need. His method stresses the organic aspect of building good soil and promoting the billions of beneficial soil organisms that are key to soil health. It's important to note that he stresses using high-quality ingredients when developing a good soil.

Using topsoil — bagged, bulk, or from your backyard — adds an important mineral and structural component to the mix. Using high levels of organic matter does not imply it is wrong. It's just higher than the widely accepted ratio of 25 percent to 30 percent by volume. Because more organic matter means more soil organisms and more plant nutrients, it can be a good approach when first filling a bed.

There are a few key differences in Bartholomew's and Lamp'l's approaches. Lamp'l uses topsoil, and Bartholomew doesn't. Bartholomew uses peat moss, and Lamp'l doesn't. Bartholomew creates a mix that is immediately ready for plants with a blend and process similar to commercial growers. Lamp'l uses organic and local materials with an acknowledgment that good soil can take years to develop. Bartholomew's blend is a specific recipe, while Lamp'l's allows for variation.

There are some similarities. Both recommend getting the ingredients together and mixing them thoroughly to fill a bed the first time. Both aim for a blend that is more than 30 percent organic material by volume. Both recommend high-quality bagged compost if you don't make your own. Both aim to make the process as easy as possible.

Gardener Scott's Mix

I'm often asked about my recipe, formula, or ratio for filling raised beds. Because organic matter is a critical component of soil health, I aim for at least 5 percent organic matter by mass, with a soil blend of at least 30 percent organic matter by volume. I acknowledge that native soil often has some organic matter in it, and that can affect how much additional organic matter is really needed when creating a soil blend in the garden. Because some of my native soil has less than 1 percent organic matter, I begin with the assumption that it is zero.

I approach my soil building as a long-term part of gardening and recognize that getting all the ingredients together before filling your beds can be cost prohibitive for some gardeners, particularly when filling many beds. Starting small by filling one or two beds and in time filling additional beds when expanding a garden is how many gardeners actually build their growing spaces. Few of us start from day one with a garden filled with all the beds we will ever have. So my approach to soil building allows for variation in time and ingredients.

Using Materials You Have on Hand

There are several advantages to using the soil and organic materials you have in your yard. If you're trying to keep things affordable, it can be a real challenge to use recommended recipes when you have to buy everything. I'm a frugal gardener, and I try to avoid buying soil ingredients if I can use organic materials I source from my landscape. The organic materials can be interchangeable, as long as they meet the minimum volume goal. Dried grass, crushed leaves, homemade compost, and worm castings from a basement bin are all viable options for me. Local sources of alpaca, cow, horse, and chicken manure add to the selection of ingredients.

Using materials from your own yard also gives you complete control over the quality of the ingredients. The expensive bagged ingredients are often screened and may be certified, but determining where they came from and if they have any contaminants may be impossible.

The materials I choose can vary through the season. A bed filled in summer might have more grass clippings. A bed filled in autumn might have more leaves. When compost from my compost bin is ready to use, it will be added to beds. As a result, my raised beds have different compositions as determined by the ingredients I had on hand when I filled the bed. To achieve some consistency, I save bags of leaves to use throughout the year and not just in fall. I have bags of dried grass for the same purpose. I keep a garbage can filled with compost that I can add, and I have one with leaf mold, too.

Keeping bags of grass and leaves from your own yard is an affordable way to amend your beds with high-quality organic materials.

The basic composition of my raised bed soil is simply this: 60 percent native soil, 20 percent compost, and 20 percent other organic materials. My blend aims for a total of 40 percent organic matter, and that organic matter can be a combination of many materials. Mixing multiple organic ingredients will make for healthier soil. I look at soil building like making a pizza. You can make a cheese pizza that is relatively bland and lacking in multiple nutrients. Or you can make a combination pizza packed with every ingredient from sausage and pepperoni to olives and peppers. Good, rich soil is like a combination pizza, packed with a variety of organic ingredients — from grass and leaves to aged alpaca and chicken manure.

Soil Composition: Gardener Scott's Mix

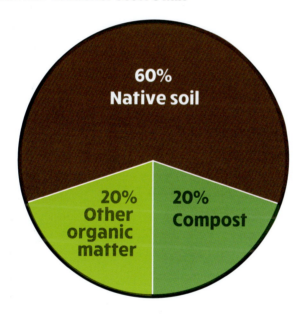

It doesn't need to be a precise recipe. It's a target, a rough ratio, a guideline. In practice, I dig up my native soil and fill my wheelbarrow about 60 percent full. Then I dump fresh compost from my bin (or a bag of high-quality compost), so that it's about 20 percent of the wheelbarrow. I finish with a blend of crushed leaves, leaf mold, grass, sawdust, manure, worm castings, coffee grounds, peat moss, ground bark, and even brewer's waste to fill another 20 percent. When I dump the wheelbarrow into the bed, I mix the ingredients together.

My wheelbarrow showing rough ratios of soil, compost, and other organic materials. Actual ingredients will vary by availability.

When I build a lot of beds for a new garden and want to fill them quickly, I'll start with a purchased bulk soil blend. I'll mix a blend that is 66 percent organic with my native soil using the one-to-one ratio described on page 117 to get 33 percent organic matter. To that I add my compost, leaves, grass, worm castings, and any of the other organic ingredients to achieve my 40 percent organic goal.

For filling a typical bed that needs 1.5 cubic yards (about 40 cubic feet) of soil, the appropriate proportions end up being half a cubic yard (13.5 cubic feet) of bulk soil with half a cubic yard of my native soil. To complete the fill, the other half a yard (about 13 cubic feet) is an equal, one-to-one blend of native soil and a mix of organic matter.

Adjust to Your Soil's Needs
Remember, because my native soil has less than 1 percent organic matter, I consider it to be close to zero when calculating the ratio of ingredients. For gardeners with richer native soil, you will need to add less organic material to achieve the target 40 percent.

Creating Your Own Blend

I make my own blend because good soil doesn't need to be purchased or made from purchased products. It just needs to have a blend of minerals, air, water, and organic matter. Most gardeners have ample minerals in their native soil that can easily be aerated and soaked with water. Simply starting with the soil you have and adding an organic component can be a successful approach. There will be labor involved to dig and mix everything together, but there can be a huge cost saving, too.

You can easily choose one of the recipes above as a starting point for developing a recipe of your own. You can use the precise ingredients of Mel's Mix. You can use specific ingredients in fixed ratios for Lamp'l's "Perfect Soil." You can use bagged or bulk products and material from your landscape for Gardener Scott's Mix. In his book *Simplify Vegetable Gardening*, my friend Tony O'Neill recommends simply mixing compost with soil dug from pathways to fill raised beds. The fact is, all of us have had success growing plants in our respective mixes. The consistent aspect of the soil recipes from these different sources is the addition of organic matter to create a rich soil with abundant lifeforms that make nutrients available to plants.

It can be difficult for a home gardener to determine what their actual soil composition is when blending soil-less mixes, native soil, and landscape organics. This is another reason I advocate getting a soil laboratory analysis completed as one of the first steps when starting a garden. Knowing how much organic matter your soil has can help you understand how to fill your raised beds.

Once loaded with a sense of your soil's composition, you may wonder how to choose a soil mix when there are so many options. If there were a single best way, we would all be doing it. Because there are many choices, it shows that there are many "best ways." What works best for me, or Mel Bartholomew, or Joe Lamp'l may not work for you. It's not until you choose a blend and begin growing in it that you'll know what you and your plants prefer. Another reason all my raised beds have different soil compositions is because I'm always trying new things to find what works best.

Gardeners don't need all the answers when creating their first soil blend. None of us gardens the same way now as we did when we first started. Experience helps us improve. A great way to develop experience and knowledge is to experiment in the garden, and experimenting with soil happens to be easy. Over time, modifying how we build our soil allows us the opportunity to develop our ideal soil.

Adding Other Amendments

Just like the ingredient selection when making a combination pizza, the ingredients for a soil blend are virtually endless. There are other materials I like to add to my mix if they're available.

Biochar: Biochar is an inorganic material that can improve soil quality. Biochar is made from burning biomass in a process called pyrolysis. Biochar is similar to charcoal, but the pyrolysis method removes the liquids and volatile gases in the organic material and leaves behind the solid portion of the biomass in a stable form of carbon. It can contain some nutrients, depending on the organic material source, but its primary benefits are to increase the water-holding capacity of soil and to provide a structure to house beneficial soil microbes. It doesn't decompose and lasts indefinitely in soil.

Biochar looks like charcoal.

I was lucky enough to work with a rancher friend who turns biomass from his ranch into biochar with his own pyrolysis equipment. His analysis of the biochar showed it to be high in calcium and potassium, because he primarily used bones as his biomass. I ran tests in many beds to determine the biochar's effectiveness. I didn't conduct soil analysis, but I did compare plant health and production. It was clear that the beds amended with biochar produced bigger and healthier plants. Many studies have shown biochar to have a positive effect on crops.

Worm castings: Worm castings are essentially earthworm manure. Like manures from plant-eating animals, worm castings can provide organic matter and nutrients to soil. As earthworms eat organic materials during their tunneling, their guts break it down and incorporate bacteria. The resulting castings are rich in beneficial ingredients.

Worm castings are typically bagged, but you can choose to vermicompost for your own homegrown worm castings.

Worm castings can be purchased from most plant nurseries, many home improvement stores, and many online sources. Large quantities can be expensive, and castings are typically used in smaller applications such as making potting soil mixes. The specialty worms for making castings are available online, and gardeners can begin vermicomposting (using worms to eat kitchen scraps and other organic materials) at home. Homegrown worm castings can be an economical way to incorporate them into soil blends.

Perlite almost resembles small, white popped popcorn.

Vermiculite and perlite: Vermiculite and perlite are inorganic materials that can be good soil amendments. Perlite is made from heating obsidian, and the result is a lightweight mineral that improves drainage and airflow within the soil. It has porous cavities like biochar, but has minimal effectiveness in storing soil nutrients and moisture.

Vermiculite is made from heating mica. Vermiculite is lightweight and effective at improving soil drainage, and it does hold slightly more moisture than perlite.

Both vermiculite and perlite are sterile, don't affect soil pH, and add no nutritional value. They don't decompose because they're inorganic and like biochar will stay in soil indefinitely. In regions

Vermiculite can resemble little brown accordions.

with heavy clay soil, adding either to a mix along with native soil and organic matter can help improve drainage that might otherwise be a problem. Bought in bulk, it can be a cost-effective way to improve soil. Even though it holds a small amount of moisture, Mel Bartholomew preferred vermiculite over perlite to counter the water-retaining benefits of peat moss.

Sulfur and lime: If soil pH is a problem in native soil — too high or too low — sulfur and lime are common amendments to balance soil pH. Sulfur increases soil acidity, leading to a lower pH. Lime reduces soil acidity, leading to a higher pH, and adds calcium and magnesium to the soil. Using elemental ingredients such as these is the preferred method for modifying soil acidity. They can provide long-lasting fixes. Avoid "tips" you see on social media for using household products. If it works, and it seldom does, organic ingredients like those will break down quickly and only affect the soil pH for a very short time.

Coconut coir: Coconut coir (coco coir) is a fibrous material made from the husk of coconuts. It is interchangeable with peat moss for improving the water retention in soil. It adds no nutrients to soil and has little effect on soil pH. Many countries do not have access to peat moss or are legislating against using it because it is not a sustainable product in their region. Coco coir is often a viable replacement. Initially a byproduct of the coconut industry, some countries are now clearing land and growing coconut orchards for the purpose of harvesting the husks to make coir.

Sold in dry, compressed blocks, coir is reconstituted by soaking it in water. Coir is initially hydrophobic, meaning that it repels water in its dry state. Once hydrated, the material can be mixed with other organic materials and native soil for a soil blend. The resulting mix should be kept moist. If the soil dries out, it can take a lot of time and water to rehydrate the coir and get it back to the point when it's most beneficial.

Coco coir stays moist, improving water retention in soil.

Peat moss: Peat moss is used primarily for improving water retention in soil, but it can also help aerate the soil. The peat moss I use comes from Canada, from manufacturers striving to produce it as sustainably as possible. Canadian peat moss is readily available throughout the United States and is an affordable option for home gardeners. That option may not be available to gardeners from other countries. Throughout Europe, peat moss is no longer available and may actually be outlawed in some places. In the regions where coco coir is produced, coir is more prevalent and is usually less expensive than imported peat.

Peat moss is dry in the bag.

Leaf mold: Leaf mold (leaf mould) is a great ingredient and can be a substitute for peat moss or coco coir. It is simply decomposed leaves. Light and crumbly, it is loaded with beneficial minerals and can hold a great amount of water. It is made like compost — with a big pile of leaves that is allowed to decompose. While it's easy to do at home, it can take more than a year for the leaves to break down completely. The dark brown forest floor is primarily leaf mold made by nature, but home gardeners can make it using fallen leaves. Fungi are the primary decomposition mechanism for the leaves, and leaf mold incorporates those beneficial fungi into garden beds.

Leaf mold resembles fine compost.

Sand: Sand is commonly used to add drainage in a soil-less mix, but it can be a problem when added to clay soils. It's a common misconception that the porosity that sand provides means that it will improve drainage when added to clay. It might do that only in very large amounts — beyond what is possible for most homeowners. Typically, clay binds with sand to create a soil structure similar to concrete, and that can make a bad situation worse. The density of the resulting sand–clay blend will be too much for plant roots to grow in easily.

Wood ash: Wood ash is the powdery residue remaining after wood has burned. It is a common amendment in many areas, but it should be used with caution. Wood ash adds calcium and potassium to soil, along with other nutrients, but it can also add salt and heavy metals. Of more concern is that it can raise soil pH. For gardens with acidic soil, wood ash can bring soil near to a neutral pH, but for regions with alkaline soil, wood ash can raise the pH beyond levels that plants can effectively grow in. Soil tests should be done before using ash. For gardeners who use wood ash, it is another amendment that can be made at home from known source material.

Filling Your Beds

You've built your raised bed, and you've chosen your soil blend. Now it's time to fill the bed. This section gives you some practical advice on when and how to do this.

When to Fill Your Beds

While you may be anxious to start your raised bed in spring, at the start of the growing season, in my opinion, the best time of year to build and fill your raised beds is in the autumn — after the busy schedules of summer have calmed down. Not only will you have used a full growing season to thoughtfully reflect on what kind of bed you're going to build and where best to place it, but you'll also be benefiting your soil.

Soil organisms and microbes need time to populate the bed and decompose organic matter to make nutrients available to plants. Raised beds built in spring and filled with soil soon after may not have had enough time for soil organisms to do their magic and release nutrients, particularly when the soil contains rough materials such as grass, leaves, and food scraps. It takes time for raw ingredients to decompose in a new soil blend. During that process, nitrogen, a critical macronutrient, is necessary for the soil organisms to function. It's also necessary for the growth of your plants. If plants are brought in at the same time as the new soil, they'll be competing with the soil life for the available nitrogen. The plants rarely win that battle, and as a result the soil may develop a nitrogen deficiency while the soil organisms use the bulk of it. Plants that are deficient in nitrogen usually have smaller leaves and fruit, slower growth, and yellowing older leaves.

Filling raised beds in fall gives soil organisms many months to build a healthy, rich, living soil and lessens the likelihood of a nitrogen deficiency the next growing season. The cumulative months of autumn, then winter, then early spring provide ample time for the soil life population to explode and break down the raw organic materials. As organic matter decomposes, nutrient levels increase within the soil.

Fall weather is still good for working in the garden and, for me, is the ideal time to fill my new beds.

There is some concern that when beds are filled too early, they end up leaching a lot of the beneficial nitrogen during winter, before the plants can use it. There are different forms of nitrogen in the soil. The primary form that plants use, nitrate (NO_3), is mobile and easily moved by water. Leaching of nitrates shouldn't be too much of a worry if the soil you build is filled with organic matter that retains water well. It is possible in regions with continual rainfall in winter that some leaching can occur, but simply covering the beds with plastic sheets or tarps can eliminate that concern. I think forgoing the early preparation of soil in autumn to offset the chance that some of the nitrogen might leach away fails to recognize the benefits that soil organisms bring with time.

If you decide to fill beds in spring, it may be necessary to account for the nitrogen concerns using fertilizers. Experienced gardeners do not include fertilizers in their soil mixes because fertilizers are not necessary when soil life naturally releases the organic nutrients into the soil. A fertilizer with nitrogen in it can bridge the gap created by a nitrogen deficiency and give young plants what they need for good growth. It can be organic or synthetic. Plants won't know the difference as they seek the nitrogen they need.

When I fill raised beds in spring, I increase the amount of worm castings I add to my blend. Though it is a small percentage, worm castings add nitrogen to the soil naturally. I still try to give as much time as possible before planting to lessen the chance of a nitrogen deficiency. Allowing at least two months between filling a bed and putting in plants can make a difference.

For even less time before planting, I add blood meal to my mix. Blood meal is much higher in nitrogen. It is not a quick-release fertilizer, and soil organisms still need to break it down, but that doesn't take many months. Fish emulsion is another alternative, but it breaks down more slowly and should be used as early as possible.

A potential problem is that it can be difficult to determine how much fertilizer is needed. Without a soil test, we don't know if there is a deficiency or to what degree it might be. It is a guess to choose the proper amount of fertilizer, and you may inadvertently feed your plants too

Spring bed filling often involves topping off the beds with organic matter.

much nitrogen. This can be detrimental to plants because it focuses the plant on growing new stems and new leaves at the expense of growing flowers and fruit. Carrots in beds with too much nitrogen will have big bushy tops and tiny, shriveled roots. Pepper plants with too much nitrogen may have lush green growth but little, if any, fruit development.

An alternative to guessing about the best quantity of organic fertilizers is to use synthetic fertilizers and follow the recommended application on the label. Synthetic fertilizers are in chemical forms immediately available to plants. Many gardeners have used synthetic fertilizers for years as part of their normal garden practice. The fertilizer feeds the plants and not the soil. Multiple applications are used at the beginning and through the end of the growing season.

For gardeners desiring to limit the use of fertilizers when building their own healthy soil, an option is to go without and then pay attention to the plants as they grow. If plant growth looks normal and they are green and strong, no fertilizer is necessary. If plants look stunted and leaves begin to yellow, an application of synthetic fertilizer can have an almost immediate impact. Until the soil life provides enough nutrients, occasional fertilizer use can help.

How to Fill Your Beds

The actual process of filling a raised bed is pretty basic. Soil is transferred from bags, heaping mounds, tarps, or wherever it is sourced to the raised bed using wheelbarrows, shovels, buckets, and hands. For premixed blends, it is simply moving it from point A to point B. There are tools required, and moving soil will take effort, but it is within the abilities of most gardeners. Soil blends can be a little more challenging, as you have to mix your soil ingredients as you're filling. Before I give you some pointers on that, let us discuss how you can fill tall beds without wasting too much money on soil.

The Bottom Layer of Tall Beds

One of the disadvantages of using raised beds is that they can cost more than other gardening methods. Don't exacerbate that concern by filling a raised bed with expensive soil or adding purchased amendments unnecessarily. Particularly in tall beds, the lower portion of the bed is too low for many roots to reach. Since the roots aren't growing that deep, the soil doesn't need to be as rich and healthy. The bottom section of tall beds can be filled with native soil and free organic materials at no cost.

This is the approach I take for my tall raised beds. I consider any bed more than 15 inches high as tall. Most vegetable plants can do well in a rich soil of 12 inches to 18 inches. Even for deep-rooted plants such as tomatoes or squash, which have roots that grow 18 inches to 24 inches long, most of the roots in our vegetable garden beds with good soil will be in the top 15 inches as they spread laterally in the soil. Below that, the soil richness is not as important and can be more basic.

My approach is to fill those lower bed levels with branches, wood chips, logs, leaves, and any other organic materials I have in my landscape. They are not part of a soil blend. They are raw ingredients at the bed bottom. As those materials go in the bed, I will add my poor native soil to fill in air gaps between them. In time, the organic matter will decompose and enrich the soil. The woody material encourages the growth of fungi, and the decomposing matter encourages beneficial bacteria and soil organisms such as earthworms. This can be a good way to build healthy soil from the bottom of the bed, while amendments such as compost and organic mulch can build healthy soil from the top of the bed.

The concept originates from the basics of Hugelkultur, a horticultural technique where wood and other plant materials form the foundation of a mounded raised bed. Translated as "hill culture," Hugelkultur has been used for centuries in Europe and more recently is a component of permaculture gardening methods. Normal yard waste, such as branches and leaves, is reused as a base material and covered with layers of organic matter such as manure, compost, grass clippings, and soil. Plants of all types are planted in the top layers of soil.

Wood chips, branches, and small logs can fill the bottom of the bed, especially tall beds.

There is little reason not to try this cost-saving way to fill tall beds. Whether you use purchased soil or free organic materials from your yard to fill the bottom, the material in the bed will be decomposing and enriching soil life. The only thing it may affect is the gardener's budget. Using a modified Hugelkultur method saves money, in addition to providing benefits with the organic additives.

Mixing and Filling with Soil Blends

If you're creating a soil blend from a recipe — whether your own or someone else's — you will need to find a way of mixing your ingredients in the correct proportions. There are a couple of ways of doing this. Putting a tarp or sheet on the ground and mixing piles of ingredients is a good option if all the ingredients in the right proportions are easy to lay out, which might be the case if you're using bagged ingredients.

Personally, I find it hard to judge exact proportions when my ingredients come from a variety of sources. I typically keep my ingredients in separate mounds or bags and mix the ingredients in my wheelbarrow as I fill my beds. For example, to meet the 40 percent goal for my recipe, I know I need two shovels of bulk soil, three shovels of native soil, and one shovel of organic material. The materials are roughly mixed as I load the wheelbarrow, and as I shovel out of the wheelbarrow into the bed they all mix together more. The way I fill my wheelbarrow gives me about 4 cubic feet of material per load.

I find that filling beds like this corresponds to how most gardeners garden. We don't have large containers with precise measuring lines, and we don't know how to measure out a cubic foot of anything, but we can match how much we put into each shovel load in a wheelbarrow. As long as we mix the ingredients using similar scoops, the exact process is flexible.

I blend materials as I fill the wheelbarrow.

If my ingredients are not in the same location — usually because my load of bulk soil is in my front yard, and everything else is in the backyard — I'll fill the wheelbarrow with bulk soil, push the wheelbarrow to my garden, and unload it in the bed. Then I'll go to the area in my backyard to dig up a wheelbarrow load of native soil and then unload it. Then I'll add bagged compost or grass or leaves to the bed and roughly mix everything with my shovel. It isn't a perfect way to blend, but I feel it's easier than moving everything to a central area, mixing it all, and then moving it to my garden to fill the bed.

In some cases, you can dump each wheelbarrow load directly into the bed from all sides without having to lift a shovel. This can work well with short raised beds, where the height does not interfere with the forward tilt of the wheelbarrow. The strength of the wheelbarrow and the weight of the soil can damage higher bed sides, though. To circumvent this, you could try building a ramp with soil or wood planks for the wheelbarrow to ride up to the bed edge. The load is then dumped from outside without touching the bed sides.

For gardeners with good construction skills, one option is to keep one side of the bed unconstructed, so you can dump the soil directly from your wheelbarrow into the bed. The wheelbarrow is loaded, pushed inside the bed from the open side, then dumped at the closed end. Each wheelbarrow load is dumped on top of or next to the previous load, and the bed is filled from the closed end to the open one. Once the bed is almost full, the fourth side is attached to close the bed, the bed sides are anchored, and the remaining space is filled with soil.

I dig native soil from an open area in my yard and can shovel it directly into my raised bed.

A wheelbarrow makes filling the bed easier.

If you're concerned about damaging the sides of the bed when unloading with a wheelbarrow, you could try keeping one side of the bed open and simply roll the wheelbarrow into the bed and unload it.

Filling through an open end can save a lot of time and effort, particularly in long or tall raised beds. However, care must be taken to stabilize the sides so they don't shift or bow during the filling process. You will have saved no time or effort if you go to close the open end, and the end board is too short because the sides are angled apart. If that happens, the soil needs to be removed and the sides repositioned, so everything can connect together.

For my taller beds, I prefer to fill them from a wheelbarrow using a shovel, whether I mix soil within the bed or fill it with premixed blends. Pushing a heavy wheelbarrow up a ramp may be beyond the physical abilities of many gardeners, and with simply shoveling, I have little worry that the wheelbarrow will fall into a bed and damage it. Shoveling takes time and is tiring, but having patience to fill a bed slowly is better than confronting the things that can go wrong. I allot a day to fill a single bed, so I do it right and don't tire myself.

For smaller raised beds, wheelbarrows aren't necessary. A 5-gallon bucket filled with soil is undoubtedly heavy, but with a few helpers a bed can be filled relatively quickly, one bucket at a time. Buckets are also effective when mixing the blend while filling. A bucket of native soil is spread into the bed, followed by a bucket of compost, then a bucket of peat moss or whatever the recipe calls for. This way, very precise ratios can be achieved. Buckets can certainly be used to fill tall raised beds, but it will take many more trips to the bed.

Amending the Soil

When the raised beds are filled, the job of managing the soil food web is just beginning. You've provided the food for soil organisms by using a variety of organic materials in the initial soil blend, but that material is finite and will be consumed in time. Without replenishing the soil's organic matter, all your efforts to create a good soil will be for naught as the organisms starve.

To maintain a healthy soil, regular applications of additional organic matter are necessary. This process is known as amending the soil, and all the same organic ingredients we use to make a soil mix are potential amendments. A key to this process is incorporating the organic matter into the soil. It needs to be added throughout the soil to be most effective.

> **Amendments and Mulches**
>
> It is important to note that soil amendments and mulches are different, even though they may be the same materials. When organic matter is incorporated into soil, it is an amendment. When it is used on top of the soil surface, it is a mulch. During the growing season, I use dried grass, crushed leaves, and straw on the soil surface as a mulch to reduce soil moisture evaporation, reduce weeds, moderate soil temperatures, and lessen the likelihood of some diseases. At the end of the growing season, I turn that mulch into my raised bed soil, and it becomes an amendment to enrich the soil.

For the same reasons I fill my new beds in autumn, I do most of my soil amending in the same season. The basic method is to add an organic amendment to the soil surface and then turn it into the soil. Tillers are a mechanical way to do this. An amendment such as compost is spread on the soil, and the tines of the tiller mix it and incorporate it into the soil. Because tillers can be difficult to use in raised beds, most of the amending is done with hand tools. My tool of choice is a garden fork.

To amend a bed, a spade, shovel, or garden fork is pushed into the soil, a large portion of

A garden fork is an ideal tool for amending.

1. Begin by pushing the shovel or fork into soil.

2. Lift the soil up.

3. Turn the spade over and drop the soil into the hole.

soil is leveraged out creating a hole, and the mass is turned upside down into the hole. (See sequence on the left.) The organic matter that was on the soil surface is now at the bottom of the hole and covered by soil that was deeper, but is now closer to the surface.

Amendments such as compost, that are mostly decomposed, will be consumed by soil organisms and add nutrients to the soil in a short time. Raw materials such as leaves, grass, and straw will take longer to break down, but once in the soil, the process begins quickly. Because it can take a long time for the rough materials to decompose completely, and because of a potential nitrogen imbalance, amending in autumn provides enough time for the material to release its nutrients before spring planting.

Soil amending is a common spring activity as well. The same process is used: spreading organic matter on the soil surface and turning it in to increase the amount of organic matter in the soil. For best results, I encourage using compost as a spring amendment and large, raw materials for fall amending. Amending with compost in spring six to eight weeks before planting allows time for the soil organisms to convert the nutrients in the compost into usable forms for the young plants.

If a soil analysis is done before amending, you can know exactly which nutrients are deficient and add them to your spring amending. In time, regular application of organic matter will provide all the nutrients plants need, and adding fertilizers should be unnecessary.

Common Soil Mistakes

Filling a raised bed with good soil is one of the primary benefits of raised bed gardening, but many gardeners make the mistake of not using that advantage and start by filling their beds with the wrong soil. Often the wrong soil is what they dig up from their landscape without amending it or what they buy in bags without looking at the ingredients. It takes time and effort, but preparing good soil is worth it. Better soil will grow better plants, which will give better results. Here are some common pitfalls to avoid when it comes to soil and filling your raised beds.

Excessive disturbance of the soil: Excessive turning and tilling of raised bed soil can disrupt and kill soil life. It can also break apart good soil structure. Adding amendments and incorporating them into the soil is important, but soil disruption should be minimized to avoid damaging the delicate ecosystem you've made so much effort to create. That is one reason why I limit most of my amending to once a year. After ample organic matter is in the soil — usually after four or five years of regular amending — simply layering a few inches of compost on top of the bed before planting can be enough to amend the beds in subsequent years. Soil organisms will gradually incorporate it.

Walking on the soil: Walking on raised low beds is surprisingly common and should be avoided, as doing so will compact the soil. Those visiting your garden may think nothing of stepping through a low bed when trying to get from one side of the garden to the other. Educate those who visit your garden to walk around the beds, and avoid stepping in your own raised beds.

Exposing the soil to the elements: Because good soil is alive, not protecting it from the effects of weather can harm soil life. It is normal in nature for soil to have plants growing in it constantly. They may be dead or dormant, but the plants provide the soil protection from the sun's harmful rays and other harsh conditions. The same premise should be applied to raised beds. Planting cover crops and using mulch protect the soil from water and wind erosion, preventing the loss of organic matter and nutrients. Soil covers help moderate soil temperatures, making the soil cooler in summer and warmer in winter, which benefits soil life. Cover crops in winter help prevent weeds from sprouting in spring and

Mulch protects the bed soil all year round.

can be great amendments when turned into the soil. Avoid having bare, exposed soil in raised beds.

Skipping the soil test: Insufficient soil nutrients can be difficult to determine without a soil test. Most gardeners fail to monitor their soil nutrition and just guess at its quality. Starting with a professional soil analysis for raised beds is a good idea and so are periodic updates. Not only does a soil test show deficiencies, but also many reports suggest how much of the deficient nutrient should be added to correct it. Tests can also show when ideal nutrient levels are reached, and annual amending can be reduced.

Not amending the soil with enough organic matter: Gardeners who begin with good soil are starting well, but they don't always continue that advantage when they fail to amend the bed soil regularly. Annual amending is a good plan to sustain soil nutrition. Healthy soil has many organisms breaking down the material, and 2 inches to 3 inches of compost, or comparable organic material, should be applied every year. After four or five years, amending can be reduced or suspended periodically because the soil should be rich enough for plants, but it should be a regular gardening activity. Feeding the soil should be no different than feeding our animal friends.

Regular additions of compost and/or other organic matter will improve the soil.

Chapter 5

Developing a Growing Plan

Like every other aspect of raised bed gardening that we've covered so far, planning what you want to grow and how you'll grow it is a key step that shouldn't be missed. Developing a growing plan for the season can make the entire gardening process easier. It's a great feeling at the end of the season when a plan has come together. A chief problem is that many gardeners aren't sure how to plan effectively.

Planning does not have to be difficult and can be accomplished with a basic road map. Educational efforts and accumulated experience can help gardeners reach a point where planning becomes second nature. Until then, and even after, following a set method, such as the standardized garden plan I give you below, is a good way to start. My garden planning process looks like this:

1) Observe the garden
2) Research gardening information
3) Determine what to grow
4) Make a plan
5) Implement the plan
6) Observe during the growing season
7) Analyze the observations and learn from the analysis
8) Modify and plan

◐ Creating a thorough growing plan will make gardening easier and more enjoyable.

This basic road map is a guideline for starting a raised bed garden and for subsequent gardening seasons. It is important for gardeners to realize that any plan should be flexible. As conditions change, the plan can change. The reason for devoting multiple steps just for observation is to provide opportunities to see what is working and what isn't and to make modifications as quickly as needed. Many of the plants we grow in a vegetable garden grow quickly enough that we often have chances to start over if things go wrong within a gardening season.

It is the modifications and shifts in our methods that can make gardening challenging, but enjoyable as well. When a plant is not growing well, gardeners should act quickly to observe, analyze, and do what needs to be done to keep the plant growing. It all begins with a plan, but remember, the garden is alive and needs constant monitoring.

Observe the Garden

The first step is to observe your garden. As you may recall, this was an important step I recommended back in Chapter 2, when you're first planning your raised beds. Taking a whole growing season to observe the way the sun moves through your yard, how animals interact with the space, how you typically interact with the space, the areas where water may accumulate, or how the wind blows through the garden — all these things may affect your bed placement and will help you anticipate problems that could crop up later.

The more you look at your garden, the more you'll see. Observe with the goal of identifying what is affecting your garden, but also look at it with no goals in mind. Just walk through the garden space. You may recognize factors in planning your garden that you hadn't anticipated. Sometimes intuition will help direct you with a bed plan that feels comfortable.

Research Gardening Information

Selecting the right plant for the right location is a basic tenet of successful gardening, but that implies that the gardener knows what makes both the plant and the location "right." Education and experience are necessary to make those determinations. There is much to learn when first starting a garden. Experience will come later, but learning the basics of plant growth and gardening tasks can start right away.

There are so many gardening tips, tricks, methods, and techniques that figuring out what is most important can be overwhelming. I suggest gardeners begin with the basics of growing plants. Quite simply, plants need light, water, air, nutrients, and heat to grow. Different plants need different amounts of these things, but everything we do in the garden is about providing plants with those basic needs.

As we learn about what plants need and what we can provide, we should modify how we garden. Say you have a shady spot, but this location doesn't provide enough sunlight for a desired plant. You'll discover that you can still grow plants in that chosen spot, but they need to be plants that grow in shade. Each garden is unique, and we should look at our gardens and find out what they offer to plants.

A shadier garden does not mean you can't grow beautiful plants. Many plants grow well in shade.

Learning everything required for a successful garden can take years. Don't be intimidated. Instead, start small and simple by learning what is needed for just your first raised beds in their first year. Ask nurseries and other gardeners what they grow and discover the best plants to put in your first beds.

You'll also realize there are many different methods in gardening, but gardeners don't need to know all of them to start. Learning a single method of sowing seeds and doing it that way will work. With time and experience, a second method can be tried, compared, and the gardener can choose a preference. A third method can come in time, but there is no hurry if the gardener is happy with how things are growing.

It's the same with how we transplant, how we mulch, how we prune, how we harvest, and how we do everything in the garden. If you learn how to do something one way before you need to do it, you'll be ready to try it when the seed or plant is in the ground. You can always look for different ways later. Just start with something simple and, if it's not working, then try something else.

Remember, we don't need to be experts; we just need to know more than we originally did to get started. Each year brings more knowledge and more success.

Where to Find Information

One of the first places to learn more about plants is a seed packet. Many seed companies include a wealth of information on their seed packets: planting depth, spacing, and temperature hardiness are commonly listed. When to sow seeds, how long until germination, and when to harvest are other important tidbits most packets include. Tags in the pots of living plants often include similar information.

An example of a seed packet for Black Krim Tomatoes.

For more specific information, nothing beats the Internet and a good, targeted search. My Gardener Scott YouTube channel has hundreds of videos on many aspects of gardening. Many gardeners have found me as a source for answers. I and many other creators and educators provide a wealth of information that gardeners of all levels can access. A search on any gardening topic often reveals dozens of videos, articles, and forum postings. Across social media, gardeners can find general information about how to grow a garden, as well as specific information about how to grow individual varieties.

My home library includes hundreds of gardening books that I've accumulated over 30 years of gardening. I began my garden learning before the rise of the Internet, when a book was the best source for gardening knowledge. I think books still have a key place in a gardener's tool kit. They are good for providing in-depth information that isn't available through videos or blogs and can be a great reference tool year after year.

Hardiness Zones and Frost Dates

Knowing your hardiness zone and your average last and first frost dates are good places to start for understanding what you can and cannot grow.

Both the USDA Plant Hardiness Zone map and the Extreme Minimum Temperature Zones map in Canada provide guidelines for what plants will survive at certain locations based on the average extreme winter temperature. This information has a particular bearing on perennial plants and trees, which we want to survive the winter. The average minimum temperature reflects 30 years of data, and the USDA Plant Hardiness Zones were recently updated in 2023. It's important to note that the hardiness zone is based on an *average* lowest temperature, and that particular temperature may only occur on a single day in winter.

Find Your Hardiness Zone Map

If you live in the United States, you can find your hardiness zone map here:
https://planthardiness.ars.usda.gov

If you live in Canada, you can find your hardiness zone map here:
https://www.planthardiness.gc.ca

My hardiness zone of 5b means that my average coldest winter temperature is –15°F (–26°C). I can grow Zone 5 plants because they are rated to that low temperature. I can also grow Zone 4b plants because they are rated to low temperatures of –25°F (–31.6 °C), and my winters are warmer than that. I may not be able to grow Zone 6b plants since they won't survive temperatures below –5°F (–20.5°C). And I definitely cannot grow Zone 7 plants, which are suitable for temperatures above 5°F (–15°C).

There are some dates that every gardener should know. They define the gardening season and influence when and how we garden. In spring, the last frost date begins the typical gardening season. The traditional summer plants we grow cannot survive frosty conditions and go into the ground after the danger of frost has passed. In autumn, the first frost date ends the season because most of those plants will be killed by temperatures near freezing.

Frost can kill many summer plants.

The average last frost date may be the most important date on a gardener's calendar. The date is based on historical meteorological data and identifies the date when there's a 50 percent chance there will be no more cold temperatures producing frost. It is also the point when there is a 50 percent chance there will be cold weather. With each subsequent day, the likelihood of frost decreases until all danger is gone.

The average last frost date is referenced on seed packets and planting guides for gardeners to determine when to start seeds, indoors or outdoors. The actual date varies from garden to garden, but using a single point of reference helps all gardeners develop a plan.

The other important date for gardeners is the average first frost date in fall. That date identifies when there is a 50 percent chance that temperatures will reach close to freezing. Of course, there is a 50 percent chance that frost will already have occurred by that date. My Colorado garden often experiences a frost before the official first frost date.

It is crucial to note that the dates we use are only reference points for basic garden planning. They are guidelines for action and not scheduled events.

Find Your Average Frost Last and First Dates
You can find your last and first frost dates at the Old Farmer's Almanac website. These dates are derived from government data sets in the United States and Canada:
https://www.almanac.com/gardening/frostdates

Use the length of the growing season when choosing plant varieties to grow. Most of our summer garden plants have a recommended amount of time that it takes for them to reach harvest. By choosing plants that can grow and reach harvest within the anticipated length of the growing season, a harvest is likely within the frost-free period. Gardeners with a short growing season may not be able to grow some common vegetables and fruits that require a longer time for maturity.

It is a common misconception that there is a correlation between hardiness zones and the last frost date in spring. The hardiness zone number has no bearing on the length of winter, how many days are below freezing, when the last frost date happens, or any other weather factor beyond the average minimum temperature. The last frost date is an average of when temperatures are warm enough for frost to be finished and does not factor in the coldest winter day.

There is also no correlation between hardiness zones and what plants can be grown in the summer garden. One of the most common questions I get from gardeners is whether their hardiness zone allows certain plants to be grown, such as tomatoes, peppers, or melons. As long as the season is long enough and the climate matches a plant's needs, any common vegetable garden plant can be grown in summer regardless of the zone number. Zone 3 Alaska can grow many of the same summer plants as Zone 8 South Carolina.

Determine What to Grow

When starting a garden, most gardeners begin with the plants they want to grow and move forward from there. Growing vegetables or flowers for cutting, or simply creating a green space to sit and enjoy the outdoors — all require different sites, bed types, and bed sizes. Selecting what to grow is strongly influenced by why you're gardening.

There are many factors to consider when choosing which plants to grow. If I know I'm growing in a raised bed, I start my plant selection by determining how much space is available for planting, one bed at a time. I look at the size of the bed, decide what the purpose of the bed is, move to what the plants will be, then figure out how many plants should be grown. The same basic approach is repeated for each bed rather than trying to plan everything all at once.

I like to group my plant selection into broad categories that match some of my reasons for gardening. These are some plants that I grow every year. They're not necessarily specific varieties, but rather types of plants that I grow. I try to stay away from recommending specific plant varieties to gardeners because all our gardens are so unique. I can suggest a tomato that does well for me in Colorado, but it might not do well for you in Florida. The okra recommended by a gardener in Alabama may not do well in an Ontario garden. The plants I like may not match your preferences.

Selecting a general category of plants is a good way to start, and below are some of mine. Once you have plant ideas in mind, specific varieties can be determined by visiting local nurseries, talking to Master Gardeners, or asking a neighbor about what they grow best.

Plants That Are Easy to Grow

Gardening can be hard and challenging, so make at least one aspect of it easy. Choose a plant for your raised bed garden that has a high probability of success because it is so easy to grow. The specific plant will vary by region and climate. It will be different for gardeners of different skill levels.

When I'm asked to suggest a good plant for kids to grow, I often recommend radishes. The seeds are big and easy to place, they germinate and grow quickly, they tend to have fewer pest and disease problems than other plants, and they are easy to harvest. For gardeners looking for quick satisfaction, radishes may fit the bill.

You should also consider the amount of time you have to maintain the garden. A single bed is easily maintained by a single gardener, but that same gardener may not have time to manage 15 beds while working a full-time job. I like having a big garden, but it takes a lot of daily effort to simply water and deal with weeds.

While they may not be challenging to grow, some plants simply take more time to manage. Garlic is planted in autumn, is watered a few times, and effectively remains dormant and needs no more gardening labor until spring. Very easy. Carrot seeds, on the other hand, need continual moisture for many days before germinating and may need light watering three or four times a day for weeks. Matching the plants with your available time may mean more can be grown with less effort.

Plants That Taste Good

In the vegetable garden, one of the reasons we grow our plants is because what we grow tastes better than what we find at the supermarket. If you grow plants to eat, you should choose a plant you actually eat. I've grown many plants for their ease of growing or how much they produce, but then at harvest found that my family didn't want to eat them. It is never a waste to grow plants because of the lessons you learn along the way, and there is always an opportunity to give away vegetables or add them to the compost pile. However, that space can be better served for plants we actually eat and, not only that, but also desire to eat. Here are some other things to consider when deciding on the plants for your vegetable garden:

- **How many of a certain vegetable or fruit do you want to eat in a year?** I like beets, but I don't want to eat beets every day. If I grew them, I might only need 15 or 20 in any given year. I desire to eat tomatoes more than any other crop, so I grow a few dozen plants that produce enough to eat, give away, and preserve. While on the topic, I also consider how much of a harvest I can freeze, dehydrate, can, and pickle. I grow some plants to eat fresh and some to preserve for later.

- **How much do certain vegetables, fruits, or herbs cost at the supermarket?** A value assessment of plants will influence what and how much to grow. Carrots from a home garden taste better

I love tomatoes, and as you can see here, I grow a lot of tomato plants.

than store-bought ones, but at my supermarket they are very inexpensive. Organic tomatoes, on the other hand, are expensive and don't taste as good as what I can grow. Instead of carrots, I could grow a couple of tomato plants that would produce a much higher-value harvest. Some plants have very high value, such as fresh herbs. They can be expensive to buy either fresh or dried. Most herbs are easy to grow, take up little garden bed space, produce ample harvests, and are easy to preserve.

- **How unique is the plant?** The pepper varieties I like are usually not available at the supermarket and can only be grown in my garden. Unique plants often have a place in my raised beds.

- **How long does the plant produce food?** A cucumber or tomato plant can produce fruit over a long period. Spinach and lettuce leaves can be harvested for weeks as they continue to grow. Potatoes take more space than some other plants, but can produce many pounds of food in a relatively brief time.

Plants with Good Production Levels

Within a given growing space, I prefer one plant over another if that plant produces a bigger harvest than another. The amount of production varies by plant. A pepper plant with steady production is better than one that produces limited fruits. For example, I love Shishito peppers because they seem to be endless during the season, taste great, and are easy to grow.

Cherry tomato plants tend to produce fruit much earlier than beefsteak tomatoes and are much more prolific. One cherry tomato plant can produce hundreds of delicious bite-sized tomatoes before a beefsteak plant grows a single one.

Fruit trees and bushes tend to be easy plants that produce abundantly. They will take time to reach a size that produces harvestable fruit, but once they do, they will be productive for years. A plum tree in a corner of the garden can produce hundreds of pounds of fruit.

Shishito peppers are a favorite in my garden because they're prolific, delicious, and easy to grow.

New Plants

It's difficult to determine what is easy, tastes great, or has high production if you don't try new plants and see how well they perform in the garden. It can be a plant type that is new, or a variety within another category that is new. The idea is to experiment a little while trying to discover a plant that could become a new favorite.

For new gardeners, this likely happens every year. At some point, we grow our first tomato plant or our first zucchini or our first strawberry. Ensure you take time beforehand to learn about the plant's needs when developing your plan to grow it, but until it's in the bed, the actual growth results will be virtually unknown. I enjoy the mystery of not being sure about what will happen, and I love it when the plant surprises me with a good outcome.

Plants That Are Easy to Propagate

If we find a successful plant in our garden, it is good if we can grow that plant again, and it's even better if we can do it at no cost. When first starting to garden, propagation is rarely on the minds of new gardeners, but there is no reason it shouldn't be. Growing a plant with the intent of saving its seeds, dividing it, or using it for cuttings adds an interesting component to gardening.

Garlic is a great plant for propagation. All the garlic I plant comes from a garlic bulb that I separated into individual cloves. The cloves develop over the course of many months into full-size bulbs. I harvest the bulbs and eat the cloves, but there is little reason not to save some of the cloves to plant in next year's garden. A typical bulb has five to 10 cloves that will grow into five to 10 bulbs, and each of those will have five to 10 cloves. A purchase of a single bulb in the first year can provide decades of garlic harvests.

Many of the fruits we harvest present seeds that can be used to grow new plants. The fruit should be fully mature to ensure the seeds are viable. Harvest a ripe tomato, and as you're cutting it up for a salad, collect some of the seeds.

Each garlic clove grows into a full bulb.

Purple potatoes are harvested next to purple okra in the purple garden I grew with my granddaughters.

Plants That Honor a Memory or Create a New One

Putting a meaningful plant in the garden adds special meaning to your beds. You can walk through the garden and easily recall a pleasant time or a loved one. If you want to grow flowers, but don't know what to choose, plant what your grandmother grew. If you remember the special treat of eating fresh raspberries in your grandfather's garden, then grow raspberries.

Making new memories can be particularly enjoyable. My granddaughters and I planted a purple garden bed. We grew purple beans, purple potatoes, purple peas, purple carrots, purple kohlrabi, and purple lettuce. Now, any time I see a purple plant I think about that special summer. Years later, they ask about some of those purple plants when I'm planting the garden.

Each gardener has their own memories, new and old, that can be made or remembered in the garden. Focusing on plants for food and production has an important place in our garden planning, but losing sight of what positive emotions and memories we gain by gardening risks turning it into just an activity or hobby instead of a passion.

Keep in mind these are simply guidelines to get an idea of what to grow when no other reason exists. And how you prioritize categories will shift based on what bed needs to be planted. Taste may be more important than production for special crops. Propagation may be more important when trying to fill out a space for the future. Identify what your priorities are and start planning.

With a basic idea of what plants you want to grow, return to the previous step to learn about the plants you have in mind. Try to cover the basics for each plant, such as:

- Best conditions for starting seeds
- Soil needs
- Light requirements
- Water needs
- Spacing needs
- Ideal duration of growing season
- Size at maturity
- What kind of harvest (if any) to expect

These and other factors will influence your decisions about which plants to grow in individual beds. Planning what to grow is always a balance of what is wanted, what will fit, and how much can realistically be grown once you've learned about a plant's needs.

Make a Plan

With a basic idea in mind of what the garden will be, put a preliminary plan on grid paper. You can also use a spreadsheet, a garden-planning app, or even a whiteboard. Just take your ideas and plant desires and document them, so you have the beginnings of a plan. It isn't important to develop a final plan yet because much can change from an initial idea to actually putting a plant in the ground.

Matching Plants to Raised Beds

One thing to consider as you're plotting out which plants go where is the bed type. The key is matching the right plants with the best bed type, as determined by you, the gardener. Some beds are better for perennials, and some may be better for vegetables, but there are no rules that say a gardener must choose planting something in one bed over another just because it is recommended. Nevertheless, here are some points to think about:

Stone raised beds can be a suitable growing space for many different plants — from long-standing trees and shrubs to annual flowers and seasonal vegetables.

Materials: Generally, raised bed materials such as wood will degrade over time and need replacing, making them best suited for annual plants that are replaced every year. Selecting rot-resistant wood, like cedar or pressure-treated wood, along with using wood preservatives, can help wood beds last much longer than a decade. If that's the case, long-lasting wooden beds can be a choice for long-lasting plants.

Durable beds made from stone and rock may never need replacing and are usually recommended for permanent plants. When choosing raised beds for trees and big landscape plants, it makes sense to start with a stone bed that will last as long as the tree is alive. However, there is no reason why a forever bed can't be used for annual flowers or vegetable gardens.

Depth: Deep beds work well for vegetable gardens, but that may not be necessary for many other plants. Some plants only need a few inches of depth to grow. Even big plants can grow in shallow raised beds if the bottom is open. When matching plants to beds, it is important to understand how much soil the plant needs for its roots.

The rooting depth of plants can be divided into three categories: shallow, moderate, and deep. Generally, shallow-rooted plants can develop roots to a depth of 12 inches to 18 inches. Moderate-rooted plants can grow to a depth of 18 inches to 24 inches. Deep-rooted plants can have roots down to 24 inches or more. These should be viewed as maximum root growth based on ideal conditions. The length of the growing season, the health of the soil, and water application will affect how long roots grow.

Most plants will grow in the space you give them. Though their ideal root growth may be many inches, they can thrive with a minimum of soil depth if the soil provides all the nutrients and water the plant needs. Think beyond the idea that roots only grow down. Roots can grow laterally as well. In my 22-inch-tall metal beds, I've pulled tomato plants at the end of the season and measured roots longer than 24 inches because they grew at an angle — downward and sideways.

Annuals versus perennials: Deciding on annual or perennial plants affects how the bed can be used for other plants. Generally in the vegetable garden, raised beds contain annual plants exclusively. At the end of the season, the beds can be cleaned up, plants can be removed, and the entire bed is ready for soil amending. For raised beds with perennial plants, after the soil is prepared initially, plants are put in place, and the entire bed will not be amended again, other than topical applications of organic mulches.

Annuals and perennials can be grown together in a bed if you don't disturb the roots of the perennials. Generally, perennial flowers, ornamental grasses, bushes, and shrubs have established clumps of roots that are deep and wide. Annual plants tend to have shallower roots that don't expand much in a single season. Feel free to add small accent annuals throughout an established perennial bed as long as you avoid planting them where perennial plants can be disturbed.

Tomato plants can grow large even if the bed depth is shorter than their maximum root measurement, like in my 22-inch-tall metal beds.

Annual flowers can add pops of color all season long.

From Sketch to Final Plan

By planning beds individually, it becomes easy to plan the garden as a whole. The basic plant selection and the number of plants for each bed are already in mind. Sketch the general shape of the planting beds and write in what you want to grow. For example, the sketch can show a rectangle labeled as "Bed 1" with "beets," "peas," "spinach," "lettuce," and "radishes" written inside. The first plan doesn't need exact measurements or spacing or plant quantities yet. It is just a way to show what you want to do in each bed. The next rectangle could be "Bed 2" with "tomatoes" and "peppers," and so on until all your beds are labeled.

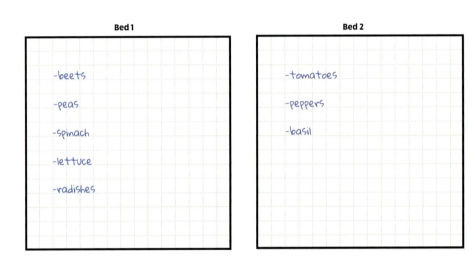

This step is about getting a visual impression of how the garden will look. With an idea of how many beds and what plants you want to grow, you can then move to how many plants will go in each bed. Based on the spacing information you've learned about the plants and keeping in mind how many you want to fit your needs, determine how many plants will fit in a bed.

For example, tomato plants are typically grown 18 inches to 24 inches apart. In a bed that is 48 inches wide, you can grow two tomato plants side by side using 18-inch spacing. The plants will each be 15 inches from the side, with 18 inches between the plants. Two more plants can be grown with the same spacing, so four tomato plants need a bed of 48 inches by 48 inches. (This assumes that the plants will grow vertically on a trellis and not sprawl into one another.) (See diagram 1 on the opposite page.)

The open space around the edges is still available to grow more plants. So a single pepper plant can be placed outside each tomato plant, between the tomato and the edge of the bed. The 48-by-48 bed now has four tomato plants and eight pepper plants. (See diagram 2 on the right.)

There may also be space to plant basil between the peppers. (See diagram 3 on the right.) By sketching plants with the recommended spacing, a plan is started.

Do this process to determine what will be grown with every plant you want. The spacing will be different for other plants, and the actual drawing will take more time with smaller plants growing closer together. The intent is to create a visualization, so the gardener has a good idea of how many plants will go into each bed and how close to plant them. The precision of the drawing is not important, unless the gardener wants it to be.

New gardeners can benefit from growing multiple types of plants in a raised bed. A couple of tomato plants, a couple of peppers, some carrots, some peas and beans, and a few plants such as lettuce or spinach can all be grown in a small space without much difficulty. The leafy greens grow well alongside peas. Beans do well in a bed with cucumbers or squash. There may not be enough plants of each to provide big harvests overall, but each plant type can teach a lot about what a garden needs and how to maintain it.

With a good vision of how many plants will be in each bed and their general placement, it may be time for a final, more-refined plan. While not necessary if the previous sketch conveys everything a gardener needs, this second-level plan is what I take with me to the garden when putting seeds or plants

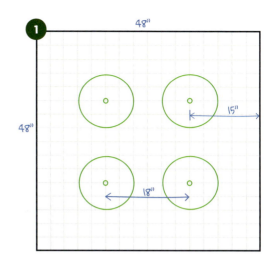

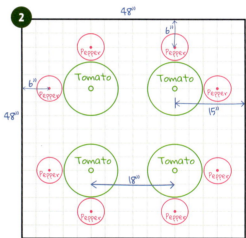

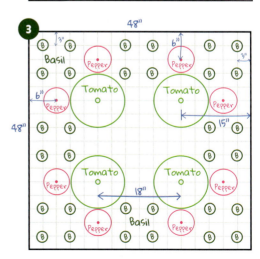

in the ground. This plan usually incorporates the correct spacing needed for each plant and is annotated with the measurements I'll use.

Old-school gardeners can do all these planning steps on grid paper. Tech-savvy gardeners can do it electronically. Many garden-planning apps use plant icons that can be dragged and dropped into an electronic raised bed that is sized to the one in the garden. The icons match the amount of space that each plant needs in the bed.

Many garden-planning apps have a library of information included in them. If you want to plant peppers, an app can give you options. Clicking on the plant icon or exploring the app's library can tell you about the plant, how it grows, how big it gets, and other basic information. Some vegetables, like peppers, have so many options that only the most common varieties are usually included. My planning app allows me to enter data for varieties that may not be in its database. Then I can use a custom icon when filling in my raised bed plan.

My planning process is a mix of the old school and the tech-savvy. I do the initial rough plan with pencil on paper. The app allows me to take the basic idea and make it precise. I can set up my plan on my computer, and then when it comes time to put seeds and plants in the garden, I take my phone out to the garden and have all the guidance I need in my pocket.

A garden planning app can be taken to the garden.

Succession Planting

The ease of planning and planting in raised beds make them ideal for succession planting. Succession planting is a gardening method that allows gardeners to maximize how many plants grow with multiple plantings in the same bed throughout the gardening season. More plants are harvested by strategically managing sowing and planting times. There are two common methods to take advantage of succession planting and achieve maximum yields.

Method 1: Extending the Season

The first method is to plan for the bed to grow plants during the entire growing season and beyond. Seeds are sown or transplants are placed in the bed in early spring, as soon as the soil can be worked and temperatures are warm enough to support their growth. Season-extending methods such as hoops and coverings can help with this (see Chapter 7, starting on page 266). Beets, broccoli, cabbage, chard, kale, lettuce, radish, spinach, and many other plants can survive when exposed to frost and temperatures near freezing, and the extra protection from the hoops and plastic coverings promotes early and healthy growth.

These plants can grow for weeks or months before the average last frost date. The goal is to plan it so the early spring plant varieties are reaching maturity and harvest when temperatures are increasing, and the garden is ready for the summer crops.

Many gardeners, particularly new ones, think of a garden as just what grows during the hot summer months. Those plants are still part of succession planting. After the early-spring plants are harvested and removed, the same beds are ready for seeds and plants that benefit from warm conditions and can't survive freezing temperatures. The summer plants such as cucumbers, eggplants, melons, okra, peppers, squash, and tomatoes go in the ground after the last frost date and occupy the same raised bed space during their normal growing time.

By choosing varieties that have fewer days to reach harvest, the beds can be ready for a

Broccoli and other brassicas, such as cabbage and kale, are great early-season and late-season plants, as they can withstand cooler temperatures.

Selective season extending can easily be done in raised beds with the help of hoops and plastic sheets.

third planting to complete the gardening year. The summer plants are harvested and removed, and more cool-season plants are grown for a harvest in autumn. The same plants that can handle cold temperatures when they begin growing in spring can also handle cold temperatures when they approach harvest time in fall. Some of them, particularly root vegetables, even taste better when exposed to frost. Using a hoop system covered with plastic increases plant choice options into fall and even winter.

By having a changing succession of plants, the beds are filled with plants longer than they would be with traditional gardening practices that tend to focus on the single warm season. The specific planting times will vary based on which plants are being grown. The benefit of using individual raised beds means that different succession planting cycles can be done in the same garden. Season-extending methods only need to be used in the beds that require them.

Method 2: Staggering the Plantings

The second method of succession planting staggers plantings to get a longer harvest period of the same plant type. Instead of planting an entire bed or a large part of a bed with many seeds or plants at the same time, the planting schedule is spread over a period of weeks. Many of the plants in our vegetable garden have specific life cycles in which they grow and are ready for harvest at peak quality within an expected time frame. When they are all started at the same time, gardeners typically get one large harvest within a few days.

By staggering the planting times, the harvests are smaller and occur over a longer period. Fewer plants are grown with each cycle. For example, two rows of lettuce seeds are sown, and two weeks later another two rows are sown. This process continues with as many rows and sowings as the gardener wants. For fast-growing plants such as lettuce, the first harvest can take place as early as a month after the first sowing, with enough lettuce to last for two weeks until the next section is harvested. Then two weeks after that, the next section is ready for harvesting. Instead of one big lettuce harvest, the gardener has daily lettuce for many weeks.

As each section is harvested, more seeds are sown to continue the cycle. As the weather changes, the new sowings can be of new plants that match the appropriate cool-season or warm-season conditions. For example, the lettuce can be shifted to warmth-loving beans. Staggering the sowing of the bean seeds as the lettuce crops are finished means that the bean harvest is extended over a longer period in mid-to-late summer. As the weather cools, the beans can be changed back to a cool-season plant for sustained, smaller harvests of lettuce, spinach, beets, and the other fast-growing crops that can handle cooler temperatures in fall.

A similar method takes advantage of expected harvest times of different varieties of a favored plant. To get staggered harvest dates of some plants such as cabbage, carrots, beans, peas, and sweet corn, you can select varieties that mature at different rates. They are all planted at the same time, but the early-maturing varieties will be ready to harvest earlier, while the other varieties are still growing. Days later, a mid-maturing variety is ready for harvest, and a few weeks after that, the late varieties complete the cycle. New plants can be planted in the space freed up with each harvest.

The grid-planning aspect of raised beds allows for precise planning of not only plants, but also planting times. When planning for succession planting, break the bed grid into sections or blocks for planting with each phase of the season. A simple way to do this is for half the bed to be planned for one crop that will be replaced by another at harvest, and the other half of the bed is planned for a different crop that will be replaced by yet another. In a few months, four complete harvests can be managed in a single raised bed.

🌱 Intensive Planting

Intensive planting is about packing as many plants as possible into your raised bed. To make this method effective, you need good planning, efficient planting, and regular plant maintenance such as weeding and thinning. Intensive planting does not break the rules of traditional raised bed gardening. It takes the classic rules, adds new ones, and creates possibilities that many gardeners never consider.

There are a few reasons why this method of growing works so well in raised beds. Because the soil is rich, it's designed for production. Though growing more plants in the same space means that more nutrients will be pulled from the soil, at the end of the season we can easily replenish those nutrients with amendments. And because our good soil retains moisture well, the higher number of plants will not take much more water than normal, especially if mulch is in place to reduce moisture evaporation. The denser grouping of plants also shades the soil and increases humidity near the surface, reducing evaporation further.

Fewer weeds appear in intensively planted beds, and the harvest can be bounteous. However, there is more planning and labor involved with this style of growing. Thinning and pruning become very important, so plants don't overwhelm one another, and when the plants are ready, regular harvests will make that task more manageable.

New Rules, New Possibilities

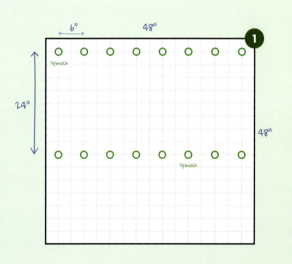

The main "rule" that is stretched to new limits with intensive planting involves plant spacing. Traditional planting methods say to space plants apart with even spacing in a row, then do it in a new row farther away. Most seed packets continue recommending this inefficient use of bed space. I have a packet for spinach that says to sow seeds 1 inch to 2 inches apart and then to thin the plants to 4 inches to 6 inches apart. The inefficiency for raised beds comes when the packet tells us to space rows 20 inches to 24 inches apart. (See diagram 1 on the left.)

Many gardeners, particularly new ones, follow this guidance without questioning it. Raised bed gardeners interested in intensive gardening ask the obvious question, "If we can plant 6 inches apart in one direction, why can't we plant 6 inches apart in a different direction?" It may not be immediately apparent to gardeners used to traditional recommendations, but with so much bare ground between the rows — premium areas for weeds to sprout up — it is natural to think there's a better way to use the space. (See diagram 2 on the right.)

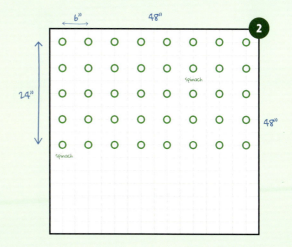

The easiest modification to traditional planting, and to get some intensive results quickly, is to fill in the open space between rows with plants at the same spacing in all directions. Six inches of spacing between plants now becomes 6 inches between rows. With 24 inches between rows, that means there is room for three more rows in the open space. By using the wonders of basic math, we have more than doubled the plants we're growing in the same space.

In the original recommended spacing, we were able to grow 16 spinach plants in a raised bed that's 48 inches wide, using 24 inches of the bed. By incorporating intensive planting, we are able to grow 40 plants in the same space. Not only have we dramatically increased how much we're growing, but also the plants will help protect the soil and reduce the likelihood of weeds sprouting.

We can take intensive gardening to another level by maximizing the recommended spacing. The seed packet for our spinach recommends spacing plants 4 inches to 6 inches, and we made our initial plan based on the 6-inch spacing. If we shift to putting plants every 4 inches, we can increase the total count to 84 spinach plants in the same space. (See diagram 3 on the right.)

That is a huge increase, but intrepid gardeners can squeeze in more. So far, we've used an easy grid pattern to plant in a block. By changing the pattern to a triangle, we can squeeze in even more plants. Using this method, we stagger the rows and use the same basic spacing in all directions. Because we're now using equilateral triangles, the rows are closer together. The 6-inch spacing between plants allows

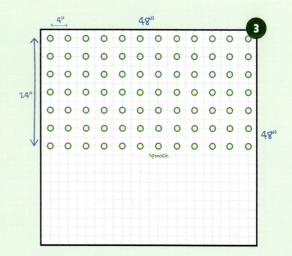

169

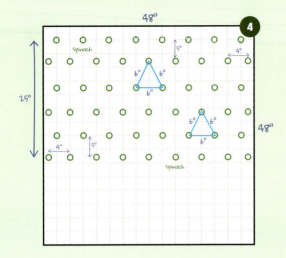

for rows that are just over 5 inches apart, and we can fit eight rows into the space that previously had five. (See diagram 4 on the left.)

It's not as big an increase as before, but the extra row when using 6-inch spacing allows us to grow 45 plants instead of 40 in the same general bed space. Generally, it can give us about 15 percent more plants. I allow for equal space between the plants on the outer edge and the side of the bed. Looking at the diagram, you can see that if you use 4-inch spacing on the edges of three rows, you could squeeze in another six plants, totaling 51 plants.

Intensive planting requires more planning and more precise measurements when sowing seeds to achieve the maximum benefits. It is up to each gardener to determine if the effort is worth it. I use the staggered planting method when I transplant seedlings because I find it easy to lay out the pots using equilateral triangles. Visually, two triangles make a diamond shape, and I line up the plants in side-by-side diamonds.

So far, we've been talking about putting all of the same plant type into a space. Intensive gardening allows for different plants with varying space requirements to grow in the same bed. In fact, different plants growing side by side is encouraged. By fitting plants into grid or diamond patterns, we can take advantage of the different mature sizes of the plants.

Instead of using 6-inch spacing for most of our spinach plants and then squeezing in extras using 4-inch spacing, we can choose to add plants to the end of the rows like bulb onions that normally use 4-inch spacing. (See diagram 5 on the opposite page.) Or, if we use 4 inches between our spinach, we can add in carrots that only need 2-inch spacing. (See diagram 6 on the opposite page.)

The diamond pattern is easy to see when the seedlings are laid out in the bed.

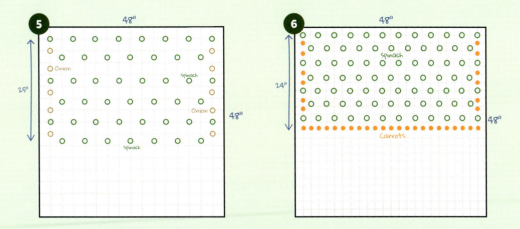

The focus changes from getting the most plants in a given space to getting greater variety in a given space. Using the same basic grid or diamond, we can fill a raised bed with plants that have similar spacing. Beans, onions, parsnips, turnips, and spinach can all fill out our plan with 4-inch spacing. (See diagram 7 below.) Cabbage, kale, kohlrabi, and lettuce can fill our bed plan with 6-inch spacing. (See diagram 8 below.)

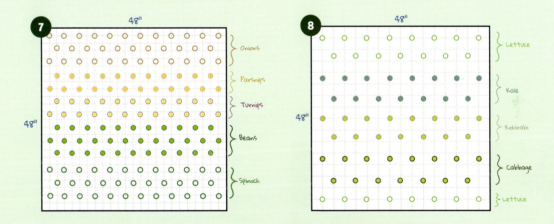

Because there are so many more plants, harvesting takes on even more importance. I stagger my harvests to give mature plants more space. I begin by harvesting every other plant in a row or grid. That means some plants are harvested young, allowing more space for neighboring plants to mature. Pairing intensive planting with succession planting (see pages 165–167) will result in maximum production in your raised beds. Of course, more plants mean more planning, especially if you add succession planting to your plan, but it can be manageable.

Schedule Seed Starting

The next part of the plan is determining when the seeds and plants are started and where. Apps can help, and many commercial seed packets include all the information needed to get the seeds in the ground. It is important to note that all seeds will not be started at the same time. Some seeds should be started indoors weeks before planting outside, so you have plants to put into the bed. Others should be started outdoors after the soil warms up. You'll need to do additional research to determine the best time for starting your seeds.

In most cases, the seed-starting decision is based on the average last frost date of the garden (see page 151). Peppers are usually started indoors 8–10 weeks before the last frost. Tomatoes can be started indoors six to eight weeks before the last frost. Beans can be started outdoors one to two weeks after the last frost date. Melons can be started indoors three to four weeks before the last frost or sown directly outdoors two to three weeks after the last frost.

Because there is so much variability with planting times, developing a plan for seed starting should take place months before any plants are growing outside. My old-school method is to take a calendar, mark the last frost date, then count backward or forward based on each plant's recommended date for seed starting. I mark the suggested sowing date for each plant on my calendar and can plan for every seed going in my garden.

Many of the garden-planning apps typically provide the suggested planting times, which makes for easy planning. You enter your last frost date in the app or you can enter your location, and the app determines the likely date for you. As you add what plants you'll be growing, the app will show the recommended planting dates. If you transfer those dates to your phone's calendar, you can have a daily reminder of what needs to be done in the garden.

Not starting plants from seeds and buying plants is a viable option for gardeners, but it doesn't eliminate the need for planning when to transplant them. The same basic process for planning a raised bed works whether you're using seeds or planning to buy all your plants from a nursery.

I still like marking up paper calendars for seed starting and garden planning, but electronic calendars and garden-planning apps can achieve the same thing.

Add Harvesting to Your Plan

One planning item many gardeners ignore or consider less important is when to start harvesting. The seed or plant information usually includes how many days until harvest after planting, or how many days for the plant to reach maturity. The harvest date should be part of the garden plan. Putting that date on the calendar is very helpful for gardeners who are unsure when to start checking for ripe fruit or ample root size.

The expected harvest date also plays into planning for succession planting (see pages 165–167). Knowing when one series of plants will be finished helps identify when the next series of plants will go in the ground. The entire sequence of planting multiple plants in multiple beds over the course of the growing season can be planned months before the first seed is started.

Implement the Plan

With a plan for what you will grow and when to plant, you can now get your seeds and plants. A general plan that includes generic plants gives flexibility to new gardeners. For many gardeners, a tomato is a tomato, and a cucumber is a cucumber. Knowing you want to grow two tomato plants or eight peppers or 20 beets is important when first looking for seeds or plants. If you plan to start your own seeds, look at the seed displays at your local garden center or nursery and choose a packet that looks good. Look for the characteristics that match your desires.

Many gardeners choose their beans, squash, lettuce, and other garden plants from the displays with only a basic idea of what they're looking for. The seeds on offer will typically be for common varieties. More experienced gardeners often seek specific varieties of plants. In this case, buying online is a better option. Unique plants with different colors, tastes, disease resistance, and production levels may only be available from online sources.

Many stores have large seed displays in spring.

Buying seeds soon after they're first available ensures you get what you want and helps solidify your growing plan. It's rarely too early to buy seeds, and knowing exactly what you'll be planting will help you do your research to determine planting times, spacing, expected production levels, and when to harvest. Many stores begin selling seeds months before the gardening season begins, and they're available online year-round.

Buying plants is also a good option and is often easiest for new gardeners. Walking through a plant center or nursery is an enjoyable experience for gardeners of all levels. Potted plants should have a plant tag that tells you when to transplant, the recommended spacing, and the plant's basic water needs. It should match what you determined when developing your plan.

With the plan, seeds, and plants in hand, it's time to get growing. Follow guidance on the seed packet, the plant tag, your planning app, or from information you gained through your research beforehand. Have pots, potting mix, and lights ready to go before starting seeds. When the start date arrives for each seed, get it in the pot and under lights. When it's time to put the seedlings and other plants in the garden, get them out there and in their beds. Methods for planting and growing will be covered in Chapter 6.

Potted plants offer a head start with planting.

Save on Seeds and Plants

Seeds can often be obtained for free if you know where to look. If you're not choosy about specific varieties, you can check out some of these resources for free or discounted seeds:

- Seed library: This is similar to a book library where gardeners can check out seeds early in the season and then, at the end of the season, return new seeds they have collected.
- Local garden club: In addition to discovering new gardener friends, garden clubs are a good opportunity to share seeds and plants between members.
- Supermarket produce and goods: While making your food, set aside some seeds to plant. Germination rates will be lower than commercial garden seeds, but the cost will be substantially less. Many dried beans and peas can be planted, as can herb seeds used for cooking.
- End-of-season sales: Stores anxious to clear out their inventory often sell seeds and plants at a huge discount a few months after they start selling them. Make note of when that happens each year at your favorite store and stock up.
- Discount stores: Discount stores usually carry value-priced seed packets in the spring and summer. The choice is limited, but bargain seeds often carry a discount of 90 percent when compared to full-price seeds. The value seeds are just as good and will grow into the same plants without the big brand name.
- Seed saving: Consider choosing plants for the purpose of saving seeds for the following year. This is a common part of planning, but is rarely a goal of new gardeners. With a little extra effort and some research on how to store and germinate the seeds, you can keep growing your favorite plants for years to come.

With a little resourcefulness, you can also acquire plants for free or at discounted rates:

- Propagation: Many plants are easy to grow and propagate for more. Years ago, I started with a dozen strawberry plants and potted up the runners as they grew. Those plants have provided hundreds of new strawberry plants that I've used in many different gardens since. Clumping plants such as daylilies and ornamental grasses are easy to split into new plants. A single plant can become dozens of plants in just a few years. You can also ask a gardener friend for cuttings or extra plants they've propagated from their garden.
- Bare-root plants: When buying plants and trees, opt for bare-root plants over potted ones. Bare-root plants are typically smaller and younger than similar plants in large pots, but the cost savings can be substantial. Within a single growing season, they can become established and within a year or two they often make up for the size difference.
- Small plants: Big potted plants with a lot of flowers cost more at the garden center, and in many cases once the flowers fade, they won't return. Buying small plants is cheaper, and as the plants grow you can expect more flowers over a longer period.
- Clearance rack: When you see bargain plants, be flexible with your original garden plan and open to changing it for affordable and available plants. Your garden plan may include a certain color or size of plant, but sometimes specific varieties may not be immediately available. I check out the clearance rack with an open mind, looking for a plant that could fit my beds. A discounted plant can still meet your plan's general intent.

Test Run Your Plan

Before putting anything into raised bed soil, I suggest a practice or test run for the garden plan. This is another observation point to see if the bed resembles what you expect. Place the potted plants in the location where they'll be planted and step back to observe. Put the seed packets on the soil for each section of the bed where they will be sown.

Even after the research and your plan has been developed, it's helpful to remember that the plan can be flexible. Once the plant is in the ground, it becomes more difficult to change the plan, so take time to confirm your expectations before you've committed. With the seeds and plants in place, take a moment to evaluate them — it may be easier now to envision how the bed will look with plants growing. Until this point, planning has been two-dimensional, and the result may appear different in three dimensions.

It's okay to change your mind about your plan at any point. When seeing the seed packets laid out on the raised bed, you may want the purple lettuce to be in front of the dinosaur kale. You may want to add two more blocks of radishes and one fewer of beets and turnips. My final planting plan has all the plants identified with the anticipated spacing, but it rarely, if ever, ends up the same when I actually lay the plants and seeds on top of the bed.

With potted plants resting on the bed in their intended spots, you get a good reference for how big they are in relation to the bed and their anticipated final size. Tomato plants will get tall and wide, but it will take a month or two to reach that point. On planting day, it may become apparent that you can sow some lettuce or radish seeds between the tomatoes. Those plants grow quickly and will be harvested before the tomatoes get too big. It's obvious when you look at the bed and less so when you plan months in advance.

Laying seed packets in the bed can help you "see" the plan.

The plan may also change when you open the seed packet and realize there are fewer seeds than you expected. I've learned that a packet of pea seeds never has as many as I want, so I make sure to buy more than one pack. If you planned for a certain number of one plant type but run out of seeds, it's okay to replace them with other excess seeds that you have. Of course, keep in mind the mature plant's size when swapping seeds at the last minute.

Essentially, your planting plan is a guideline to get the plants you want where you want them. It doesn't need to be a hindrance with only one outcome. Be flexible and happy with what you put in the ground. I don't recommend starting the growing season with too much stress because the plan you worked so hard on had to be tweaked. Use this as an opportunity to learn from the planning process, which will inform the next year's planning.

I try to envision the mature plant size when laying out pots for planting.

Observe during the Growing Season

The planning process does not end when the plants are in the ground. In many ways, it is the beginning of the planning process for the next gardening year. The garden is alive with activity above ground and below, weather changes every day, and insects, good and bad, show up — all these things and more affect how your plants grow.

Learning to observe is a critical component in becoming a good gardener. Of course, we can never see everything and often we are overloaded with what we observe. Rather than trying to absorb everything that is happening and trying to make sense of it, focus on the gardening aspects that seem important in the moment.

If you are unsure about how you should water, make a point of noting how you do it and observe the results. If you water in the morning, do you notice any feedback from the plants? Plants can speak to gardeners if we understand their language. When a plant wilts, it is telling us that it does not have enough water, or that it has too much, or that the temperature is too high, or that the wind is too dry. If you water and the plant wilts, test the moisture level of the soil to see if it is dry at root level or saturated. If the plant perks up at the end of a hot, dry, windy day, it may be telling you it is okay, but was stressed by the weather.

The same goes for thinning and pruning, mulching, soil quality — any aspect of gardening, really. Note how you're doing it and observe the result. Choosing just one or two practices or methods and focusing on that is an incremental approach to becoming an expert gardener. You can also focus on just one or two raised beds.

Also, try to observe the plants you've chosen and how well they do in your garden. Plants do best when all their needs are met. Very few gardens can give all plants everything they need. Note which plants do best in your garden and which do worse. They may be different varieties of the same plant type, or they may be completely different plants. I know that Black Krim tomatoes do great in my garden, but Brandywine tomatoes suffer. I also know that cucumbers do great for me, but my okra struggles.

I work in the garden with a hat on and gloves at the ready.

Note how plants do over the course of the season. Do they start off strong, but begin to wither in the heat of summer or when a particular pest appears? Do they start off slow during early cold months, but bounce back when the temperatures warm? Because so many factors affect plant growth, try to recognize what is happening in your garden and what effect it has on plants of all types. The same influence may have no impact on certain plants and be catastrophic for others.

Go beyond the plants and observe your own activities in the garden. Make note of what you enjoy and what you don't. Look for anything that adds stress to your gardening day. If something causes pain, by all means stop doing it. I wear gloves because I don't want to damage my skin and a brace when I lift heavy things, so I don't hurt my back. I wear a hat to protect my head from the sun.

If something brings you joy, then do more of it. You began your gardening journey with specific ideas of why you wanted to do it, and those reasons need to be acknowledged and observed regularly. Take time to observe what it is that has the most impact on you. Just as our garden plan can be modified as we observe it in action, we can also modify our reasons for gardening once we get outside and start growing plants.

Last, don't ignore things happening in the garden just because you don't understand them. Instead, pause and observe the events. You don't have to make sense of what you see, but you can look for clues, effects, results, mysteries, and anomalies. The observations are purely for accumulating data for later. There are many things about gardening that aren't understood until much later. Analyzing what you observe comes next.

Analyze the Observations and Learn from the Analysis

The observations at all phases of planning and growing plants pave the way for learning much about gardening. The observations may show things that are simple and easily understood, making modifications easy. They may be complex and require months of research to understand and longer to implement changes in the garden. The intent of collecting the observation data is to improve how we garden and how well our plants grow. Without analysis, the observations are worth little.

It's important to note that observation and analysis are continual processes in the garden. Don't stop with just one or two observations in the garden. Make regular observations and couple the information with a timeline of the plant's growth during the gardening season. Does the observation appear to show problems with the plant, soil, water, raised bed, an animal, or anything else that could be harmful if not acted on? Or does the observation identify something that might benefit from modifications that can be made in the future?

Because the garden is alive, some actions are more critical than others to keep it afloat. Observations are simply things that the gardener sees and wonders about. The analysis is what determines whether it has the priority that requires action sooner or later. The problem for new gardeners is that the analysis may take time to research and act upon and it may not be fast enough. The nice thing about being a seasoned gardener is that we've experienced the results of many of those stalled decisions and learned from them.

For effective analysis, consider where it happened, when it happened, and how it happened before you start trying to determine why it happened. The context of the observations can help show any patterns, trends, or relationships within the garden setting. Oversimplifying an event is a common issue with many gardeners, particularly new ones. Avoid glazing over an observation and just analyzing the surface appearance with a simple answer. The simplest analysis may end up being correct, but the thing you observed may also be pointing to a deeper issue. Instead of jumping to an easy conclusion, begin to peel away the layers and try to find the root cause that isn't initially apparent.

The analysis of observations requires that we interpret what we saw or experienced. We develop a theory, to ourselves, for what may have happened and then we take what we know and what we can research to address that theory. Based on results, a new theory may emerge, and we may need to interpret the data differently. Experienced gardeners may find this process fast and easy due to years of accumulated knowledge. New gardeners may struggle with issues they don't understand.

One of the best things about gardening is that gardening networks, both online and in person, are easy to access for better understanding. In any group of gardeners, there are many common experiences they have encountered. Shared experiences often make for an easy resolution, and unique experiences are educational for all. My local garden club has gardeners of all levels who help one another with gardening information specific to our environment. Master Gardeners are a great source to ask questions about why something happened in the garden. Established garden clubs are another. YouTube videos are an area I favor.

Here's an example: Say you have a problem with yellow leaves on your tomato plants. Incorrect watering, either too much or too little, is a common reason for yellow leaves and is a problem many gardeners have experienced. There are some tomato diseases that cause leaves to turn yellow. Nutrient deficiency is another possible cause. Some insect pests can cause yellow leaves. They can also be part of the normal aging of a tomato plant.

Because there are so many things that can cause yellow leaves, the analysis should look beyond the first possible reason. This is the "peeling-away-of-the-onion" aspect of garden analysis. If you check your soil moisture level and determine you don't water enough, start watering slowly and deeply on a regular basis. This may correct the problem. Continue to inspect the plant for other causes. If the plant growth slows with lower leaves yellowing while new leaves at the top are bright green, it could be nitrogen deficiency in the soil. If there are spots on the leaves or obvious leaf damage, investigate the possibility of disease or pests.

As something unexpected happens, investigate throughout the garden and compare observations. Are all the plants in the same bed showing a problem, or is it just a single plant? Look for environmental factors that influence the area in question. I once had a row of young boxwood plants I was growing into a hedge. Two of the plants on one end were stunted and not as healthy as the others. Observation and investigation showed that those plants were being shaded by a fence early in the day. My analysis was that the troubled plants received substantially less sun than they required. It took time to develop that theory after eliminating other possibilities, but I stand by it as being the most likely.

There are a few possible reasons why the tomato has yellow leaves. Analyzing the issue and trying different corrective measures will hopefully get you to the bottom of the problem.

When recognized early enough, corrective action may solve the problem within the same growing season. Moving plants to a new location, increasing or decreasing watering, adding nutrients, fighting pests, and protecting plants from weather are all actions that can be taken immediately after observing and analyzing what is happening in the garden.

Delaying corrective action is not necessarily a bad thing even when plants suffer or die. That is the reality of gardening. Sometimes plants die, even if we've tried many things or nothing at all. Experience helps us identify when there are more important things to do in the garden and to accept negative outcomes that have lower priority. In many ways, it is sacrificing some plants so others will thrive.

Don't assume that all observations will be of things that are wrong and need to be fixed. Many more observations are of the things that are working. The same analysis process should be followed for good activity. When a plant grows tall and green and is loaded with fruit, it is not time to sit back and assume everything the gardener did was right. Analyze why it is tall and green and loaded with fruit, especially if it hasn't happened before. What were the factors that can be repeated in other areas of the garden?

The key is to observe and analyze continually in the garden. I think some of the best gardeners are the ones who are always wondering *why* and then taking time to research to be able to explain the why. One of the reasons I've been successful teaching gardening to the public is that I asked and answered why so many times that I can now share the answers comfortably.

Modify and Plan

Any garden issues should be addressed during the growing season, whether for immediate action or for future modification. Even high-priority items that require a quick response — such as pests, diseases, or nutrient deficiencies — identify potential problems in the future if the corrective action isn't repeated. Much observation should be done with an eye toward garden planning in the following year and subsequent years.

Continual garden observation throughout the garden season may identify trends when analyzed at the end of the season. During the few years when there are no pests or no severe weather, it can be easy to just look at the results of what was done and determine that the soil, irrigation, and plant selection made all of the difference. It could be that the garden success wasn't caused by what was done, but rather it was caused by what didn't happen. Time and experience help with our decisions, but thorough analysis of all factors, present or not, helps develop the experience.

Begin planning next year's garden by looking at each plant of this year's garden. If your plan included two tomato plants, everything about those two plants can provide useful information. Did they grow as expected? Did you get the harvest you hoped for? Did they taste as good as you wanted? Would you grow them again? Analyzing each plant in each garden bed helps lay the groundwork for future planning. You may find that you grew too few of a favorite plant and want to grow more next time. Maybe you liked what grew, but you didn't eat or preserve it all, so next year you'll sow fewer seeds.

Basic garden chores such as watering and weeding should be part of the observation and analysis. Was the gardening year as easy as you hoped? If it took longer to water the garden than you expected, begin thinking about how you can make it more efficient. If you spent excessive time pulling weeds, do the analysis for why. You may have noticed that the mulched raised beds had fewer weeds than the ones with bare soil and can plan to mulch more next time.

The basic question throughout the season and particularly at the end is, "What should be different?" Seeking to improve every aspect of gardening is part of the journey every gardener experiences. Because there are so many different ways to garden, and so many different plants, and so many unique influences on our gardens, there is no single best answer for every gardener when confronting that question. What is different from one year to the next will be different for everyone. We have control over some of the differences, and those are the ones we should include in our planning.

It's okay if the answer is that the garden shouldn't be different for the next year. If everything is working well, there is little reason to change it just for the sake of change. If a plant grew well and produced well, then keep it in the garden plan and grow it again. This is how experienced gardeners learn to have an easy and productive garden. We find what works and keep doing it. Many gardeners grow the same plants in the same beds year after year because they've determined that is the best way to do it.

I occasionally do things differently just to confirm that my previous process was good. After years of growing a favored variety of zucchini or tomato, I'll plant something new and compare the results. If the new plant compares favorably, it may make it into the new garden plan; if not, it won't be repeated. If changing the soil or irrigation or how I plant something makes a difference, then I can analyze why and decide if a change is needed with my planning. It all becomes more knowledge to build gardening experience for the future.

Some seasons I focus on the gardening tasks that I do the same way from year to year and see if anything could be different with minor changes. I'll analyze how I water my garden and seek to improve it the next year with a new wand or different timing or longer soaking. I try it a certain way, observe the effectiveness, analyze the results, and determine if I'll do it the same way next season or not. It is similar with how to start seeds, how to transplant seedlings, and how to prune plants. Trying out a new technique may offer a better way of doing things.

Tips for Documenting

Key to observing, analyzing, and experimenting is documentation. Documenting helps retain the gardening wisdom that shouldn't be lost. It's nice to recognize what is happening in the garden, but the data should be recorded. Every gardener should have some form of a garden journal. It can be a folder of papers, a notebook, or an electronic file. The journal can include the initial garden plan, how the beds were planted, how the plants grew, what weather trends developed, which pests were problems, how much was harvested, and any other observations that the gardener deemed important. Drawings and photos can be part of it.

A journal records both successes and failures. Having a log of those lessons helps prevent them from happening again. A journal is also a great way to start the next garden's plan. When sitting down to determine what to grow and where, a review of the previous year's journal can reveal what you were thinking months before and what you wanted to do differently.

Over time, a review of many years' worth of journals can be insightful. When I choose to try something new, it surprises me to find that I may have already tried it years before. Philosopher George Santayana famously said, "Those who cannot remember the past are condemned to repeat it." There may be no place where that is more true than in the garden. There is much about gardening that we do and then forget as we do more.

Raised beds are particularly suited for a garden journal. Each raised bed is an individual space for documenting the plants and soil within it. Because of how we plan and plant each bed, it is already in a format that can be recorded for future review. Trends quickly become apparent when comparing results between different beds in the same year or between different years within the same bed. Successes signal what should be repeated as part of the next season's plan. Failures or problems indicate the potential need for change.

The journal can include whatever each gardener wishes to record. I recommend tracking weather and pests over the years to recognize trends that might be missed. I also recommend keeping track of specific plants, where they were grown, and how well they grew. It is easy to dedicate a page in the journal for each bed, with each page documenting the same data.

The journal should also include a section for observations taken during the season, whether they resulted in corrective action or not. Anything of note should be in the journal. Many things we see today can be happy memories in future years. I know the date I started my Master Gardener training because I annotated it in my garden journal 20 years ago. I can see when I had visitors to the garden long after I'd forgotten who stopped by and when.

These days, much of my observations and annotations are on video. I use my YouTube videos to educate other gardeners and I include some views and comments about my garden that are educational but also intended for me personally, as a kind of video garden journal that I can reference in the future. I can see the progress of my garden planning and building by reviewing my own videos and comparing the changes over time. I find it helpful to see what has happened in earlier gardens as I look to the next plan.

There are many different journals that can be purchased from nurseries or online seed companies. Most of them contain pages for basic recordkeeping: calendar pages, grids for drawing a planting plan, sections for taking notes, and a list of plants. These journals are a good place to start, especially if you have little experience documenting a gardening season. Many seasoned gardeners eventually create their own personalized journal to document the information they deem most important.

Make Your Own Garden Journal

Many garden journals allow for drawing the season's plan and then offer a series of pages for information in one of two formats: a single page for each plant with the applicable data, or a page as a calendar date with space for filling in what happened that day. This may be enough to meet the basic needs of a typical gardener, but I prefer to include that information and more. On the following spread, I've given you examples of page masters from a personalized garden journal that meets my needs.

These two pages show sample garden journal entries for an individual plant profile as well as a summary of a growing season's milestones and highlights.

Plant Profile

Plant name: _____

Color of flower or fruit: _____

Size at maturity: _____

Sun and water requirements: _____
_____

Special needs: _____
_____

Source (and cost): _____

Date seeds were started: _____

Seeds started indoors or outside: _____

Bed it was planted in: _____

Seed depth and spacing: _____

Germination rate: _____

How many days to germinate: _____

Plant spacing: _____

Date when flowers and fruit appeared: _____

Date when harvested: _____

Amount harvested: _____

Pest or disease issues: _____
_____
_____

Special observations: _____
_____
_____

Changes for next time: _____
_____
_____

Season Milestones and Highlights

Date: _____

Important weather: _____
_____
_____

New gardening techniques: _____
_____
_____

Key observations: _____
_____
_____

Pest appearance and effects: _____
_____
_____

Disease appearance and effects: _____
_____
_____

Fertilizer and amendments: _____
_____
_____

Important events: _____
_____
_____

Successes: _____
_____
_____

Failures: _____
_____
_____

Ideas for next year: _____
_____
_____
_____
_____
_____

Chapter 6

Growing in Raised Beds

Common gardening practices are not ignored in raised beds. Some may be easier, some may be more difficult, but sowing, watering, mulching, thinning, pruning, weeding, and harvesting are all typical tasks that still need to be done. Some chores are unnecessary in raised beds, such as tilling and hoeing rows. Other tasks, such as trellising, are normal activities. Growing plants takes effort, even in raised beds, but figuring out the best ways to do it isn't hard.

Generally speaking, raised beds help keep common tasks orderly and manageable. The first bed is weeded until only desired plants remain, then mulch is added to fill in any gaps, and then the soil is watered. Then the second bed is weeded, mulched, and watered, and then the third. If the gardener is interrupted or delayed, it is easy to know which beds are done and which still need attention.

Separating the mundane gardening tasks into individual raised bed events makes for easy scheduling. Gardeners with limited time but big gardens can plan which activities are done on which days and be assured that everything will be accomplished over time. My weeding plan sometimes unfolds over a period of days, with one or two beds finished each day. The plan runs concurrently with a mulching plan, a seed-sowing plan, and a planting plan. Different tasks for different beds on different days, but it all is planned and completed.

Developing a foundation of basic raised bed gardening information helps make the whole process easier and more manageable. The methods of sowing a seed or putting a plant in the ground are not complicated, but there are tips, tricks, and recommended techniques that are more successful than others. Learning the best methods for irrigating your beds, pruning plants, and maximizing harvests will help you take advantage of the benefits of raised beds. Each

◀ My garden in full production.

garden and each gardener is unique, so every gardening tip may not be the best for you, but learning, practicing, and choosing what works for you will keep gardening enjoyable and ultimately successful. The guidance that follows can help you make the most of your raised beds.

Planting in Raised Beds

With a plan in place and everything ready to go, planting seeds and plants can be one of the easiest aspects of gardening. As I mentioned in the previous chapter, I like to lay out all of the seed packets and potted plants in the space they'll occupy before planting anything. This is the time to modify the garden plan, before the plants are growing in the beds.

With everything in place and the locations confirmed and approved, it's time to get them in the ground. The garden plan should include the recommended spacing, and that's how I begin. For seeds, I space and plant a few different ways depending on the size of the seed or plant and the initial spacing. Potted plants and bigger seeds are easier to see and place in the soil. It is more difficult to select individual small seeds for precise placement.

Raised beds make the work easy because you can sit on the bed's side or kneel next to it as you plant seedlings and seeds. Precise spacing is easy because the bed sides offer an exact starting point. Place a ruler, tape measure, or a stick with markings at the desired interval on the soil surface. On some beds I hammer small nails into the wood and run twine between the nails to create a perfect straight line for planting.

Plans can be modified right up to planting time.

I use twine strung between nails to make straight lines and grids for exact planting.

Before You Plant ...

Before you plant your seeds and seedlings, make sure the temperature is just right. Plants do best when the soil temperature is warm. If it's too cold at planting, they can be stunted, may not grow well, and may die. Check the soil temperature with a probe thermometer and only plant certain plants when soil temperatures are above the following minimums:

- Plant cool-season plants, such as beets, kale, peas, and spinach, when the soil is at least 50°F (10°C).
- Plant summer plants when the soil warms to at least 60°F (15.5°C).
- For certain plants such as tomatoes and peppers, wait until the soil is at least 70°F (21°C) before planting.

Before planting, I also recommend you install trellises and/or any support structures needed for protecting your plants. Waiting to install a trellis or hoop system after plants are big often results in damage to the plants, as the system could bend or fall and break stems, branches, and leaves. Put these structures in place as part of bed preparation. Seeds and plants can then be planted around a trellis and allowed to grow up it with ease and no threat of damage. In-place hoops are ready to support plastic and insect mesh to protect young plants as soon as they're needed. See pages 232–242 to learn more about trellising, as well as Chapter 7 for information about how to use hoops and trellises to protect your plants from pests and the elements.

Check your soil temperature with a probe thermometer before planting anything.

There's no threat of damage to your plants when hoops and trellises are in place early.

Sowing Seeds

A rule of thumb is that a seed should be buried to a depth that is two to three times its width. So a bean seed is planted deeper than a carrot seed. The recommended planting depth on seed packets is close to the rule of thumb. There are several methods of sowing a seed, but with all of these techniques, it helps to start with bed soil that is already moist. I prefer to start watering the soil in the raised beds for days before the seeds go in.

One method is to dig a small hole to the appropriate depth. The hole can be made by pushing a tool or finger into the soil to the appropriate depth. You then drop a seed into each hole and then cover it with soil. Seeds can be sown individually with this method. For a group of seeds, dig multiple holes with the recommended spacing between them. I prefer to make a grid of holes to fill out the space, drop a seed into each hole, then cover all of them with soil at the same time. (See sequence below.) I make sure to use a plant marker to identify each row or block before I place the seeds, so I don't lose track of what I'm planting.

1. Make a hole with a finger or a tool, such as a dibble.

2. Continue making all the holes in the grid or row.

3. Drop the seeds in the holes.

4. Cover the seeds by brushing soil in the hole.

For another method, the hole is not dug beforehand. Instead, place a seed on top of the soil at the correct spot and with the right spacing, push it into the soil with a finger or stick to the proper depth, then cover the seed with soil. This can be one of the fastest ways to sow a block of seeds: All the seeds are placed on the surface with the appropriate spacing and then pushed down into the surface one after another and covered with soil. (See sequence below.)

1. Place the seeds on the soil in a grid.

2. Push all the seeds into the soil, finishing the grid.

3. Cover the seeds with soil.

For planting multiple seeds in a row, dig a small trench in the soil to the appropriate depth. A shallow trench is easy to make by dragging the tip of a trowel across the soil. Place seeds in the trench at the recommended spacing and then cover all of them with soil. This can also be a quick way to sow multiple rows of seeds at a time. Dig several appropriately spaced rows of trenches. With all trenches dug, drop the seeds into each trench and then cover the whole area with soil. (See sequence below.)

1. Scrape parallel rows of trenches at the proper depth and spacing.

2. Drop the seeds in all the rows.

3. Scrape the trowel across the rows to fill in the trenches.

For a no-digging method, place seeds on top of the level soil and then cover them with enough soil to bury them to the desired depth. This method works well for seeds that are broadcast across the surface and then thinned later on. Before spreading the seeds, loosen the soil of the bed slightly by scraping the surface with a trowel or by lightly running your fingertips back and forth across the surface. This gives the soil a texture that will keep the seeds from shifting. Then sprinkle the seeds across the soil, and loosely drop more soil onto the seeds. (See sequence below.)

1. Loosen the soil surface with your hands or a tool.

2. Drop the seeds on the soil.

3. Cover the seeds with a light layer of soil.

A dibble creates holes for seeds at precise depths.

The seed size and planting depth influence which method to use. Big seeds such as peas or beans tend to be planted deeper, as much as 2 inches deep. Making holes ahead of time with a tool like a dibble is effective. A dibble is a small tool with graduated marks that makes holes with consistent depth. With all the holes formed, simply drop a seed into each hole and then cover the seed with soil.

Medium seeds such as radishes and beets are usually planted about a ½ inch deep, and the trench method works well. This method is best for when there is flexibility in actual planting depth, so the trenches don't have to be dug to an exact depth. Ideally, the spacing between seeds can also vary slightly, since dropping seeds from fingertips will not give exact spacing.

For small seeds such as lettuce or carrots, the planting depth is usually much less. It can be challenging to get exact spacing, so the seeds are broadcast across the surface as evenly as possible by dropping them from fingers. With the area covered by seeds, they can either be lightly rubbed into the soil with fingers, or the entire space can be covered in a loose layer of soil.

Fingers are great tools for seed planting.

The fingers can be very effective seed-planting tools. All seeds can be pressed into the soil with fingertips. Fingers can be used to make a hole. I often use my fingers to create a trench if it is only half an inch deep. I have more control when sprinkling soil across the surface when I use my hands and fingers.

Once seeds are in the ground, they should be watered. Soil will settle around the seeds during the first watering, and moist soil is the kickoff to germination. Regular watering is needed to keep the soil moist. It should not be allowed to dry out, especially for seeds that are shallow.

The flow of water should not be so strong as to wash away soil and the seeds, but should be light, like a mild rainfall. Using a watering can or water wand with a sprinkler head works well. It is better to lightly water the surface, allow it to soak in, and then lightly water again than to try to drench everything all at once.

New seeds need an initial good soak and then regular, light watering. Watering wands with sprinkler heads will deliver a light but thorough watering.

Label Your Plants!

It's a good idea to label all your rows or grid squares when sowing seeds. Because so many plants can be grown side by side in raised beds, the simple task of labeling plants takes on more importance. Too often, gardeners think they'll be able to remember what they planted, but when hundreds of plants in multiple varieties suddenly fill a bed, it can be difficult to tell which plants are growing where. Take the time to label plants as they go in the ground, so their identification is easy. The labels should have the type of plant and variety as a minimum.

Be sure to label seeds right away to avoid any confusion.

Blank plastic plant tags are available at garden centers, nurseries, and numerous online sites. You can also make durable plant tags from items such as plastic bottles, aluminum cans, and even the slats from old window blinds. Durable materials such as plastic and metal can be reused for more than one season and are great for labeling general plant types to identify areas of your raised bed. You can also use leftover Popsicle sticks for specific varieties that may only be planted once. Use a pencil or specialized waterproof garden marker to label the tags. Standard permanent markers will fade in sunlight.

Hardening Off Plants

Before planting seedlings that were grown indoors or in a greenhouse, these young plants should have a period of time to acclimate to the outside conditions in the garden. This is called "hardening off." The seedlings have been grown in a sheltered, controlled environment with consistent temperatures and no wind or harsh sun. To put the tender plants directly into the garden with harsh conditions during both day and night may stunt plant growth and could damage or kill the young plants.

Hardening off gradually exposes the plants to the conditions they will encounter in the garden. Over a period of days, they experience increasing sun, wind, cool nights, and whatever else will confront them outside.

Begin the process by putting the plants outside in an area protected from wind, but exposed to morning sun. The early sun is less damaging, and most plants can handle a couple hours of exposure for the first day of hardening off. After that exposure, the plants are returned indoors under lights.

Over the next few days, expose the plants to ever-increasing time in the sun. On the second day, put the plants outside in the morning and give them a few more hours of sun. On the third day, extend the exposure into the afternoon. The goal is to have the plants outside all day on day five or day six. Each night, you should bring the plants indoors.

It is important to monitor the plants and water them regularly. If they look stressed or begin to wilt, take it as a sign that it is time to return them indoors. The specific number of hours in the sun is not as important as keeping the plants alive as they are hardening off. Exposure to a breeze can help strengthen the stems, but excessive wind can cause damage, so avoid putting them out on windy days.

By the end of a week, you should begin to expose the plants to cooler overnight conditions. The day before I plan to transplant them into a raised bed, I'll place the plants in position, in the beds they'll occupy, for an entire 24-hour period. Transplanting puts stress on plants, and hardening off helps reduce the weather stresses that could make it worse.

There is some labor involved as plants are taken outside and returned inside each day. It's easy to do with just a few potted plants but can be a major exercise with multiple trays of plants.

Initially, plants should have some protection from harsh sun and wind. You might set them next to a wall.

Bring plants back inside after brief sun exposure.

Place the pots in the bed a day before transplanting.

You will also need to have spaces both inside and outside for the plants. The effort is worth it when all your plants survive transplanting and begin to thrive in the garden. Many of us have transplanted plants without hardening off, only to find many of them dead or severely damaged on the first day they were exposed to nonstop harsh sun.

Once the plants have spent an entire day and night outside without obvious negative effects, they are ready for planting. They can remain in pots for many days after the initial hardening off if conditions change, or you're not ready to plant yet, but try to avoid waiting too long. The plants will grow better in the good soil of a raised bed.

Planting Seedlings and Plants

For transplanting seedlings and potted plants, appropriately spaced holes must be dug to a depth that matches the pot size. The hole should be at least as deep and as wide as the pot that the plant is currently in. Slightly wider is good. When the potted plant is placed in the soil, the surface of the pot soil should match the bed soil. To get a precise hole, dig it, then place the pot in it, then dig again as needed. As with seeds, it helps to start with bed soil that is already moist. Watering the soil in the raised beds for days before the plants go in makes it more likely that it will be moist at root level.

A concern that many gardeners overlook is that the soil dug from the holes needs some place to go. Have a bucket ready, so the soil dug from the holes can be placed in it. Alternatively, dig a hole and heap the soil in a mound elsewhere in the bed. Some of the soil will be used to fill the gap between the root ball and the edges of the hole.

A hand trowel is suitable for digging most holes. A useful tool that many gardeners like is a Hori Hori knife, which is similar to a trowel, but with sharpened edges. Bigger plants in bigger pots may need a spade to dig the hole. For small plants, hands and fingers are useful tools to scoop away loose soil to a suitable depth.

With the hole dug, you can remove the plants from the pot. Do not pull or yank the plant because that can cause plant damage.

Place the pot in the hole and look for the soil surface levels to match.

Instead, knead the sides of the pot gently to loosen the soil edges. Gently squeezing it from all sides is usually enough to separate the soil from the pot. For bigger pots and stiff plastic pots, rest the pot on the ground and roll it while applying pressure from above. This should be enough to loosen it, but be careful not to damage the stem.

Cradle the plant with your hand by putting your hand on the top of the soil, with the stem resting between your index and middle fingers. Don't squeeze the stem; just support the soil surface with one hand as you turn the plant and pot upside down. Pull the pot away from the root ball with your other hand. With the soil loosened, the pot should lift easily. (See sequence below.)

A Hori Hori is a great tool, but watch out for sharp edges.

1. Dig a hole deep enough for the roots.

2. Squeeze the pot to loosen its soil.

3. Cradle the plant's stem between your fingers.

4. Gently remove the plant from the pot.

5. With two hands, place the plant in the hole.

6. Fill the hole and firm the soil.

Set the pot to the side while you continue to cradle the plant upside down, and then use both hands to flip the plant upright and place it into the pre-dug hole. Have one hand underneath the root ball and use the other hand to help guide the plant into the hole. Again, resist holding or squeezing the stem. If you must adjust or tug the plant, it is better to use the leaves to do so.

Using fingers or a trowel, fill in the space between the root ball and the sides of the hole with soil. Gently firm down the soil around the plant, adding soil as needed to maintain the surface level. Use one hand to hold the plant steady and erect while filling in the hole. (See sequence on the left.)

After the plant is in place, it is time to water — long and deep enough to reach the roots. Beginning with moist soil aids in the water reaching a suitable depth. As with seed planting, it is better to start with multiple light waterings than one big quench. A key difference is that seeds are usually planted at less than an inch deep, so the initial watering can be light and easy, but for transplants the soil needs to be moist much deeper.

Bare-root plants such as strawberries or asparagus are easy to plant by using holes or trenches. I like using a slightly different method. Place the plants at the recommended spacing on the bed surface. At each location, stab a trowel into the soil and pull back on it to create a hole. Place the plant in the hole and then pull out the trowel. That causes the soil to fall back against the roots. Firm the soil around the roots, adding a little more soil if needed, then water the soil well. (See sequence on opposite page.)

Alternatively, you can dig a deep trench suitable for the plants. A strawberry trench is typically 3 inches to 6 inches deep, and an asparagus trench can be 12 inches deep. Plants are laid in the trench at appropriate spacing, roots are spread out, and then the trench is filled in with soil. As with seeds and seedlings, water well after the bare-root plants are in the soil.

1. Stab the trowel to the appropriate root depth.

2. Pull the trowel toward you to make a hole.

3. Place the bare-root plant in the hole and remove the trowel.

4. Firm the soil around the roots.

Successful Succession Planting

As you learned in Chapter 5, the ease of planning and planting in raised beds makes them ideal for succession planting. Succession planting is a gardening method that allows gardeners to maximize how many plants grow with multiple plantings in the same bed throughout the gardening season. More plants are harvested by strategically managing sowing and planting times.

When extending your season potential by growing a spring and fall crop in addition to the main summer crop, particular emphasis on the bed's soil can make a positive difference. Full amending of the soil should be complete before the first crop is planted because amending the soil mid-season may cause a nitrogen deficiency as new organic matter begins to decompose. A good, rich soil that's full of life should be able to support three cycles of planting.

If not amending the soil, or if the soil is still being developed, you can strategically use fertilizers to make up for any deficiencies. Early, leafy crops such as lettuce, spinach, and kale can benefit from extra nitrogen. Excess nitrogen should be avoided with root crops and fruiting plants such as beets, carrots, potatoes, and tomatoes in favor of fertilizers higher in phosphorus and potassium. Most vegetable garden plants, including melons, peppers, and squash, can benefit from balanced fertilizers with an equal distribution of N-P-K.

Each of the growth cycles should be treated as a distinct and separate growing season. As soon as the soil has thawed in the early spring and can be easily worked with a trowel or shovel, sow seeds for beets, kale, lettuce, peas, radishes, and spinach. Transplant broccoli, cabbage, and cauliflower seedlings because they can take longer to germinate and grow to size. Choose plant varieties that have similar maturation times with the intent that you will begin and then complete a harvest within a couple weeks.

In late spring or early summer, with the first harvest complete, clean up the bed by removing any remaining plants. If you're still building your soil, you can add an inch or two of well-decomposed compost to the surface. However, avoid digging and fully amending the bed because the soil life is already established and ready for another round of plants.

Adding a top layer of compost is a good idea after the first harvest is done.

Treat the bed as you would for any summer planting. Sow bean, cucumber, melon, and squash seeds. Transplant eggplants, peppers, and tomatoes. Put the normal heat-loving plants into the bed and tend to them over the growing season. To get a third succession planting cycle, plan to complete the summer harvest in late summer or early fall. If you are content with a long summer growing plan, you can end the succession planting with this second cycle and let all of the plants grow until killed by frost.

For planting fall crops, remove all the summer plants when the harvest is complete and sow a new round of seeds. Consider transplanting brussels sprouts, broccoli, and cabbage. You may need to prioritize your fall crop over an extended summer crop. It can be mentally challenging to pull a productive indeterminate tomato plant in favor of beets, kale, or spinach.

When the long growing season is finally complete in late fall or early winter, clean out the plants in the bed and amend it well. Based on the successes you encountered or failures that led to new knowledge, begin developing your succession planting plan for next year.

If you choose the second method of succession planting — staggering plantings to get a longer harvest period of the same plant type — start by planting just a portion of the raised bed. Sow seeds for plants such as arugula, beets, cabbage, carrots, lettuce, peas, radish, and spinach in one-quarter or one-third of the raised bed. These types of plants can be harvested throughout their life cycle, from small to large. As individual plants mature, you can harvest only the ones that are ready and allow others to grow.

Carrot, beet, and radish seeds are sown in late summer.

Wait two to three weeks and sow another round of seeds in a second portion of the bed. Wait another two to three weeks and do it again in another section. Within a couple of months, you will have a bed filled with plants in various stages of growth. Harvest some beets small to serve as baby beets in a salad, while allowing others to grow large for fall storage. Harvest carrots when you need them without filling your refrigerator produce drawer from a big harvest. As you pull plants or do a more complete harvest, continue to sow seeds in the bare spots to keep the bed filled. With the final harvest, the bed is ready for amending.

Annual culinary herbs are something I recommend for succession planting. Basil, chervil, cilantro, dill, fennel, and parsley can all bolt when temperatures get too hot, so use succession planting to replace older, woody plants and maintain a fresh supply of young, tasty plants. Some of these herbs such as cilantro and dill are often grown to maturity to harvest the seeds for culinary uses, so you can leave some of these plants in place.

Watering

Proper watering is critical to the success of a garden. It begins when the plants are first put into the soil, and consistent moisture is needed during the growing season for plants to grow normally. The roots are the part of the plant that absorbs water, and unless the water reaches the roots, the plant simply can't access it. Applying too little or too much water can affect the plants adversely. Too little water, and the soil can dry, damaging or killing plant roots. Too much water can drown plants by limiting access to oxygen.

It is important to check soil moisture regularly. A soil moisture meter is a tool for seeing whether the soil is moist or dry. You insert the meter's probe into the soil and get an immediate indication of the soil's moisture level. They can be accurate, but I've found that many inexpensive meters lose accuracy quickly.

Personally, I find the finger test to be an effective way to determine soil moisture at no cost. To do a finger test, physically push your finger into the soil to see if it feels wet, dry, or just right. You can dig a small hole in the raised bed to different depths and use a finger to check for moisture down to root level.

For large-scale consideration, grab a handful of soil and squeeze it. If it holds together, it usually doesn't need water, and if it falls apart, it does. If it drips from the pressure of your squeeze, the soil is too wet, and an extra day between irrigation is probably advisable.

Moisture meters offer a general idea of soil moisture.

A finger can easily detect moisture.

Soil that is too dry does not hold a shape when squeezed.

Soil that is too wet will glisten and form a ball.

Saturated soil will drip when squeezed.

Evenly moist soil will hold its shape but break apart when pressed.

How Much Water

Determining how much water is the right amount for plants can be one of the most challenging aspects of gardening. There is no single application that is appropriate for all plants. Most garden plants will grow well with 1 inch to 1.5 inches of water per week during the growing season. That water can come from rain or supplemental irrigation. Maintaining a consistently moist soil is the goal.

There are several factors at play when it comes to deciding how much and how often you need to water your plants, such as weather and climate, root

Learning how much and how often to water is a challenging aspect of gardening, and it often requires you to closely observe your plants and how they react to the water you give them.

depth, plant size, the stage of the plant's life cycle, and soil quality. You have control over much of it as you observe your garden, recognize the changes in plants as they grow, and adjust the water amount accordingly.

Weather and climate: Rain, wind, and temperature are all important factors in figuring out how much to water. We don't have control over the weather, but we can use it to modify our watering plan. Rainfall of an inch or more may mean that the beds don't need to be watered for a few days. A light rain that does little more than wet the surface of the mulch has little impact and shouldn't be a substitute for your regular irrigation plan.

Heat and wind have an enormous impact on soil and plants. Sunny, windy days may require extra water because the soil dries out, and plants wilt. On these days, plants will need more water to grow and thrive. Cool, overcast days may have less evaporation and less plant stress, so regular irrigation may not be needed. Plants grown in early spring require much less water than those grown at the height of summer.

The frequency and amount of water could also depend on your general climate. In dry regions, water needs may be higher because soil moisture loss through evaporation can be high, and plants may lose more water through transpiration. Transpiration is the process where the water absorbed through the roots is distributed throughout the plant. Cells in the leaves open and close to release or retain water vapor. This evaporation of plant moisture draws more water into the stem and leaves. In dry conditions, more water vapor is lost from the plant, requiring more water to be available for the roots to absorb.

In wet and humid regions, soil can remain moist because there is less evaporation of the soil's moisture. As relative humidity of the air increases, transpiration decreases. How often the plants need enough additional water to support plant growth is reduced when the humidity is high.

The impact of weather and climate highlights one disadvantage of raised beds. Raised beds are exposed to weather on all four sides in addition to

Collect Rain

Saving water may not seem important to everyone, but many of us have to pay for the water we use. Every wasted gallon of water has a literal cost associated with it on our monthly bills. If you pay for your water, consider adding rain barrels to your yard to collect rainfall. You can collect a little more than half a gallon of water for every square foot of roof space when it rains one inch. Fill rain barrels and use them, along with rain, to reduce how much valuable water you use from your hose.

If you don't have access to rain barrels or are limited in how many you can have, you could try to design your garden area to take advantage of rain from your roof. Build low raised beds near the house and direct downspouts into the beds. Thousands of gallons of water can be directed from roof runoff, and the savings can be big.

Directing downspouts into beds can help water your beds.

exposure on the surface, all of which increases the likelihood of soil moisture evaporating. Elevated beds warm faster than those lower to the ground, and warmer soil evaporates sooner. Even in beds with solid sides, the exposure to wind and sun dries the soil edges, and that can wick away some of the interior moisture. As a result, raised beds can require more frequent, deeper watering to account for that moisture loss.

Root depth: The depth of the roots also influences how much water is needed. Deep-rooted plants may need more watering, particularly in sandy soil. The plant may only need an inch or two of water each week, but, as explained above, the raised bed may need two or three times that to replenish what is lost through drainage and evaporation and stay moist.

Shallow-rooted plants, particularly new seedlings, have their roots close to the surface and usually benefit from light watering more often. Deep watering isn't as necessary because the roots aren't deep. Instead, frequent watering

Light pooling allows water to drain deeper.

207

is required to maintain enough moisture for the roots close to the surface. The top of the soil is the first to dry out in the sun, and the top inch or two can be dry when the rest of the soil is moist.

Plant size and spacing: A good rule of thumb is to equate the amount of water a plant needs with its size. The bigger the plant, the more water it requires. The total plant mass should be considered as well because many small plants may need as much water as one big plant. In raised beds, that holds true, but because more plants are usually growing close together, some factors vary from traditional in-ground beds. If plants are crowded together, there may be more shading on the soil from the plants and less evaporation. This could result in less water needed than if the plants were spaced farther apart.

A plant's life cycle: Plants need different amounts of water at different times in their life cycle. Seeds and young seedlings will benefit from consistent watering to keep the soil evenly moist. Frequent, light irrigation may be necessary in the early days of germination and plant growth to keep the soil from drying out. In my dry Colorado conditions, I water new seeds in the early morning, again in the late morning, again in the midafternoon, and again in the early evening. Extra watering may be needed if the day is particularly hot and windy.

Once plants are established and growing well, regular deeper watering is better to promote deep root growth. The frequent, light watering needed early on can lead to shallow root growth later in the plant's life. Even for shallow-rooted plants, it is advantageous to grow roots as deeply as possible. Roots too shallow can stress the plant during dry periods when the soil surface dries out and the roots begin to die.

During flowering, older plants will need more water than before. And during fruit set and up to harvest, plants may need the most water of their lives.

Soil quality: Soil quality affects how well the soil retains moisture. Over the course of a growing season, roots can grow long when conditions are good. Soil rich in organic matter holds onto more moisture than soil with a higher mineral component, which causes water to drain faster. The depth of the amended soil should also be considered when determining how much and how often to water. Physically checking the soil's moisture, with a meter or a finger, is a good way to learn how the organic content correlates to soil moisture retention.

Always Use Mulch

Mulching has many benefits, but reduced soil moisture evaporation is the one that can save you money. Less evaporation means that you water less often. Efficient mulching can greatly reduce a bed's water needs and reduce how much you spend on water.

How to Water

Grouping plants by water requirements is the most effective way to ensure all the plants in a bed get adequate water and can be a distinct benefit of raised bed gardening. Hydrozoning is the practice of irrigating efficiently by planting a bed with plants that have similar water needs. This irrigation method can save water and allow for a vegetable garden in areas that are prone to drought because wasted water is minimized.

In a hydrozoned bed, shallow-rooted plants are watered at a rate suitable for those plants. Watering will be different in this bed than in a bed with all deep-rooted plants that have higher water needs. However, when plants with differing water needs are planted in the same bed, the gardener needs to take care not to give all the plants in the bed the same amount of water. Light watering is enough for the shallow plants, but not the deep ones. Conversely, deep watering to reach the root level of the deep-rooted plants will moisten soil well below the root level of the shallow ones.

This is a hydrozoned bed with plants that are grouped by their watering needs. Matching plants by their water needs helps ensure multiple plants thrive.

Hand watering allows for plants with different water needs to be planted in the same bed. Knowing which plants have higher requirements, I can apply more water to that section. For intensive plantings in a raised bed, it often happens that plants will grow at different rates and reach different sizes at different times. Hand watering ensures each plant gets what it needs.

Hand watering with a hose and watering wand is my preferred method of irrigating my raised bed garden. I use a water wand with a nozzle that distributes the water in an even, light flow. Hand watering with a wand is also very efficient when starting seeds because the water can be broadcast across the bed surface, ensuring the entire bed's soil stays evenly moist.

The biggest criticism of hand watering is that it can be labor and time intensive. Dragging a hose through a big garden with many beds can take a long time. Personally, I don't see this as a disadvantage because the time allows me to get up close and personal with each bed and every plant. I have the opportunity to see problems before they develop and care for the plants individually.

Watering wands provide easy, even watering.

Drip irrigation is a very efficient way to get water directly to plant roots. Drip emitters can be installed with specific flow rates that can be tailored to each plant. The emitter regulates how much water reaches the plant's roots. Within a single bed, plants with different water needs can be planted side by side, and the emitter ensures that one plant gets more water than the other. The water is only applied where the emitter is installed and can be directed to the root zone of each plant.

There are different types of emitters for different purposes. The drip emitters allow the water to drip out at regular intervals or to seep into the soil. Micro-sprinkler emitters act as miniature sprinklers that spray water across the soil. The emitters can be installed along a length

Individual water lines of a drip emitter system can run to each plant.

of poly tubing to create a line of dripping water, or lateral tubing can branch off poly tubing with emitters at the end of the lateral line.

The main supply line runs from the water source, often a faucet, to the garden. Poly tubes branch off from the main trunk into each raised bed. Within a raised bed, the water supply line can run along one side or through the middle of the bed, and lateral lines run to individual plants for directed water flow. The lines and emitters can be modified to match the plants growing in each raised bed.

Small, elevated micro-sprinklers can water a bed by spraying water across the soil.

The system can be challenging to install for gardeners unfamiliar with all the components, though many DIY kits are available. Different-sized tubing, pressure regulators, filters, valves, and emitters are integral parts of the irrigation layout. The system can be run by a timer for easy scheduling. I think gardeners should still inspect beds and plants regularly to ensure that the drip irrigation is working as planned. Overwatering and under watering are still possible with an automatic system.

Soaker hoses, or drip hoses, are an easy option for gardeners. The hose is designed to deliver steady drips of water along its length. Made with material that seeps water or as porous irrigation pipes with small holes drilled

Soaker hoses exude steady drops of water along the length of the hose.

in them, they distribute water along the length of the hose. Some common soaker hoses available in garden centers are made from recycled rubber. I use hoses that are covered with fabric sleeves.

The hose can be snaked around the bed and between plants to get water to root zones, but it also drips water between plants where nothing is growing. Soaker hoses are better at providing a slow rate of water to a large area than drip emitters that water a precise zone. Most soaker hoses are designed so multiple hoses can be attached to one another in line. They can be an effective hands-off way to irrigate a large area.

The biggest limitation of soaker hoses is that the amount of water dripping varies along the hose. Water pressure is higher closer to where the soaker hose is attached to the water source. Water comes out of the hose at the beginning of the line easily and forcefully. As it flows along the hose, the water pressure decreases, with less water seeping out. The far end may only produce intermittent drips. This means that the soil at one end of the hose gets more water than the other end.

Multiple water lines can direct water to your plants.

Within a single raised bed, a soaker hose can be an efficient way to distribute water evenly because the hose can be placed so that it covers the entire surface. Connecting multiple hoses and running them between beds is not as effective because much water is lost as the hose continues to seep in the space between beds. An alternative is to set up a drip irrigation system and use small soaker hoses designed for the poly tubes instead of drip emitters.

Sprinklers are a common irrigation method in the landscape, but less so in raised beds. Small sprinklers with adjustable patterns can be placed in beds and keep water within the bed. Larger overhead sprinklers can water large areas, but much water is wasted when it falls on the sides of the beds and in the paths between them. Water continually soaking the sides of a wooden raised bed may also hasten the breakdown of the wood. If a large area of plants includes some raised beds, sprinklers may be a good option. In my pollinator garden, I use an overhead sprinkler to water all the flowers and to get water to my stone

Watering using an overhead sprinkler is suitable for large areas of plants.

and metal raised beds in that area. I'm not worried about wasting water between beds because there are plants growing all around them.

Because sprinklers deliver a consistent flow of water, they can be difficult to adjust for beds to get different rates of water. Even though the flow closest to the sprinkler tends to be higher than at the end of the stream, all of the beds receive similar amounts of water. That means some plants may get more than they need, and others might get less. Sprinklers work best for areas with plants that have similar water needs.

Raised beds can be made to be self-watering. Wicking beds are self-watering raised beds designed to water plants from below the soil surface. A sealed reservoir at the bottom of the raised bed holds water, and when the bed is irrigated it is through tubes that replenish the reservoir. Special soil blends absorb water from the reservoir and moisten the soil through capillary action. The idea is to create a relatively hands-off approach to irrigation.

With a full reservoir, the soil stays consistently moist at lower levels as it absorbs water. In practice, the moisture levels within a wicking raised bed are usually inconsistent. The lowest levels can be saturated with water while the top of the bed is dry. A well-designed wicking bed ensures the soil is evenly moist at root level.

Regardless of the irrigation method, it's important to stay attuned to your garden's needs. A common error is when gardeners set their irrigation system in early spring and never make any changes until the system is turned off in the fall. The amount of water plants need can change daily, and as we learned earlier, there are times during the gardening season when more or less water should be part of the irrigation plan.

Look for Discounted Irrigation Systems

Keep an eye out for drip irrigation systems at yard sales and thrift stores. Some pieces are often missing, but you can get most of the big components at a greatly reduced cost. It's cheaper to replace a few lines and emitters than to buy a brand-new system. And let your gardener friends know you want to try drip irrigation. They may share old components when they upgrade.

When to Water

Knowing when to water your garden is important. Generally, water early in the day. Cooler morning temperatures mean less evaporation. It tends to be calm in the morning with less wind and that reduces evaporation, too. As the water soaks into the soil, the plants take it up right away and begin the day strong, turgid, and ready to confront the stresses of a hot day. It is normal for plants to slow growth and wilt when it is hot or windy. With adequate soil moisture, plants will perk up quickly when conditions cool.

Watering in the early evening has similar advantages. Plants may be stressed from a hot day and will benefit from an application of lifesaving water. Much plant growth happens at night, and soil with adequate moisture levels can provide all the water and nutrients needed by the plant. With a moist bed in the evening, plants can use the water as soon as the sun rises. Gardeners with a regular day job may find evening watering better because they can focus on the garden and plants as they calm and relax after a day at the office.

Gardeners typically choose an either-or plan with morning or evening irrigation, and that is usually enough, but watering when the plants require it is important regardless of the time of day. A quick check of the soil can determine if watering is needed. In cool seasons, watering may take place days apart. During the peak growing season, water may be needed every day. On a hot summer day with a lot of wind, two irrigation cycles per day may be needed, in both the morning and the evening.

Early evening watering is cool for both the gardener and the plants.

Mulching

Mulch is a material that is applied to the soil surface. Amendments are added into soil, and mulches are added on top. In the garden, we use two types of mulch: organic and inorganic. Organic mulch comes from material that was once living. Straw, leaves, grass, hay, wood chips, and compost can all be used as organic mulch. Inorganic mulch material has no organic component. Gravel, ground rubber, and plastic are typical inorganic mulches.

The ability to mulch each raised bed individually is a great advantage to gardening in raised beds and should be embraced by gardeners. I vary the mulch in each of my beds based on the plant types in it, the irrigation I use, the time of year, and the reason for mulching. Some of my beds have straw mulch, some have pine needles, some have wood chips, and some have a combination of materials.

The primary reasons I mulch are to reduce soil moisture evaporation, to provide an organic food source for soil organisms, to moderate soil temperature, and to suppress weeds. Additionally, mulch reduces soil compaction, reduces nutrient leaching, and can help avoid fruit contact with bare soil. Mulch is often used to reduce soil erosion, but that is rarely a need with the level surface of a raised bed.

Generally, I apply mulches after plants have started growing and the soil has begun to warm. If laid down too early, a thick mulch can inhibit the growth of small seedlings. The common practice is to sow seeds, allow them to germinate, and when the plants are a few inches tall, apply a light layer of mulch to the soil surface. As the plants grow, more mulch is added until the soil surface is covered. The depth of the mulch usually corresponds to the size of the plants and the benefits desired.

When transplants are put into the ground, you can spread a thicker layer of mulch across the soil right after planting and watering. It helps to leave room around the plant stems in

Pine needle mulch still allows strawberry runners to root.

Mulch after planting, but leave some open space around stems.

Wood chips can be good for perennial beds.

the beginning to ensure air and water reach the roots. For small plants, the mulch can interfere with growth, so leaving a gap between the plant stem and the mulch gives it room to grow.

A few inches of mulch in a raised bed are enough to suppress weeds, reduce evaporation, and moderate soil temperature. In my vegetable raised beds, my mulch depth tends to be between 2 inches and 3 inches. The mulch layer is shallow because much of that material will be incorporated later as amendments.

Around my fruit trees and in open landscapes, the mulch is much thicker. The primary reasons for mulch in those areas are weed suppression and reducing soil moisture evaporation. The mulch is at least 6 inches thick in these areas. I use a chunky wood chip mulch that decomposes slowly and will not be worked into the soil as an amendment.

Mulch Materials

The choice of mulch material is influenced by the bed location and the plants growing in it.

Wood chip mulches: Wood chips, bark, and shredded hardwood mulches are long-lasting and can be an attractive garden component. They stay in place and are less likely to wash away in heavy rain or blow away in heavy wind. For raised beds with perennial flowers, ornamental grasses, flowering shrubs, or fruit bushes, a chunky mulch keeps maintenance to a minimum. Periodically, additional mulch is added because it will settle and break down in time, but little more effort than that is needed. I also use wood chips around my raspberry plants.

Cheaper Chips

There are a few places where you can look for free or discounted wood chips. Many of the same companies that offer compost often have industrial chippers and sell bulk wood chip mulch at reduced costs. You could also contact local arborists and ask for wood chips. They typically have to pay to dump the chips they get from pruning trees in a local landfill. If you see tree trimming and chipping in progress, ask the foreperson if you can have them. They are often glad to dump them in your yard for no cost. (But consider offering a gratuity for their efforts.) You can also check out ChipDrop at getchipdrop.com. ChipDrop acts as the middleperson between arborists and gardeners. Sign up and get wood chips delivered to your house for free, though a small gratuity for the crew is encouraged. You don't have much say in how much you get and when they arrive, and you may get more than you wanted, but the extra chips can always be saved or shared. Lastly, check for bargains on bagged wood chip mulch. Bags with tears are often available at a discount, or wait for end-of-season sales.

Pine needles: Dried pine needles or pine straw are good mulch options for beds with perennial plants because they last a long time before decomposing. Water drains easily through them, and they are very effective at weed suppression and moisture retention. They are also great at keeping fruit off the soil. I use dried pine needles around my strawberry plants. They are easy to spread and a great way to reuse organic material in the landscape. Contrary to popular misconception, pine needles are not acidic and will not lower the soil's pH.

Pine needles bind together for a stable mulch.

Mulching Vegetable Raised Beds

In vegetable garden raised beds, the soil is worked regularly during transplanting, amending, and garden cleanup. Wood chips and pine needles that end up buried in the soil can cause a nitrogen deficiency at root level as they break down. This can interfere with the growth of your vegetables. To reduce this likelihood, gardeners who use chunky mulch in vegetable beds should remove the mulch completely in spring, then sow, plant, and reapply the mulch when plants are big enough that their growth will not be affected by the mulch. Personally, I avoid that concern by not using those long-lasting mulches in my vegetable garden beds.

Instead, I focus on lighter organic mulches, such as grass clippings, crushed dry leaves, and straw, in my vegetable garden raised beds. They are less of a problem when buried because they decompose quickly and add organic material to the soil.

Dried grass clippings: Dried grass clippings are the first type of mulch I apply to my raised garden beds. Light and easy to spread, I sprinkle a shallow layer of the clippings shortly after sowing seeds. A light layer up to ½ inch thick helps reduce soil evaporation during seed germination, but it is not so heavy that it interferes with seedling growth.

Fresh grass clippings can clump and interfere with small plants, so it's best to dry the grass first. After mowing the lawn, spread out the clippings and allow them to dry for two or three days before using as a mulch. I store bags of dried clippings so I can use them year-round. Avoid using clippings from grass treated with herbicides for weed treatment because chemical residue may remain on the blades and interfere with vegetable seedling growth.

As plants grow, I add more grass clippings. Applying a dried grass mulch 2 inches thick is effective for small plants 6 inches tall or more. The biggest issue with clippings is that they can shift and blow away in areas with strong winds. The sides of a raised beds help keep them inside the bed, but they often need to be respread to cover bare spots. I regularly reapply clippings during the early stages of seedling growth.

It is better to mulch with dried grass clippings than fresh, green clippings.

Doesn't Get Cheaper than Free!

Use the organic materials in your yard for free mulch. Crushed leaves and dried grass are easy to collect, save, and use when needed. They're also easy to find on the sidewalk in many neighborhoods. However, you'll want to ask the homeowner if any herbicides were used on them. Not only will using these free materials in your raised beds save you money, but also you'll be saving the materials from a trip to the landfill.

Dried leaves: Crushed, dried leaves are slower to break down than grass and work well as an organic mulch. They are ideal to mix with grass clippings. Whole, wet leaves can compact and inhibit water and air movement in soil, but when dried and crushed, the leaves work very well. By themselves they are susceptible to blowing away in strong wind, but when combined with grass, the two materials bind together well and stay in place much better. As seedlings grow, a combination of materials 2 inches to 3 inches thick is more effective than either material by itself.

A blend of grass and leaves makes a good mulch.

Straw and hay: Straw is the mulch I use the most in my vegetable garden beds. Along with hay, it is easy to apply and is very effective as a mulch. For plants that are bigger and growing well, applying a layer of straw or hay 3 inches to 4 inches thick reduces soil moisture evaporation, moderates soil temperature, reduces the likelihood of weeds, and virtually eliminates problems with soilborne plant diseases. More mulch can be added as plants grow because it will settle and break down over the course of the growing season. Under my melons, squash, peppers, or tomatoes, I use straw by itself or layered on top of dried grass clippings and crushed leaves to a depth of 6 inches.

Straw is an easy, effective mulch.

When it comes to straw bales, look for clean stalks and avoid excessive seed heads.

I have some concerns when using bales of straw or hay. There is the possibility that it can be contaminated with herbicide residue that can affect vegetable plants. Asking the seller about that possibility is advised, but I've found that few if any of the stores know the source of the material and whether it has that potential. To reduce the risk, I age my straw bales before using them. Most of the potential contaminants will break down when exposed to sun and weather. I buy my bales the year before I plan to use them, leave them in the open, exposed to all types of weather, then use them a year later.

There is also a good chance that the bales will have seeds from the plants used for the hay or straw. Hay is a field grass that's a food source for farm animals, and seed heads are common. Straw is a byproduct of cereal grain production, in which grasses such as wheat, barley, or rye are harvested for the seed heads and the remaining stems are baled as straw to be used as animal bedding. Some seed heads will be baled along with the stems.

The result is that unwanted seeds can be introduced to raised garden beds. Hay mulch has a high probability of sprouting grass weeds. There is less likelihood with straw mulch, but it is still common. A mulch depth of 4 inches to 6 inches is usually enough to limit the chance of seed germination and growth, as with other weeds. Mulching with shallow layers of hay or straw increases the possibility of weed growth. Luckily in raised beds, it is easy to see the grass seedlings emerge and then pull them from the bed, but if gardeners are not vigilant, the bed can quickly be overtaken by the weed growth.

As with grass and leaves, a light mulch such as straw is susceptible to shifting in high wind. To get the benefits of the different mulch ingredients, I like to mix them all together. Grass, crushed leaves, and straw have different lengths and thicknesses, and can create a mulch that lets air and water through, while resisting the likelihood of blowing away in wind or washing away in rain. By itself, straw needs reapplying, like the others.

Light straw by itself can shift in strong wind.

A blend of materials makes a much stabler mulch.

Gravel: Gravel and pebbles last the longest of any mulch and may be suitable for perennial plants in areas that require no cultivation or regular maintenance. Landscapes designed with xeric (drought-tolerant) plants are often mulched with gravel. A multitude of colors, sizes, and textures can add a nice visual element to the bed. These long-lasting mulches are best suited for raised beds that are not used for vegetable gardens.

Gravel is effective at reducing erosion in mounded beds and can add visual flair.

Plastic: Synthetic mulches are a possibility in raised beds. Black plastic is effective at warming soil, conserving moisture, and limiting weeds. According to research plots by scientists with the Agricultural Research Service and Clemson University in South Carolina, red plastic mulches boosted tomato yields by up to 20 percent. Plastic can be cut to the size of the raised bed and used for more than a single year. It does need to be removed to amend soil, but can be laid down before planting, with seeds or plants placed in slits or holes cut in the plastic.

Plastic mulch is not as common in home gardens and is more often found on commercial farms.

Plastic mulches tend to be good for heat-loving plants. Eggplants, peppers, melons, squash, and tomatoes benefit from warm soil temperatures, and the plastic supplies that. In regions with hot summers, the soil temperatures can rise too high with black plastic, so adding another organic mulch on top to moderate the temperature is effective and advisable. Clear plastic is not recommended as a mulch because the access to light, warm soil and moist conditions can be ideal for weed growth underneath the plastic. Using clear plastic can be good for warming soil early in the year but should be covered with organic material to reduce weed seed germination.

Cover crops: Using living plants as a mulch is a great option practiced by more experienced gardeners. Cover crops are plants grown to cover soil for the same benefits as other mulches. An additional benefit is that the plants can be incorporated into the soil to add nutrients, particularly nitrogen, that aren't as prevalent in other organic mulches. They protect soil and improve soil fertility. Because of that nutritional benefit, they are also known as "green manure."

Several different plants can be used as cover crops. Legumes, such as field peas, clover, and hairy vetch, can add nitrogen to the soil. Cover crops with big roots, such as daikon radishes (white radish), are effective at breaking apart dense soil. Grasses, such as winter rye and winter wheat, can grow quickly after the main growing season and add good organic matter to the soil when incorporated in spring. Cover crops can provide shelter and food for animals and insects, above ground and below. Hairy vetch is one of the first flowers in spring for bees and butterflies. I use a blend of Austrian field peas, winter wheat, collards, hairy vetch, daikon radish, and yellow mustard to get varied benefits from the different plants.

The type of mulch affects the effectiveness of irrigation methods. The same thick mulch that covers soil and reduces soil evaporation can hinder the movement of water and stop it before it reaches the soil. Dry mulch is likely to absorb light rain before any reaches the ground. When watering plants, the gardener should account for the mulch to ensure that water flows through it or that irrigation systems are placed under mulch so water flows on and into the soil surface.

A bagged blend of cover crop seed is a great option for growing a living mulch.

Thinning Plants

Ideally, every seed we sow would germinate, and every transplant would thrive in our raised beds, but the reality is that much of what we plant doesn't grow. To overcome the possibility of failed germination or early death, most gardeners sow more seeds and plant more plants than they plan to grow. Instead of sowing a single seed in a hole or pot, we sow two or three. Some small seeds can be difficult to sow exactly where we want them, and we end up with more on the ground than we need.

These seedlings are clumped together and will need to be thinned. Growing backup plants provides options for choosing the healthiest seedling.

We may want a nice straight row of carrots spaced perfectly apart, but the tiny carrot seeds rarely fall where we wish and more drop to the soil than we plan. The result is carrot seedlings growing too close together and outside our desired row. The lettuce seeds we broadcast across the surface germinate where they fall, often in clumps or randomly distributed. Having extra plants in the ground provides backups for the ones that die or fail to thrive.

Pests, fungal diseases, and inconsistent watering are leading causes of early plant death. But when things go right, there is little plant death, and too many plants end up growing in the designated space. Good soil, ample nutrition and light, and proper watering exacerbate the overcrowding problem as most of the plants grow well. At some point, overcrowded plants will begin competing for those needs, and the resulting deficiencies can cause some or all the plants to suffer, be stunted, and fail to grow to maturity.

The solution is counterintuitive. Some plants must die so that others will live. By selectively removing plants, gardeners leave behind the plants that are more likely to survive and thrive. The strongest plants remain. The process we use is called thinning, thinning out, or pricking out. It is the deliberate removal of some plants growing too close to others.

If I'm starting seeds indoors, I typically sow two or three pepper or tomato seeds in each cell of a 72-cell planting tray. If only one seed germinates in each cell, I'll have 72 plants, but if most of them germinate I'll have more than 200, which is too many for my needs. By choosing just one seedling in each cell of my seed-starting tray, I maintain manageable plant numbers while ensuring the strongest and best seedlings go in my garden.

The same process is used in the garden when direct sowing seeds. When too many seeds germinate, some of the seedlings are removed to leave one or two with the correct spacing. Many seed packets direct gardeners to intentionally sow more seeds than needed, with guidance to remove some of the seedlings to get better spacing for the adult plants.

The first time to consider thinning plants is once they form their first set of true leaves. The first leaves on a seedling are cotyledon leaves; the second set are the true leaves. That second set of leaves shows that a root system is established and that the seedling is beginning to grow strong.

We want the strongest plants to remain, and that may be easier to determine after they have their second true set of leaves. When two seedlings are growing side by side, remove the

The first set of leaves is the cotyledon leaves.

The second set of leaves looks different. These are the true leaves.

Look closely for plants growing too close together.

Cut out the weakest-looking plants.

Continue thinning the bed.

weaker-looking of the two. A quick visual analysis is usually enough to determine which one looks taller, bigger, or stouter and is the better candidate for survival.

Thinning should also be done with a specific spacing in mind. Carrots are typically sown ¼ inch to ½ inch apart, but mature carrots do best when spaced 2 inches to 3 inches apart. Lettuce seedlings may emerge a few inches apart, but the final spacing should be 8 inches to 12 inches. Beet and chard seeds are actually small fruits with multiple seeds in them, and numerous seedlings will emerge together. Thinning out our seedlings takes gardeners from poorly spaced, random, and clumped seedlings to an orderly arrangement that maximizes production.

Thinning plants does not need to be a single event, with the final spacing determined after the first round. Thinning out is often best done in phases. When seedlings are clearly growing too close, remove the weakest. As the remaining seedlings grow stronger, retain the strongest that is close to the desired spacing. Before the bigger plants interfere with one another, do a final round of thinning.

By working in phases you can have intermittent harvests of some of the young plants. Many vegetable garden plants can be eaten at all phases of growth. Carrots, kale, lettuce, peas, and spinach can all be pulled when small and added to salads. Baby beets are simply beets harvested early before reaching full maturity.

The grids in this bed are overgrown.

After thinning, the squares may not look much different.

However, many plants were removed from the two squares, as this photo shows.

How to Thin

Once the sacrificial plants are identified, there are a few ways to remove them. The simplest method is usually to pull the seedling from the ground. Grab the small stem and pull straight up to reduce the chance of your interfering with nearby seedlings. Alternatively, cut the seedling at ground level using sharp scissors or small pruning shears. Cutting the seedling is preferable if pulling might possibly interfere with the roots of the other seedlings close by.

Once the small plant is removed, just drop it on the soil surface to become mulch. If you're thinning out a lot of plants, add them to a compost pile. Pulling and dropping can be fast and efficient. Because thinning can happen many times, eventually, bigger plants may need to be pulled or cut if it is apparent they are interfering with other plants. I add the big ones to my compost.

In late winter, many trees have dead tips that should be trimmed away.

Pruning off lower branches of tomatoes reduces pest and disease issues.

Pruning

Pruning is the selective removal of parts of the plant that are no longer needed or desired. Removing a branch, leaves, flowers, or fruit by selective pruning is done with the goal of benefiting the plant. When I prune my plants, I do so with the "four Ds" in mind. I remove plant parts that are dead, diseased, damaged, or disorderly.

Dead, diseased, and damaged branches and leaves are no longer providing beneficial photosynthesis and could present opportunities for pests or disease to enter the plant. Removing them makes for a healthier plant and could prevent the problem from spreading.

I consider a plant part disorderly when it interferes with or impedes the growth of itself or another plant or when it presents a hazard to people and property. This is often seen with tomato plants in the vegetable garden. An indeterminate tomato plant can quickly grow and overwhelm a bed, choking out other plants and blocking pathways. By selectively removing tomato branches, it can be controlled without causing problems.

Selectively pruning out some flowers and developing fruit can encourage the plant to produce more flowers and fruit. For many plants, removing some parts of the plant can open it up to more sun, which stimulates the formation of flower buds, encouraging maximum fruit production.

Particularly with fruit trees, removing branches to shape the tree can provide a structure that is appropriate for maximum fruit yields. The three primary shapes are open center, central leader, and modified leader. (These general shapes are illustrated below.) I use all three with different fruit trees in my garden. Additionally, specialized pruning can achieve decorative shapes for hedges, topiaries, and espalier trees.

Espalier is a pruning method to shape fruit trees.

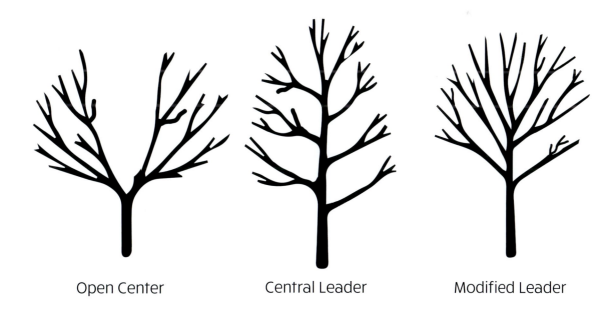

Open Center — Central Leader — Modified Leader

These are common pruning tools. From left to right: hand pruners, bypass loppers, anvil loppers, and a folding pruning saw.

Tools

The most-used pruning tool in my garden is a set of hand pruners. Like a set of robust scissors, they cut through most of the stems and branches in my vegetable garden. For thicker stems or branches, such as those of trees, loppers are long-handled tools that provide a bigger blade and extra leverage to make the cut. For very thick branches, pruning saws are made with sturdy blades and angled teeth that are designed to quickly cut through the wood. For some pruning projects, I'll use all three on the same plant.

Weeding

Just as seedlings can compete with one another for limited soil resources, other plants in a bed can compete as well. A problem arises when many of the competing, unwanted plants seem to grow faster and bigger, and they overpower our desired plants. The unwanted plants are weeds. Weeds are simply any plants growing in a location where you don't want them to be. Many consider dandelions, bindweed, or purslane to be weeds, and they can be, but lettuce, peppers, and even tomatoes can be weeds if they're growing in the wrong location.

The Raised Bed Advantage

There are several advantages to raised beds for preventing and controlling weed growth. Tilling in-ground soil can increase weeds because buried weed seeds are brought to the surface to germinate and grow. The reduced soil disruption in raised beds limits the likelihood of weeds sprouting from those dormant seeds. The height of the soil in a tall raised bed can also inhibit annual weeds that might be growing in pathways. Because of the clearly defined growing area, any weeds that appear can be easier to see and pull. My bed height is designed for sitting when pulling weeds, and if they do appear, I can comfortably pull them without bending over.

However, there are some limitations. The soil brought in for filling beds may be loaded with weed seeds. As well, weeds may not be as easy to see in a large garden plot overflowing with plants. Experienced gardeners can still see them when they emerge and bend down to pull them, but that may be more difficult for new gardeners. In short beds, weeds can invade from the pathways. Gardeners who don't till the ground and who mulch their in-ground beds can expect a similar amount of weeds as raised bed gardeners following the same practice.

> **Raised Beds and Invasive Plants**
>
> It is easy for some plants to escape an in-ground garden bed. A common example is a mint plant that quickly overwhelms a garden to become the primary plant. The confines of a raised bed help to keep plants where the gardener wants them. Many of the invasive plants in our garden spread by roots as they extend below ground or by the stems rooting when they fall to the ground, but when those types of plants hit the sides of the raised bed, they're stopped with nowhere else to go. If you decide to grow invasive plants, it's important to build the bed high enough that roots can't escape or build the bed with a bottom that limits them.

Eradicating Weeds

I first determine if a plant is in the proper location before deciding if it is a weed — regardless of the plant type. I allow many plants to grow that others may consider to be weeds. Dandelions provide food for many pollinators and animals, and I let them grow around my raised beds. Many native plants surround my garden because they support native wildlife. They are not weeds to me if they grow outside my raised beds.

Any plant that is growing inside my raised beds is a weed if it isn't a plant I put there as part of my garden plan. The same plants that I allow to grow elsewhere are immediately pulled if I see them appear in a different bed. I've removed tomato plants, asparagus, and many herbs as

I let many native plants grow right up to my beds.

Only one of these plants is not a weed.

weeds because they appeared as seedlings in a bed that was planned for other plants. It is common in the garden for fruit or seed pods from the previous year to fall to the ground and their seeds sprout when temperatures warm the next year.

Removing the unwanted plants from our beds is called weeding, and weeding is commonly considered one of the worst garden chores. It doesn't need to be a tedious task. As a regular part of garden maintenance, it can feel like it's in the same category as watering plants. The primary reason weeding can be challenging is that gardeners wait too long to do it. When small, most weeds are easy to remove, but when left to grow, they can explode in population and require extensive effort to remove.

The easiest way to manage weeds is to pull them as soon as they emerge, just as we would when thinning plants (see pages 223–226). Mulching raised beds also reduces the likelihood of weed seeds germinating and makes weeds easy to spot when they first start growing. They pull easily in moist soil, and I make it a practice to water my raised bed and pull out the small weeds I see at the same time. I'll take a few minutes to sit on the bed, inspect my plants, and pull what doesn't belong.

A key to early management is proper plant identification. Many gardeners are afraid to pull small plants because they are unsure whether they might be the plants they desire. Many seed packets include a picture of what the seedling looks like. That is helpful. Make a point to observe the seeds as they germinate and then as the seedlings grow. It is easy to note the similarities in the seedling size, color, and leaf shape when many are sprouting in the area you sowed seeds.

With practice, it becomes easy to note when something looks different. In a block of radish plants, seeing similar plants with rounded leaves helps identify them as radish seedlings. If another plant emerges with different leaves or in a different color, it is a weed. Don't wait until it gets bigger to try and identify what it is. Save the effort of removing a big plant by plucking it from the soil while it's still small. You don't need to know what a plant is to decide if it's a weed; you just need to know what it isn't. If it isn't what you want, get rid of it.

If the plants get bigger before being identified as a weed, removing the plant by digging is better than pulling. The stem of many weedy plants can break when pulled, leaving the roots in the ground. Often those roots continue growing and will sprout again. Use a trowel to dig out the whole plant, including its roots. Long, specialty weeding tools can make the task easy for long-rooted weeds.

A hoe is the traditional tool for chopping and digging clumps of weeds in a garden. Long-handled hoes can be difficult to control in a tall raised bed, but there are short-handled hoes that work well while the

A cultivator claw tool can clear weeds easily.

gardener sits on the edge. Short weeding tools with sharp ends can slice through the soil and remove weeds quickly and effectively. A cultivator claw tool can disrupt the soil surface and pull out dozens of small weed seedlings.

Herbicides are an option for killing weeds, but I use them as a last resort for pernicious weeds that don't respond to digging and keep coming back. Be sure to read all the directions and safety information before using any chemical in the garden. Only use herbicides as directed. Many gardeners avoid using herbicides in the vegetable garden because the chemical residue may contaminate and kill plants near the target weed.

If weeds are a big problem and everything needs to be removed (including the desired plants), you can cover the bed with a clear plastic sheet to kill all the plants in the bed. In a process called solarization, the plastic initially traps heat and moisture underneath. That encourages germination of the weed seeds in the bed. The plastic sheet also keeps additional water out and heats up the soil. Over a period of weeks during the summer, the solarization process kills the plants and keeps new ones from growing. The design of raised beds makes this method easy because the plastic can be sealed around the bed edges.

It is important to note that all weeds should be cut or removed before the plant flowers and sets seed. The seed head of some weedy plants can contain thousands of weed seeds. Once weed seeds are allowed to spread, it can be very difficult to eradicate them. Get rid of weeds as early as possible and never let them stay in the ground long enough that they can propagate.

Trellising

Traditional gardening methods encourage gardeners to grow horizontally with plants sprawling across the ground. Big backyard gardens end up looking like small farms to accommodate the amount of space needed to grow big plants. Pumpkin patches occupy large areas because each pumpkin plant can require 10 lateral feet, or more, for the vines to grow big enough to support the bulbous pumpkins. Cucumbers, squash, and melons are notorious for how much space they require in traditional gardens.

Vertical gardening is a great option for growing more plants in a smaller space because the lateral requirements are shifted upward. A plant that grows 4 feet across the ground may only need 6 inches or 8 inches of space for the roots and main stem that anchor it in the ground. Instead of having one plant every 4 feet, vertical growing allows that plant to grow 4 feet skyward, freeing up space around it. Another plant can be grown a few inches away, also growing vertically.

The key to vertical gardening is the use of trellises. Trellises can increase the number of plant possibilities by shifting from horizontal plant growth to vertical plant growth. Trellis is both a noun and a verb. A trellis is a structure that supports plants as they grow, typically a framework that allows the stems, vines, or leaves to be secured to it. To trellis is to train a plant with a trellis, often by weaving it through the trellis or attaching the plant to it.

Raised beds are ideally suited for trellises. The design of raised beds allows for trellises that can be anchored to the sides or buried in the soil within. Posts can be placed outside a column of beds and wire strung between them to support all the plants along the way. A bed can be placed next to a fence, and the fence wire or wood can be used as a trellis. I have hoop trellises that are custom-made to fit my beds and I interchange their use based on what I'm growing each year.

The sky is the limit for vertical growth when you're using trellises.

An elevated structure can be stunning when covered in leaves and flowers. The visual impact is a good enough reason to use trellises. In the vegetable garden, trellises not only allow for more plants in a small space, but they also make the plants easier to harvest. The fruit hangs from the plant at eye level, or close to it, and becomes more obvious than when the plant sprawls across the ground and needs to be lifted to reveal the fruit.

An added benefit is that trellising can reduce plant disease. Increased air circulation around elevated plants lowers humidity around the plant parts. Fungal diseases need moisture to grow, and drier leaves can prevent them. Other diseases reside in the soil, and getting plants off the ground reduces exposure to certain pathogens.

It's easy to see fruit on a trellis.

Trellis Design

The structure of the trellis is quite variable and can be built to match the growth type of the plant. Its primary purpose is to provide a strong support to hold the plant. As plants grow, they become increasingly longer, wider, and heavier. That's not a big problem when they spread along the ground and have the earth to support them, but when grown vertically, the trellis should be designed to support the plant in all phases of growth, particularly the weight of the full-grown plant. For plants that produce fruit, the size and weight of the fruit also need to be considered when making a trellis.

The size of a raised bed and the material it's made from can add strength to trellises. Wood and metal trellises are often easy to attach and secure to a sturdy wooden bed. Trellises can be buried within the raised bed, and the weight and depth of the soil add stability. Newer metal modular raised beds are often offered with trellises designed and fitted for those specific beds.

Trellises from Free and Recycled Materials

Like your raised beds, you can make your trellises from free, recycled materials. Tree branches, recycled fencing, and old fence posts can all be used to make trellises at no cost. Scrap metal and wood are often available for free from construction sites. They may be placed by a dumpster, or you can ask the foreperson.

You can also check out home improvement stores that sell donated materials. My area has a Habitat for Humanity ReStore. All kinds of construction materials, new and slightly used, are available at a fraction of the original cost. These materials can be used to make beds, trellises, paths, and much more. Some cities have thrift stores with separate sections for donated building materials.

A trellis can be as simple as a long bamboo stick that guides the growth of your plants. Sticks can be pushed into the soil soon after transplanting, or they can be pushed into the soil at the appropriate spacing for your plants and then seeds are sown at their base. Choose bamboo based on the mature height and size of the plant. Thin bamboo a few feet tall is good for peas and peppers. Thicker bamboo 3 feet to 4 feet long can be suitable for beans. Sturdy bamboo sticks 6 feet long can be strong enough for tomatoes.

A common trellis consists of a crossbar supported by two posts. The basic design can be small and made with bamboo or similar sticks, or it can be tall and wide, and made from sturdy lumber and posts. The structure is constructed to

Bamboo is a strong support.

Twine hanging from a crossbar supports plants.

anchor secondary material that supports the plants. Trellis nets made from nylon, polyethylene, and polyester stretch between the sides and top, and plants grow up the nets. Similarly, wire mesh fencing can be stretched between the posts for stronger support.

A similar trellis design uses the same side posts and top piece, but lengths of twine are suspended from the crossbar. Twine pieces are secured at the top and drop down to the plants. Beans, cucumbers, peas, and even tomatoes can climb the twine as they grow. The plants with tendrils will grab onto the twine, and beans will curl up it, but other plants will need to be trained to grow around the twine or be fastened to it. Tomato clips and small plant support clips work well to hold plants to the twine as they grow vertically.

Wooden lattice covered with ivy or honeysuckle is a classic garden image. So is a metal arch over a garden path supporting climbing roses. Both can be used in raised beds. Securing lattice work to the back of a raised bed allows the plants within to grow up it. I have two sturdy raised beds that anchor the bases of an arch, and the vining plants in the raised beds grow up the arch.

I have many different types of trellises in my garden to support different plants. An easy and rustic trellis for beans is built from three or four small tree branches or thick bamboo stakes that are connected at the top to form a pyramid. Taller and sturdier branches can support a single indeterminate tomato plant as it grows.

One of my strongest trellises is the base of an old bunk bed buried on end within a raised bed.

A tomato clip attached to twine supports this tomato stem.

A buried bunk bed frame becomes a sturdy trellis.

This horizontal cattle panel is a long, stable trellis that will support dozens of plants.

My bell trellis is a favorite feature in my garden.

The metal slats that supported the mattress can now support my plants. It is ideal for cucumbers. At the end of the season, the trellis is pulled from the soil, stored, and is ready to be used again the following season.

My preferred trellises in the vegetable garden are made from cattle panels. Cattle panels are a type of livestock fencing. Along with hog panels and sheep panels, they can be repurposed into a sturdy trellis. The four-gauge galvanized steel panels are strong enough to support any garden plants. Sold 16 feet long and 50 inches wide, they can be cut and bent to make a variety of trellises.

The simplest cattle panel trellis follows the basic netting design, but the strength of the steel doesn't require a top support. Eight-foot-long wood posts or metal T-posts are driven into the ground, and the cattle panel is attached horizontally to them. For best support, at least one post should be used in the center of the panel. I use this trellis as a permanent support in my low, concrete block raised bed. The base of the panel is about 2 feet from the soil surface, which puts the top at about 6 feet high. I train my plants onto the trellis, and it can support dozens of cucumber or tomato plants loaded with fruit.

Functionality is the primary reason for trellising plants, and most gardeners don't mind the wood or metal posts that are doing their job to support plant growth. Basic trellises don't always add a positive visual impact in the garden, but they can. With stain and paint, they can be made more appealing. For extra expense, carved metal trellises can provide stunning visual appeal in the garden. It is possible to have both functionality and positive aesthetics.

Selecting a Trellis for Your Needs

It's important to consider your own reach and the mature size of the plants growing on your trellis when choosing one for your raised beds. With a bed about 12 inches high and a trellis that's 6 feet tall, the total height is 7 feet. That is fine for tall gardeners like me, but it may be too tall for some gardeners when it comes time to harvest the tomato plants that grow past the top.

To avoid needing a ladder in the garden, there are a few options for deciding how to trellis tall plants. One is to grow both vertically and horizontally on a trellis. Cucumbers, squash, and tomatoes can be trained to grow at an angle up a trellis like my horizontal cattle panel. The vine can be 12 feet long but because it is growing at an angle, the final height might only be 6 feet. All the other plants are trellised similarly, so there is adequate spacing between them.

Pruning the plants to fit the trellis is another option to keep plants under control. This is generally a good idea for all trellised plants, so they don't overwhelm the trellis, but it can be more important if the trellis or the gardener is too

Unpruned tomatoes can overwhelm a bed.

When pruned, they are manageable and shouldn't overwhelm the trellis.

short for the full mature size of the plant. Trimming off the primary growing tip is enough to stop additional growth on the vine. That can stimulate side growth instead. Additional pruning may be necessary, but gardeners can trim any plant to fit a trellis.

The type of trellis can also depend on whether the plants growing on it are annuals or perennials. Our vegetable garden plants tend to be annuals that only grow for one season. However, perennials such as clematis, honeysuckle, jasmine, and roses may grow on the same trellis for many years. Trellises for perennials need to be constructed of long-lasting materials for the long haul because replacing trellises can damage plants. Strong anchoring and sturdy materials ensure that the vining plants have support for years. Trellises for annuals typically don't need to be so robust and can be portable for use in different beds in different years. Cucumbers, gourds, squash, and tomatoes can be grown on trellises with less permanent materials that allow for replacement between seasons.

How to Trellis in Raised Beds

Trellising plants means attaching them to a vertical support. Even for plants that naturally grow tendrils that curl around supports, it can be beneficial to physically connect the plant to the support. For plants without those natural anchors, an attaching mechanism may be necessary. Matching plants that need trellising to a proper trellis can make attaching easy.

When placing trellises on and in raised beds, always consider sun and shade. Plants in front of the trellis should receive the most sun, while plants behind it may receive very little. Typically, trellises are placed at the back of a bed, so most of the plants in the bed receive sunlight. I often take advantage of the shade to grow plants that will bolt with too much sun. For example, I typically place my bunk bed trellis in the middle of the bed to support the cucumbers and just behind it, I plant lettuce, radishes, and spinach that can benefit from cooler conditions and less light during the heat of summer.

When installing a trellis, it helps to have some access all around it to work with the plants and the supports. For raised beds set beside a wall or fence, the trellis should be placed in the bed so it's not flush against the vertical surface. As plants grow up a trellis, it helps to distribute weight if they can grow on both sides. A flush trellis means all the plants are growing on one side, and that can add stress and weight that the trellis can't support, pulling it away from the wall.

Allowing space behind a trellis, even just a few inches, gives room for plants to grow and room for fingers to work attaching stems to the trellis. Consider mounting the trellis using a bracket that is attached to the fence or wall. A minimum of 6 inches should be enough for most plants. The plants will be distributed more evenly, which reduces the chance of a potential imbalance.

One-sided trellises can work well for flowers or ivy. Freestanding trellises should have access from all sides. This latter type of trellis benefits fruiting plants, since multiple sides allow for more potential harvest as the fruit can hang from the front, the back, and the sides.

With the trellis in place, sow your seeds or transplant your seedlings close to the base. The vertical growing allows plants to be spaced closer than recommended for open beds. Instead of several feet between plants, they can be grown inches apart as long as the plants are directed upward as they grow.

The basic process of trellising often involves weaving the plants through the trellis structure. For lattices, wire fencing, cattle panels, and other grid structures, as the plant grows, the stem is directed from the front of the trellis to the back and then again to the front when the plant has grown longer. Weaving plants achieves a similar support as plants that use tendrils to grab onto the trellis. The plant becomes closely connected to it. In some cases, the plant may need to be directed along vertical twine until it reaches the trellis structure.

When using arch trellises, weaving can be quite effective. Arch ends are anchored in the

Free-standing trellises are great because they can be easily accessed from all sides.

This plant has been woven in and out of the cattle panel trellis.

Plants are woven in and out of this arch structure — in this case between two narrow raised beds, creating a unique and whimsical pathway.

middle of raised beds. Vines are planted on the inside of the arch, and as the plant grows it is directed to the outside of the arch. The growing tip is then trained back toward the inside, and when it gets even bigger it is trained back out. The primary stem follows this weave to support the plant, and branches that grow out from it can be woven through the trellis or allowed to grow on the outside.

With regular weaving, there may be little need for additional clips or ties for the main stem. The size and weight of the plant are enough to hold it to the trellis. The branches that extend from the stem usually benefit from extra attachments. Branches and leaves tend to dangle and drop down and can tear away from the stem. To maintain vertical growth, the other plant parts may need to be attached to the trellis.

One of the simplest connectors is basic garden string or twine. Jute and cotton twine are easy to cut and tie, but can degrade and break down in sun and weather. Twine made from nylon and polypropylene tends to last longer and can be reused from one season to the next. Metal wire and plastic zip ties hold well, but the rigid material can cut into stems and may cause damage.

To attach plants to trellises, cut your string or twine long enough for the ends to be tied. Form a loop that wraps around the plant and the trellis. The loop should be loose enough for the stem to continue growing and widening. A loop that is too small can strangle and cut into the plant when it grows bigger, causing damage. Bigger is better. When I attach the twine, I prefer to add a twist to form a figure eight. This creates two loops, one that circles the trellis support, and one that circles the plant stem. The entire loop can slide up and down both the trellis and the plant and doesn't hinder growth.

A similar method for attaching the twine is to wrap one end of it around the trellis support and tie it in place, allowing the other end to fall toward the ground. This can be an effective way to pre-position the ties. Twine is anchored to the trellis at many different points early in the season. As the plant grows, the trellis twine is already in place and can be connected to the plant as it spreads up and across the trellis.

Clips and clamps are other good ways to connect plants to trellises. Some vine support clips resemble small spring clamps. The small handles are pinched to open the end. The tip squeezes around the trellis, and the open center loosely holds the stem in place. Clips like these are generally used to anchor plants to stakes, cages, netting, and small hoops.

Tomato clips, which are very effective with tomatoes but can be used with other plants, too, are designed to clamp to twine between the center hinge, and the open end wraps around the plant stem and clicks closed. For netting and twine trellises, this type of clip can be attached at multiple points along the stems to firmly support the plant.

Plastic tomato clips hold stems well.

The initial clip or clamp can be connected to the plant close to its base as an anchor spot, particularly when using dangling twine. As the plant grows, more clips are connected. If the plant sags or growing tips fall and stop growing vertically, it may be time to add more clips. Horizontal growth can be supported as well. Tomato plants will send out suckers that grow horizontally. Securing both vertical and horizontal vines can spread a large plant over a large area with multiple pieces of twine connecting it to the trellis.

A popular trellising method for tomatoes is called the "Florida weave" or "stake and weave" method for supporting plants in a row. Large stakes are anchored into the soil or attached to the ends of a raised bed. Instead of securing the plant vertically with twine, it is anchored horizontally. One end of the twine is tied to a post. It stretches laterally across the front side of the plant stem until it reaches the next plant, where it is moved to the back side and then at the next plant the twine is moved to the front. The twine weaves between the plants. At the other stake the process is reversed, so the twine weaves between the plants, sandwiching the stem front and back. (See sequence on the next page.)

1. Begin by tying the twine to a stake.

2. Run the twine behind the plant.

3. Then run it in front of the next plant.

4. At the opposite stake, reverse the process so the twine sandwiches the stems at the front and back.

The first level of support for a weave method like this bolsters the plants a few inches above the soil surface. As the plants grow, another level is woven between the stems 6 inches to 8 inches higher. Each layer of twine is loose enough for the plants to grow and not be restricted. With multiple levels of support, the horizontal twine effectively holds the plants vertically. Lateral branches can be trained around the twine or attached using clips.

Harvesting

So much of our time is spent observing, planning, planting, watering, and weeding that the simple act of harvesting often gets forgotten, or at least it becomes a low priority. For many gardeners, the harvest is the goal of the season, and for many of those same gardeners the harvest is less than it could be.

A primary reason the harvest doesn't happen when it should is that gardeners are not sure how to tell when a plant is ready. It can be a challenge to identify a ripe fruit. It can be difficult to know how big a carrot root is when it's buried in the ground. It can be confusing to decide what is the right color for a pepper.

One key is to start learning about each plant's harvest before seeds or plants go in the ground. Read the seed packet, the online description, or the plant tag. In almost all cases, you'll find a guideline for harvesting. Some sources show how the mature plant, root, or fruit should look. At a minimum, the information should include how many days it takes for the plant to reach harvest or maturity.

Signs a Plant Is Ready

Researching what each plant should look like and taste like is important — I can't emphasize this enough. How big should it be, and what color is best? Having an idea of what will happen soon after the days to harvest date arrives, you can spend time with each plant observing the changes as the harvest approaches. Changes and maturation can literally happen overnight, so when you think the plant is close, check it every day.

These "Hillbilly" tomatoes are almost ready to harvest.

Different types of tomatoes will look different when ripe.

"Days to Harvest" or "Days to Maturity"

The number of "days to harvest" or "days to maturity" may seem straightforward, but in my experience it adds to the general confusion. The problem is that there is no consistency between growers as to what those timelines mean. Some seed companies list how many days from when the seed is put in the ground until the recommended harvest point. Other seed companies start the clock after the seed has germinated, and the seedling is growing with true leaves. There can be a difference of many days between the two for seeds that take longer to germinate.

For plants put in the garden after being started from seeds indoors, there is a general consensus that the timing begins after the plant is transplanted into the garden. The "days to harvest" clock starts when the plant is in soil and sun, and the roots are beginning to get established. Make note of this date and add the expected days to identify the date in the future when you can harvest. Days to harvest is usually more helpful than days to maturity because we harvest many of our plants before they reach full maturity.

An additional consideration that confuses the whole matter even more is that the suggested days are usually based on optimal growing conditions in a greenhouse. When everything is optimum — ideal heat, light, water, and nutrients in a pest-free environment — that's how many days the plant will take to reach harvest. Very few gardeners have ideal conditions in their gardens. Heat, cold, wind, humidity, inconsistent watering, and pests are some of the factors that can stress a plant and affect how long it actually takes to produce a harvest.

The days to harvest and days to maturity measures are helpful when putting plants in the garden, but they should be considered general guidelines and not precise predictions. I think of those as the minimum number of days to grow the plant before thinking about a harvest. I remember that that number is how long it will take under ideal conditions, and since I don't have those in my garden, I know it will take longer. It may be a day or two longer or a week or two longer. Each year is different based on the actual factors that affect plant growth in that season.

Taste: An easy way to determine when a plant is ready to harvest is to taste it. Pinch off a lettuce leaf, pull a carrot, cut off a cucumber. If the size is satisfactory, the color looks right, and the taste is pleasant, it's ready to harvest. If any aspect isn't quite right, wait a day or two and try again. When it's good, it's good. With experience you'll learn to incorporate firmness, texture, and hue into your decision. In time, you'll be able to look at a plant and guess pretty closely if it's ready to harvest. Even then, I taste one first before harvesting everything.

Dig one up: Root vegetables and bulbs can be among the most difficult to discern their readiness. For these types of plants, simply dig one up. Even when my garlic leaves look perfect, I dig up a bulb to check for sure. I always dig up a carrot or two before starting the harvest. Potatoes and sweet potatoes are a bit more challenging because they don't have individual roots, but you can dig a hole near the plant and then gradually move away more soil until you reach the tubers and roots to check their size.

These peppers may look ready, but the Feher Ozon on the left will turn orange and the Alma on the right will turn red.

Color: Color is a big factor for many of the plants we grow. Peppers are among the easiest to identify and one of the most misunderstood. Ripe peppers will change from green to another color. Many bell peppers and chili peppers turn red when ready to harvest, but because so many of them are green at the supermarket, it's easy to assume that is the right color. Peppers, like many crops, can be eaten while they are immature, but there can be wonderful flavor development when allowed to ripen and change color.

Size: Size is a factor for many plants, but bigger isn't always better. Cucumbers and squash are often sweet and tasty when they are young and small. They can grow much bigger, but a monstrous fruit often lacks sweetness and is tough or fibrous. Melons often have a precise size, and when the fruit reaches that size, it is ready to harvest. Most root crops can be eaten at any size, with smaller ones often being sweeter.

Completing the Harvest

Once you get the first harvest, check the plant every day until the harvest is complete. For fruit-producing plants, harvesting a single fruit is enough to stimulate the production of more flowers and more fruit. The fruit already on the plant will ripen quickly. It is amazing how a small cucumber or zucchini can become full-sized in a matter of hours.

Crops that are usually harvested all at once don't have to be. You can harvest a portion of the carrots and come back the next day to harvest more. The longer root vegetables stay in the ground, the bigger they get, and you can get the size you want by choosing when to harvest. Over a period of a few days, you can get an idea of the effects that time has on the crop quality. Harvest some of the potatoes and leave others in the ground for a later date. The soil can be a good place to keep crops as a storage method if indoor space is limited.

Most gardeners have heard they should harvest in the morning, after the dew has dried. The idea is that many vegetable plants taste sweetest in the morning after a cool night. The heat of the day can dry out some plants and affect the flavor. Use that time as a guideline, but harvest when you have time. Many gardeners are busy in the morning with school or work. Early evening is a good time to harvest if that's when you can. It's close to dinner time, and so the harvest can be used fresh in the kitchen.

It may seem obvious, but plants should be regularly harvested during summer. It is common for gardeners to wait too long to harvest or completely miss harvesting ripe fruit or mature roots. Delaying the harvest of ripe fruit by just a day may give hungry birds and other animals time to eat it themselves. Leafy crops can lose sweetness and become stringy if left on the plant too long. Some plants, such as cucumbers and squash, may stop producing new fruit completely if old fruit is allowed to stay on the vines.

Hot summer temperatures can cause many of the plants that grew well in the spring garden to send up flower stalks to set seed. This is called bolting and changes how the plant grows. When a plant bolts, its energy goes into flower development. The taste and texture of leaves and roots will change, usually becoming tough and bitter. Harvest plants before they bolt, as soon as you see a flower stalk develop. Pull them once they start, unless you want to save the seeds. If you're succession planting, bolting plants indicate a good time to clear the bed and move to the next phase of your plan.

Avoiding Food Waste

Some of our harvests go to waste because they spoil before we can eat it all. If you learn to preserve your harvests, you can eat everything you grow. Freezing, dehydrating, canning, and jelly making are some of the ways to preserve your crops to eat later in the year. Good-quality harvests can last on the shelf or in the freezer for months and not be wasted.

Of course, one key is to grow more of what you normally eat. While it's enjoyable to grow new varieties of vegetables, it doesn't always lead to savings if the crop is not part of your normal diet. Replacing the food you buy with food you grow is the goal. The savings come from the money you don't spend at the supermarket because you're growing what you eat at home.

Chapter 7

Managing Problems in Raised Beds

Every garden, regardless of whether it's filled with raised beds or not, occasionally experiences problems such as diseases, pests, and powerful forces of nature. Given the segmented and architectural nature of raised beds, they offer distinct advantages when it comes to these problems and more. They can also help northern gardeners extend their seasons, protecting plants from cold temperatures at both the beginning and end of the growing season. This chapter will explore some common garden issues and how raised beds can help you manage and mitigate many of the problems you may encounter.

The Wonders of Hoops and Trellises

A key tool in managing the curveballs nature throws at us is a secure hoop or trellis system that's anchored in your raised beds. As we saw in Chapter 6, trellises help the gardener take advantage of vertical growing, but those same trellises can be used as structures that hold up row cover fabric, netting, and other materials to protect your raised bed plants from pests, extreme weather events, and frost. You can also install hinged or removable hoops or other supports, which act like a tent frame over your raised beds.

◐ Ladybugs are beneficial predatory insects that keep aphid numbers in check. Creating a healthy garden that encourages their presence is one of the best tactics for managing harmful insect pests.

To avoid possible damage to plants, I place my hoops or trellises in the raised bed and then sow seeds or transplant seedlings. Without special care, putting the structure in place after everything's planted can lead to plant damage as the ends are moved into position. When choosing a trellis or a hoop system, consider how easily you can work with plants when it is in position.

I love it when my tools and garden structures can play more than one role in the garden. Trellises may be placed with the intent of supporting plants as they grow, but trellises can also support the cover materials needed to protect those same plants. The cover material can be elevated above the plants early in the season before the small plants cover the trellis completely. A trellis strong enough to support a heavy plant can easily support row cover fabric or plastic sheets.

My favorite trellis is made by bending cattle panels into long hoop structures that fit in the raised beds. The rigid metal holds its shape and is strong enough to support anything that covers the bed. The thin metal frame is ideal for using spring clamps to secure the cover materials. The frame's weight and rigidity are enough to hold it in place in the bed without the need for additional supports or anchors.

I use cattle panel hoops throughout my garden, and they are my favorite type of trellis because of their versatility.

If you choose to use a system of individual hoops instead, hoop supports can be made from plastic, PVC, wood, or metal. A common garden hoop is made from PVC Schedule 40 pipes from home improvement centers. Sold in 10-foot lengths, 1-inch and 1½-inch pipes can be easily bent into hoops that fit 4-foot-wide raised beds. A piece of wood, like a 1-inch by 2-inch strip, is screwed or bound to the hoops with light rope or heavy twine, forming a semirigid structure. Protectant covers, such as plastic sheets or netting, drape over the hoops.

PVC pipes are easy hoops to install and use.

Metal electric conduits make similar hoops. The metal tubes are 10 feet long and ½ inch wide and can be bent to form a hoop to fit the raised bed. While PVC will degrade over time when exposed to the sun's UV rays (and even UV-resistant PVC will need to be replaced periodically), metal conduits should never need replacement and can be used year after year. They hold the curve of the bend well and can be stored in a shed or garage when not used.

Metal conduits make great tall hoops that are very sturdy.

Hoop systems will need to be anchored in the bed or securely attached to the bed. Cover materials such as plastic can block airflow to retain warmth, but that ability also means they can act as sails in strong winds. Many gardeners have seen their hoops, covered with plastic, blowing out of the bed and across the yard in gusty winds. Taking the time to anchor the hoop system can save that disappointment.

Light hoops made from plastic tubing or PVC pipes are more likely to shift or blow away and need the best anchors. My preferred method of securing these hollow hoops is with pieces of rebar. I insert a 2-foot length of metal rebar into the soil to a depth of 1 foot. The end of the hoop slides over the 1 foot of rebar that rises above the soil. The ends of the hoop tend to push outward, and that exerts enough sideways force to secure it on the rebar and anchor it well. (See sequence on next page.)

1. Hammer pieces of rebar into the bed soil on opposite bed sides.

2. Slide one end of the PVC pipe over the rebar on one side.

3. Bend the pipe toward the other side of the bed to form a hoop.

4. Slide the other end of the pipe over the rebar.

5. Tension will hold the pipe in place.

Metal pipe straps also work well. Galvanized pipe straps are semicircular metal pieces made to hold pipes flush to joists and walls. They can be screwed into the wood of a raised bed. The ends of the hoops, either PVC or steel, are slid into the pipe straps anchored to the bed. The hoops can be mounted inside or outside the bed. I prefer inside mounting because the sideways push of the hoops holds them against the bed sides for extra support.

Rigid trellises and hoops can be pushed directly into the soil for anchoring. Metal prongs on the trellis ends or the steel ends of the hoop pushed into soil 6 inches or more are usually enough to hold the structure in place during windy conditions. If it's supporting plants, too, 6 inches should also be enough to keep the structure in place as plants grow and put weight on it.

Metal pipe straps can also hold PVC and metal hoops in place. Secure the pipe straps a few inches below the top of the bed.

Once you start using hoops and trellises, it soon becomes apparent what advantages they give your garden — such as better pest control and weather protection. I also like the double bonus of hoops that can become trellises for vertical gardening as the season progresses. Trellises and hoops may not have been a part of your plans when deciding to build raised beds, but they're a worthy addition for managing various issues that can arise in the garden.

Diseases

Spots on leaves, wilted and stunted plants, disfigured stems and leaves, discoloration, powdery appearance, lesions on flowers or fruit, oozing stems, leaf curling, and slow death are just some of the signs that your plants might have a disease. Plant diseases are caused by bacteria, fungi, or viruses. Once plants get a disease, it often seems that the gardener is in a constant battle to save the plant. Depending on the disease, defeating it may be a lost cause. Keeping plants healthy is an important step in preventing disease, and raised beds are a major tool in a gardener's arsenal.

We tend to know what healthy plants look like. Vibrant green leaves, steady and strong growth, and consistent flowering and fruiting are normal in a healthy garden. When blemishes appear on plants and fruit or unusual colors begin appearing on the plant, it is often the beginning sign of a disease. Regular observation in the garden helps us identify when a plant no longer appears normal. Recognizing how the appearance is different, what part of the plant is affected, and the pattern of the infection are important in identifying the potential disease.

Common Diseases

Common symptoms of bacterial diseases include oozing on the stem or fruit, lesions on leaves, crusty areas on the plant, discoloration of the plant's tissue, or sudden collapse of the plant. Viral diseases often produce mosaic and mottled leaves, leaf curling, vein yellowing, ring spots, yellowed leaves, or stunted growth.

The most likely plant diseases in your garden are fungal. There are more than 20,000 different species of fungi that affect plants, and about 85 percent of diseases in our garden plants are due to fungal infections. The most common symptoms of fungal diseases are white powder on leaves, dark lesions on stems, the yellowing and withering of the plant, or rings on the leaves along with spots on fruit.

Some fungal diseases are relatively common. It seems that most gardeners confront powdery mildew and blight in the vegetable garden — both are fungal diseases that affect many different plants.

Powdery mildew: Powdery mildew affects more than 10,000 plants. It commonly looks like white powder on the leaves, stems, and buds of plants. It usually doesn't cause severe damage, but it can make a plant look unattractive. The spores that cause powdery mildew can travel easily in the wind, and when a spore lands on a plant it can quickly cause infection. Unlike many other fungi, powdery mildew doesn't need moisture to infect a plant and even thrives on warm,

Powdery mildew is a common disease.

dry days. Poor air circulation around plants is a leading factor for infection. The height of raised beds and the selective pruning of lower branches can improve air circulation. Along with organic mulches, these factors can lower the likelihood of infection.

Blight: There are different blights that can affect plants, frequently infecting tomato plants. Early blight is a fungal disease that begins as small, brown lesions on leaves. As they grow, the lesions begin to look like bullseye patterns, then the leaf turns yellow, then brown, before it dies and falls off the plant. Fruit may be saved before it becomes infected. Late blight is a more serious disease that can cause complete defoliation and collapse of the plant within 14 days. Lesions can appear anywhere on the plant and often have a light halo ring around them.

Once blight is identified, acting quickly by removing infected leaves can keep it from spreading. The leaves should be burned or bagged and thrown out in the trash. Diseased plants should be pulled out and destroyed. Keeping foliage dry by increasing air circulation and limiting overhead watering can reduce the likelihood of infection. Again, an organic mulch can reduce the risk of spores bouncing from the soil onto the plants.

Different blight diseases affect most gardens. The photo on the left shows signs of early blight on a potato plant. The photo on the right shows late blight on a potato plant.

Identifying and Dealing with Diseases

While powdery mildew and blight are common, there are many other diseases that can infect garden plants. Some, such as black spot disease, only affect roses. Bacterial diseases, such as fire blight, affect fruit trees. Mosaic viruses can infect beets, cucumbers, tomatoes, and petunias. The key to identifying them is to first recognize that something doesn't look right with the plant and then use research to try to identify what the problem could be.

Raised beds tend to make diseases easier to spot because the plants are higher and closer to your eyes for observation. Planning for proper plant spacing and regular pruning can improve airflow around and through the bed, reducing disease exposure. Without regular pruning of branches, high and low, plants could be susceptible to both airborne and soilborne plant diseases. If disease problems develop, one of the easiest long-term fixes is to avoid growing the susceptible plants in that affected bed until the disease is eradicated. Many diseases can remain in soil and plant debris for years and can infect plants later. There may be chemical or organic controls available to deal with diseases, but plant separation is usually part of the treatment. One of the best advantages of raised beds is that quarantining infected beds is easy.

Plant varieties that were infected and other plants in the same family are susceptible to that and similar diseases and should be planted in different beds each year. Regularly moving plants into new beds after a disease hits the garden, otherwise known as crop rotation, reduces and may eliminate the possibility of infection. Not rotating crops could mean a gardener continues the problem each year rather than isolating and eliminating it. Thankfully, using different beds at different times is easy with raised bed gardening. Each bed is a distinct planting space that can be tracked and planned for.

Pests

Pest control is an inevitable part of gardening, so inspect for plant pests often. Most pests are most active when plants are growing big and temperatures are warm: adult insects are laying eggs; young larvae are devouring tender leaves; and animals are eating tasty vegetation. Recognize when leaf damage appears and search out the culprit. Make it a regular task to lift up leaves and look for any insects and eggs. Note when fruit has holes or looks deformed.

There are many options for how you deal with common pests. Some gardeners immediately reach for a chemical pesticide to kill unknown insects. Others take a hands-off approach and let nature deal with potential pests. Most gardeners tend to try organic control methods as a primary approach and resort to chemicals when other controls don't work.

Integrated Pest Management

I practice Integrated Pest Management (IPM), an approach that focuses on environmental impact and uses a combination of control methods with the least possible hazards. Two keys to IPM are identifying and understanding the life cycles of pests. It doesn't preclude the use of pesticides, but that tends to be a last resort, and there are many other control measures that take place first.

Not all insects, animals, and weeds actually require control. While some estimates consider as many as 3 percent to 5 percent of insect species to be "pests," the USDA reports that less than 1 percent of insects are considered harmful. The great majority of insects are beneficial or neutral. Automatically spraying a pesticide on an unknown bug may cause future problems because you're also getting rid of any beneficial predatory insects that can help control the few actual harmful pests. Ladybug larvae may be scary-looking insects that elicit a spray from unknowing gardeners, but these ugly beasts are ravenous when they encounter aphids.

Monitoring and identifying pests are important steps in IPM. By knowing what insects are on your plants, you can determine what control measures to take — *if* control is even needed. Setting action thresholds will help you decide when action should be taken. A single insect

Ladybug larvae are great garden allies because of their voracious appetite for aphids.

257

pest rarely requires a response, and many innocuous pests can be on plants with little harm. The best default response is often to wait and see if pests really pose a problem.

My primary IPM action is to work to prevent pests from becoming a threat in the first place. I plant a great variety of flowers, grasses, and herbs that attract predatory insects. I have birdhouses and water features throughout my garden to attract the avian allies that eat bad bugs. I place barriers around and over my beds to keep out pests. I learn the life cycles of common pests in my area and adjust planting schedules to disrupt the likelihood that they'll appear when my plants are most susceptible to damage.

When insect damage appears, identify the pest and then take appropriate action. Much of the time, removing the pest from the plant and killing it is enough to reduce potential problems. Dealing with insect pests when the number is still in single digits can prevent or reduce future infestations. When I detect a single potentially harmful insect, I remove it, kill it, and look for signs of eggs on the plant. Half a dozen squash bugs or cucumber beetles are easy to spot when they first appear and can easily be caught and squished or bagged for disposal.

If monitoring, identification, threshold determination, and prevention fail to be effective, then a control measure can be determined. It may involve trapping, physical removal, biological control, or possibly targeted chemicals. If the insects do gain a foothold and begin damaging plants, summer is the time to set traps to reduce their numbers. Encouraging or purchasing beneficial predator insects is appropriate for insects that are prey. Treating plants with diatomaceous earth (a silica-based powder) or neem oil will work for susceptible insects.

Chemical control is an option, but one I recommend as a last resort. Most pesticides are nonspecific and will kill good bugs as well as bad bugs. Targeted chemicals to deal with specific pests can reduce the likelihood of disrupting beneficial garden life. Thankfully, I've never had to resort to broadcast spraying a nonspecific pesticide over my plants because any major infestations are kept in check by the actions I take to keep wildlife in my garden.

Mitigation Methods

Prevention efforts to keep pests away from plants are easy in raised beds and help reduce the need for future, additional control measures. Aphids, caterpillars, grasshoppers, squash bugs, and many other potentially harmful pests can't do damage if they can't reach plants.

Row covers: Just as hoops and trellises can be covered with plastic to extend the gardening season (see page 266), they can be covered with materials for managing garden pests. Row covers are designed primarily as an effective barrier method for protecting plants. They can add a few degrees of plant protection during cool nights in spring and can deter many insect pests seeking to attack plants early in the season. It is a physical barrier that keeps insects from reaching plants. A plastic sheet holds in more heat than a row cover, and it also can act as a solid barrier to pests of all kinds that want your plants as food.

A cover needs to be in place as soon as seeds or plants are in the ground, so trellises and hoops should be installed before any seed sowing or transplanting is done. Some insects, such as adult flea beetles, will lay their eggs near the soil surface or on stems or leaves in the spring. The larvae develop underground and emerge about a month later to feast on young seedlings. We want to keep the adults of insects such as these from finding and laying their eggs on our plants in the first place, so we need to have covers in place before they first appear.

Covers can allow sun and water through while keeping insect pests out.

Protected plants receive little or no damage from pests.

Many insect pests live in the soil as part of their life cycles. They may live in the soil through the winter and emerge as larvae in spring to attack plants or lay eggs as adults. If a bed had insect damage in the previous year, it is important to identify the pest before using row covers or plastic as a barrier. If the pest was an insect that overwinters in soil, the covers won't keep the pests out and instead will trap them inside the hoops with the plants they love to eat.

Row covers are synthetic fabrics, often made of polypropylene, that can stay in place for many weeks because the fabric allows air, sunlight, and water to reach plants and won't overheat them. They can easily be cut to size for a perfect fit over the raised bed. For many vegetable garden plants, they can stay in place until harvest to completely prevent insect infestations. It is a common misunderstanding that all garden plants need pollination to grow well. Beets, broccoli, cabbage, carrots, lettuce, radishes, spinach, and many others are harvested long before flowers develop, and none of them need pollination.

Other plants such as beans, eggplants, peas, peppers, and tomatoes are self-pollinating and don't require pollinators either. They can remain covered during the growing season if specific insect pests are present and need to be kept away from the plants. Using row covers for those plants is common while they are young and starting to flower. When they are bigger, the weather is usually warm enough and the plants are strong enough that insect protection is less important.

Pollination is, however, needed for cucumbers, melons, peas, squash, and similar fruiting plants. That means beneficial pollinators need access to the plants once they start flowering. Row cover fabric needs to be removed or opened to allow insects to reach the plants during the day. The beds can be covered at night for the warming benefits.

Bird netting: Barriers such as bird netting can be used over the same hoop or trellis structures to protect flowers and fruit from animals. Bird netting is a heavy-duty mesh that keeps bigger animals away from plants while allowing insect pollinators access. Clamped to the support structure, the netting does not interfere with plant growth and can easily be rolled up or removed for plant maintenance and harvest. While designed for birds, netting can be effective at keeping rabbits, deer, and other critters out of your raised beds.

Cattle panel hoop trellises: Cattle panel hoop trellises can deter animals without the need for netting. The openings are big enough for my hands to reach through, but they are small enough to interfere with a deer's snout. I've had plant tips eaten by deer that grew outside the metal hoops, but the animals have never reached inside. They are also effective at deterring my dogs from jumping into the raised beds and can support netting to keep birds and smaller animals out of the bed.

Welded wire fencing: This type of fencing is a lightweight barrier that deters many pests. I use wire fencing bent into hoops, such as my cattle panels, over the strawberries in my narrow raised beds. The barrier deters deer from eating the strawberry plants and allows my vining flowers to grow through the fencing and up my garden arches, which are full-size cattle panels. The fencing is also strong enough to support bird netting to keep the birds from eating the fruit.

Bird netting on hoops helps keep fruit undisturbed by larger pests.

Cattle panel hoops do double duty as trellises, too.

Sticky traps will quickly attract insect pests.

Insect traps: Removing pests from plants and keeping them separate until they die are easy with commonly available traps. I like to use yellow sticky traps staked to my raised bed or dangling from a hoop for the few occasions I need to deal with insect pests. As the name implies, a sticky trap is a piece of cardboard covered with glue, and when an insect walks or lands on the trap, it gets stuck. They are nontoxic, easy to set up, and a single trap can catch hundreds of bugs.

Sticky traps are indiscriminate, and any insect that touches the surface will be caught, even beneficial ones. Because of that, I only set them up when I know I have an infestation, and I am careful to place the traps near only the affected plants. Once the pest population falls, the traps can be removed and thrown away with the bugs attached.

There are a number of DIY traps you can make to deter insect and animal pests. One of the most effective is simple cardboard. Lay a sheet of wet cardboard at the base of your raised bed and see what you catch. Many pests seek out cool, dark locations during the day before they attack plants at night. In the morning, lift up the cardboard and dispose of the pests underneath. You may be surprised by the numbers of snails, slugs, mealy bugs, earwigs, and even termites.

Weather Protection in Raised Beds

Hoops and trellises can help protect plants and beds from weather extremes. Few gardeners have climates and weather patterns that provide consistent conditions from one day to the next. For most of us, there is a storm around the corner that could threaten our plants. Planning and constructing with the weather in mind can make a big difference when the worst happens.

The structures and appropriate anchoring of hoops and trellises should match the possible weather extremes. When we think of our growing season, we often envision garden days that are sunny and calm — maybe with a light rain or slight breeze. For many of us, those days are the anomaly. Rain falls, wind blows, and the sun shines, but occasionally it gets worse. We have rain that turns into a deluge. We have wind that blows away anything that's not tied down. We have sun harsh enough to burn our skin and the leaves of our plants.

If built for day-to-day weather patterns, most hoop or trellis structures can handle an occasional variation that is stronger than normal. It isn't until the rare extremes occur that we can adequately judge the structure's true strength. I encourage gardeners to anticipate the worst possible weather situation and build accordingly.

Wind

The biggest weather event many of us have is strong wind. Poles, posts, sticks, and pipes that are used for trellises usually need additional anchoring. This isn't because the material of the trellis isn't strong enough, it's because it may not be strong enough when covered by plants and exposed to high winds. Plants covering a trellis catch the wind in the same way a sail does. Strong wind can push, bend, or break trellises that aren't strong enough when covered by plants.

With proper anchoring, trellises can be used as windbreaks to protect tender or small plants. Large, tough plants on a sturdy trellis can block the strong wind that can damage other plants behind it. A trellis can support fabric panels or mesh sheets to reduce the effect of wind on the plants behind it. Hoops and trellises covered with plastic can protect plants from cold temperatures and the strong winds that often accompany snow storms.

Precipitation

Heavy rain is a problem in many areas during certain seasons. The rain may be strong enough to damage small plants and can also pose problems if the rain

A tarp offers quick protection from heavy rain.

I cover large garden areas with hail cloth, anticipating thunderstorms.

can't drain quickly enough and saturates the soil. Heavy-duty plastic or polypropylene tarps can be very effective at shedding rain from raised beds. Supported by trellises or hoops, the tarps protect the plants underneath and divert the rain, so it doesn't saturate the bed soil. Thick plastic or canvas sheets can be pre-cut to fit beds and supports, and the covers are held in place by strong clamps.

Thunderstorms in summer can be very intense with strong wind, heavy rain, and hail. For some of us, they are the worst weather events we face because of the multiple damaging forces. Anti-hail netting, or hail cloth, is a sturdy woven material designed to withstand steady hail and keep it away from plants. It has some effectiveness at dissipating rain and reducing the effect of wind, but its chief aim is to block and divert hail. Trellises or hoops supporting hail cloth need to be extra strong because the weight of large amounts of hail can stretch the netting and topple weaker structures. I have hail cloth over a large area of raised beds continually during the peak of thunderstorm season.

Sun and Heat

The sun may be the most destructive weather force that we face. While rain, wind, and hail can damage plants when they are extreme, the sun can affect plants even when it isn't particularly extreme. A hot summer day can be enough to disrupt normal plant production. Without enough water and when exposed to strong sun, plants can wilt and then encounter worse leaf damage. Above 90°F (32°C), pollination can cease, blossoms can fall off plants, and fruit set decreases. Some plants and fruits can get sunscald in full sun, damaging the tissues.

Shade cloth provides varying levels of protection from harsh sun, depending on the shade percentage of the cloth.

One of the most effective controls against severe sun is shade cloth. Shade cloth is a woven netting made to block a pre-determined amount of sunlight. Typically, shade cloth that blocks 40 percent to 50 percent of the sun is enough for home gardens during the peak of summer. It is a lightweight material that can be supported by trellises without additional anchoring.

The mere presence of dappled shade can be enough to keep plants from bolting, enhance pollination, and prevent damage to plants and fruit. Different levels of shade cloth can be used to achieve varying levels of sun blockage. A cloth of 30 percent shade may be enough for gardens needing minor shading, and a thicker cloth of 60 percent shade may be beneficial for areas with prolonged and intense sun.

Season Extending in Raised Beds

The concept of extending the gardening season is to create an environment that is warmer and better for your plants. Air temperatures below freezing can adversely affect many plants, but if that cold air can be kept away from the plant or warmed up, the plant may avoid damage. Extending the season typically happens at the beginning of the growing season, when there's still a chance of cold nights damaging young plants and affecting germination. As you'll see, it can also be employed near the end of the season, to keep plants growing for weeks longer.

The most common way to extend the season is to cover plants on cold nights. Soil warms up during the day as the sun shines on it. The warm soil releases its heat as the air temperature cools. By covering the plants and trapping that heat at night, the air around the plants is warmer, and they are protected from frost. The next day, the soil warms up again and recharges the air with more plant-saving heat.

Depending on the cover material, many degrees of protection can be obtained. When the outside air temperature is close to freezing, a few degrees can mean the difference between life and death for a plant. Colorado State University conducted studies many years ago on the effectiveness of different covers. The results were one of the first things they taught me in my Colorado Master Gardener training.

Floating row covers, a material that is typically woven into long sheets of varying weights, are used to keep pests away from plants and protect plants from wind and weather. Depending on the specific material, row covers can provide up to 10°F (5.5°C) of protection. That means, when the outside air temperature is close to 32°F (0°C), the air around the covered plants is closer to 42°F (5.5°C) — well above the temperatures that can cause damage.

Covers made from 4-mil or 6-mil plastic, the common size of rolled sheeting that's available at garden centers, can provide 3°F (1.6°C) to 6°F (3.3°C) of frost protection. That may not sound like a lot, but it can make a difference for plant survival when outside air temperatures approach freezing. Using clear or slightly opaque plastic supported by hoops allows sunlight into the bed to warm it during the day and trap some of that heat when the air cools. Adding an aluminum space blanket over the plastic sheet at night reflects and retains so much of the ground heat that, in the Colorado studies, it prevented the plants from

Plastic covers can protect the soil and plants inside from frigid temperatures.

Ideally, plastic sheets should be large enough to extend over the bed sides.

Spring clamps allow easy opening and closing.

freezing when outside temperatures dropped to 0°F (−17.8°C). Mylar survival blankets also offer similar protection.

Lightweight covers can be placed directly over plants to provide protection, but if the plastic or fabric touches a plant during frigid temperatures, it can get damaged at the point of contact. Ideally, the covers should be supported above the plants using hoops or trellises. Typically, the hoops are placed 3 feet or 4 feet apart and span the width of the raised bed. The cover is placed over the hoops and needs to be big enough to extend down to enclose all sides, creating a kind of tunnel.

The plastic sheeting should completely cover the bed, and the edges should be sealed as much as possible to eliminate airflow in and out of the bed. The cover can be stapled to a wooden raised bed or weighed down with bricks, boards, or stones around the edges of the bed. The edges of the plastic sheet can also be buried in soil. I like to use spring clamps to secure the plastic cover firmly to the hoops.

The covering is effective at holding warmer air around plants during cold conditions. Heat builds up during the day, and as the temperature drops outside the covering, the warmer air is retained. It is important to note that season extending with a plastic covering is used just at night and during cold days to warm plants, and the plastic needs to be removed during sunny and hot days to avoid overheating and potentially damaging the plants.

Greenhouses can reach very high temperatures, well over 100°F (37.8°C), if they don't have ventilation to remove hot air. Our hoops

The plastic sheeting can be rolled up during warm, sunny days, allowing for ventilation.

and plastic covering act like a mini greenhouse, and the temperatures can rise quickly without ventilation. Simply opening the ends of the bed covers or rolling up the plastic on the sides is enough to quickly moderate temperatures by allowing cooler outside air in. A big reason why I like spring clamps is that I can quickly unclamp the plastic, roll it up to allow air in, and use the clamps again to hold it out of the way. I have complete control over the ventilation.

On warm spring days, open both ends to allow complete airflow across the bed and soil. On cool sunny days, open one end or side slightly to allow some cooling air in while also allowing the soil to warm. On cool overcast days, the cover can remain closed to hold in the warmer air because the lack of sun reduces the chance of overheating. When the nights are cold, ensure the cover stays completely sealed. There is effort involved to monitor garden temperatures, and open and close the cover each day, but that effort can add weeks to the growing season. The warmer conditions not only protect the plants from frost but also enhance seed germination and early plant growth.

End-of-Season Extending

Most of the focus of season extending is at the front of the growing season to keep plants warm while nights are still cold. However, the same structures can be used at the end of the season to keep plants warm as nights start getting cold again. End-of-season protection can extend the season enough to get the last harvests that might otherwise have been lost if the plants were exposed to frost. The same hoops and plastic work well for this as well as the trellises that may already be in place for plant support.

Hoops and plastic coverings are usually placed for protection in early spring and then removed during the summer months. To get late protection, the hoops are put in place again and remain until temperatures are too cold for the plants to benefit from a few degrees of warmth and their season has ended.

Anticipating the size of late-season plants, you'll want to ensure that your hoops are tall enough to cover your plants. The 10-foot-long pipes are good because they form a hoop about 4 feet tall when bent inside a raised bed that is 4 feet wide. That height may seem to be too much for young plants in spring, but it can be just enough to cover the bigger plants loaded with fruit ready for harvest. Having hoops all the same size allows them to be stored easily and then brought out for use when needed.

Of course, the size of the hoops can be modified to any height. A big reason I like cattle panel trellises is that I can cut the panels to form hoops of any height from 2 feet to 6 feet above a 4-foot-wide bed. With additional support, cattle panels can even make hoops that are 8 feet tall. Once the panels are cut to size, they become rigid hoops that can be reused every year. I have a collection of cattle panel hoops that I rotate into my garden into different beds, depending on the height I need for that season. Shorter hoops allow for easy installation of plastic sheets, row covers, or bird netting for protecting short plants throughout the growing season. Taller hoops are primarily used as trellises and are ideal when plants need a quick plastic cover to protect them on cold nights.

➲ I cover plants like peppers and squash at the end of the season to buy extra time for the fruit to ripen.

Chapter 8

Preparing for the Next Growing Season

Over the course of the calendar year, different tasks and activities will be needed for your raised beds — both in maintaining the beds and preparing for the next growing season.

Many of the garden activities described in this chapter have a "best time" for when you should try to accomplish them. Spring may be better for some, while fall may be a better time for others. Much of the timing is subjective, though. My recommendations are relatively standard based on when many gardeners do these same things, but they aren't universal.

My tasks also align with my calendar year in Colorado, where I get four distinct seasons. My summers are short and hot, and my winters are long and cold. Autumn tends to introduce change gradually over a long period, while spring is a roller coaster of changing temperatures with dramatic variation and few stable, warm days. If you're a gardener in a region without four seasons or with four seasons but ones that are shifted in the calendar, you'll need to modify your yearly schedule of gardening tasks. My brother lives in Arizona, a state that gets four seasons but ones that don't have the same extremes that mine do. Summer is so hot in Arizona that vegetable gardens are impossible to manage in that season, and gardeners rarely try without extensive measures to control shade and cooling. The growing calendar is shifted in such areas, with fall, winter, and spring being the primary growing seasons. Vegetable garden plants are started in fall, grow through winter, and finish in spring before the intense heat of summer.

◐ A view of my garden as it winds down in the fall.

Cool-season plants grow with little concern about bolting, and the plants that like warm conditions do best in spring.

Changing a year-round schedule of raised bed gardening activities to match your garden is recommended. Start with the basic layout of a typical calendar year, but modify it based on your preferred gardening methods and the plants you choose. Even my own plan is modified for different plants, different times, and different reasons.

Reviewing how you garden and how you plan and schedule your garden tasks should be a regular part of establishing your gardening methods. I used to do all my soil amending in spring until I learned more about amendments and soil life and decided I could get more benefits in fall. I also recognized that some beds didn't get amended in spring because so many gardening tasks were competing with one another. The same scheduling issues weren't happening in fall and more time was available to get the beds done, so I shifted my amending to the autumn.

In essence, there is no single recommendation for which specific tasks should be done and when. Instead, the recommendations in this chapter are meant to prompt gardeners to develop a list of tasks and think about when they should do them, so the most important activities are not forgotten or ignored. I do the same things at the same time each year because it helps ensure I have a successful garden. I recommend other gardeners develop a similar consistency.

End of the Growing Season (Fall)

The harvest is finished, and the garden is starting to wind down. While this time of year often marks the end of the growing season, I begin preparing for my next gardening year. Because the plants have been harvested and most gardening chores such as weeding and watering are no longer necessary, the time I was spending growing plants can now be redirected to other raised bed tasks. It helps that the days are still warm enough and long enough to get work done well.

This is a transition time because some plants will still grow in cooler temperatures and may be weeks away from harvest. Others have completed their life cycles and lie dead in the beds. Still others are best planted in the fall. Part of garden planning is anticipating these differences when deciding which plants will go in which beds. When all the plants in a bed die at the same time, the bed is ready for the next phase. If some plants are dead and some will still be alive for weeks more in the same bed, it has an impact on your activities.

Fall Planting

Some of the plants that benefit from fall planting are alliums, the plant group that includes onions, shallots, leeks, and garlic. Garlic should be planted in fall, usually October or November. Shallots and onions also benefit from fall planting. Because they take months to reach maturity and then harvest, succession planting is not an option, and they should be planted in dedicated beds. The soil should be amended with organic matter before planting because there will not be another opportunity to do it before harvest time. I plan the raised beds for my garlic plants at the same time I plan my tomatoes, peppers, and squashes because those are the plants that will be killed first by frost. Their early finish will free up the space for my alliums.

For raised beds in the landscape, crocuses, daffodils, tulips, and other spring-flowering bulbs go in the ground in the fall for spectacular color in spring. Many shrubs and perennials benefit from fall planting, too. Coreopsis, echinacea, heuchera, hostas, mums, ornamental grasses, and many others do well in cooler temperatures, when the soil is still warm enough for root growth. There are fewer competing weeds, fewer insect pests, and less soil evaporation, all of which aid in their establishment.

Planting cover crops, or green manure, is a good choice for covering garden soil and developing organic matter to add to the soil. Starting these plants in late summer or early fall as vegetable garden crops fade and beds are cleared gives many of them time to grow and establish before severe cold temperatures arrive. Annual ryegrass, winter rye, radishes, and oats

As the growing season wraps up, plants in your beds will die at different times. Anticipating when each plant is done for the season and how it will affect your end-of-season activities are important parts of planning.

Garlic is ideal for fall planting.

Cover crops, such as hairy vetch and winter rye, can be started while the main garden is still productive.

can all grow well in cool conditions and add organic matter and nutrients into the soil when they die. Legumes such as clover, hairy vetch, and winter peas do the same, and they add nitrogen to the soil as well. Typically, the cover crops are mown down in late fall or early spring when they're grown in open ground, but in raised beds you can dig and turn the plants into the soil after they're dead.

Fall is also the best time to divide many of our perennial plants. Alliums, astilbe, daisies, daylilies, hostas, irises, and salvia can be divided in fall. The new divisions can be planted in other raised beds, and they'll begin growing in conditions that are less likely to stress the plants. While formulating your raised bed planting plan, try to anticipate how many more plants will fill your beds each fall from this method of propagation.

In the absence of rain or snow, continue to water your beds until the ground freezes. Fall-planted plants will benefit from consistent moisture, and many of the bulbs and plants will establish root systems needed for winter survival. Roots of already-established perennial plants are actively growing in fall even if the foliage has faded or turned brown. Soil life requires water to live, and soil microbes and fungi will benefit and increase their populations in moist soil.

Before it turns too cold, dig up and store tender bulbs such as cannas, dahlias, and gladiolus. Wait until the first frost damages the leaves. Frost halts plant growth and helps the bulbs to begin drying. Cut the plants within 6 inches of the top of the bulb and then dig out the roots using a spade or garden fork, avoiding cutting through the bulbs. After removing the soil from the bulbs, you can store them inside until spring.

New Raised Beds

The end of the growing season is my preferred time to add new raised beds. Grass and other plants are entering dormancy in fall. Placing new beds on top of the dormant plants increases the likelihood that the plants will quickly break down, decompose, and become part of the new bed soil. Many landscape plants are pruned in fall, and the cuttings and small branches make for a good addition at the base when filling new beds. Dried leaves raked from your lawn help ensure the bed has a good foundation of organic materials. When filled with a good blend of soil and organic matter, the beds will be ready for spring planting when warm weather returns.

Building beds in fall is good planning for the next growing season.

Final Harvest

One of the last activities for autumn is the final harvest before the ground freezes. Root vegetables can remain in cold soil as a storage method and be harvestable for months, but when the ground freezes, they can be difficult to dig out and their texture and taste will be different. At some point, it may be too cold to get in the garden comfortably, so harvest the brussels sprouts, chard, kale, spinach, and any other crops under hoops while you can.

Bed Preparation

The best thing for a new spring garden is to prepare the beds the fall before. It takes time for the beneficial soil microbes to enrich the soil health, and the extra months between fall and spring can make a big difference in their development. For new raised beds, filling them with good soil in fall ensures better soil for the plants growing in spring.

For the raised beds already in place, fall is the first opportunity to clean up the beds and begin preparing them for spring planting. With the final harvest done, weeds and dead plants should be removed and added to the compost pile. Any fruit resting on the surface should also be removed. Many insect pests will overwinter in the plant remnants in our gardens. Removing roots, stems, branches, leaves, and fruits can lessen the possibility that those pests will return.

Any diseased plants or plant materials should be removed from the garden completely. Bag diseased plants and dispose of them in the trash. Diseases can be transferred to other beds if the material is added to a compost pile.

As part of plant cleanup, collect the seeds from the plants that produce them and that you want to continue growing. Faded flowers, herbs, and fruiting vegetables all produce seeds that are ready to collect in fall. Like plant division, part of your planting plan should include the possibility of seed collection. Sometimes it helps to group plants in a bed for the intent of seed saving, so the activity can take place at the same time with multiple plants. When the seeds are bagged, the rest of the bed is ready for cleanup.

Remove most stakes, trellises, and hoops. Raised beds will not need these structures in winter, and extreme weather can damage them and hasten their breakdown. Instead, remove them and store the materials in a shed or garage protected from rain and snow. Storing trellises can add years to their usefulness. Because my cattle panel trellises are so sturdy, I may leave them in place to protect the plants that will be in the ground through the winter, such as garlic, from digging animals. My PVC and conduit hoops are stored.

After cleaning up the beds, soil amending is next. This is covered more thoroughly in Chapter 3. Add compost and other organic materials to the soil surface. Generally, 3 inches or 4 inches of compost is spread on the soil in raised beds and mixed into the top 10 inches to 12 inches of soil. In the absence of cover crops, light mulches such as straw, grass, and crushed leaves can remain in the beds and get turned into the soil along with other amendments. Turning the soil incorporates the organics and becomes food for the microbes.

Alternatively, the organic materials can remain on the soil surface as mulch and be allowed to break down over time. This is an easy approach and can work well in established beds with soil known to be rich in nutrients. Soil organisms, primarily earthworms, will eat and decompose the material and enrich the soil. No-dig gardening ensures little soil disruption, with nature doing the work of a gardener who manually turns their soil.

Top off existing beds with compost after cleaning up the bed.

With raised beds cleared, cleaned up, and amended, it's time to mulch the soil. Soil should be protected throughout winter to avoid wind and water erosion, to reduce the likelihood of weed seeds landing on bare soil during windy weather, and to add a barrier between soil life and harmful UV rays. Living mulches, such as cover crops, achieve the same benefits and can be an alternative to straw, leaves, or grass mulch, but I like to use both. Whether you're using living plants such as cover crops or organic covers like straw or leaves, at a minimum, these mulches are intended to protect the soil through harsh winter weather. By using organic materials, you get extra benefits from these mulches because they can also be turned into the soil to enrich it and feed soil organisms in spring.

Fresh pathway mulch is beneficial and makes the garden look good.

Fall is a good time to clean up and mulch pathways between raised beds. Perennial weeds should be removed before winter because they are among the first plants to thrive in spring. Thick mulch such as wood chips in paths can virtually eliminate erosion and weed problems. With rains and winter snows, the mulch will settle and create stable conditions for walking and working in the garden in spring.

Bed Maintenance

I generally save major raised bed repairs for spring, anticipating that harsh winters will hasten the breakdown of new wood. Wood that obviously needs replacing can wait, but boards that are still usable but aged can benefit from attention in fall. Loose boards should be anchored with new screws before they pull away completely. Dry wood looking like it might crack soon can benefit from an application of linseed oil or tung oil to protect it for another year or two.

Inspect your metal beds. Any loose bolts should be tightened. Painted surfaces with nicks or scrapes should be touched up to prevent the onset of rust. Any rusted areas that are obvious should be sanded and painted or treated with rust-reforming paint. Temporary metal beds can be disassembled and stored during winter.

Offseason (Winter)

With beds cleaned up and mulched, there is little to do during the winter months. Depending on the severity of winter storms, a small amount of maintenance can help.

Strong winter winds can shift and blow away mulch. On clear, warmer days, adding mulch to bare spots is a good excuse to spend time in the garden.

> **For Those with Mild Winters**
>
> Season extending may be a possibility for regions with mild winters. Keeping hoops in place and covered with plastic can keep the soil warm enough for soil microbes to live and feed on soil organic matter, but the reduced sunlight in winter is rarely enough for plants to thrive. They may stay alive, but growth slows dramatically. See page 270 to learn more about extending the growing season.

Plant Protection

For the same reasons soil in raised beds warms faster in the hotter months, it will also freeze faster in winter. For raised beds with perennial plants, this can stress plants that are used to more gradual rates of freezing in open ground. Gradual freezing allows perennials a longer period to enter dormancy, while fast freezing may damage or kill them. Consider covering beds with tarps or plastic sheets for unexpected or extreme freezing conditions before plants have moved into dormancy. A thick mulch can also help moderate the temperature change.

Tender plants can benefit from protection and covering in winter. Roses can be covered in burlap, and rosemary may benefit from being covered with leaves as insulation. Once plants are dormant in late fall or early winter, anticipate when extreme freezing conditions will arrive and insulate the plant before harsh weather hits. Note that snow is an excellent insulator that maintains a constant temperature at or slightly above freezing. In regions with regular snowfall, keeping the snow in raised beds can be as effective as other methods for protecting plants.

Draining Out the Water Supply

Before freezing conditions set in, turn off the water to any irrigation systems and blow the water out if it doesn't drain easily. Disconnect hoses and drain them, but be sure to first fill a few watering cans for plants that are not dormant yet. Winter watering may be needed during warming trends before it gets cold again, particularly in dry regions. When temperatures rise above freezing for sustained periods and soil begins to thaw, drench the raised bed soil early in the day so the water can moisten the roots of perennial plants, bushes, and trees before another soil freeze. Be sure to drain any hoses before freezing weather returns.

Planning for the Next Growing Season

Take this quiet season to plan your spring and summer gardens. With the beds cleared and no (or very few) plants growing, you can see the bare bones of the garden. I spend much time outside in my wintry yard envisioning what I want my garden to look like when it's actively growing. Many plant varieties are decided on when snow covers the ground. You can refer back to Chapter 5 as you develop your new growing plan.

The snow acts as insulation against freezing temperatures, so if you have regular snowfall, be sure to keep it on top of the raised beds.

Winter is also a good time to acquire new garden tools designed for raised beds. Around the holidays, you could ask family and friends for garden tools you wouldn't normally buy yourself. In late winter, many stores begin to stock up on spring supplies and early sales can ensure you get the tools that sell out quickly.

A downy woodpecker stops by this suet feeder in winter for a high-energy meal.

Backyard Birds

If you're trying to attract birds to your garden, clean and fill bird feeders. Many of the birds in our gardens do not migrate and remain throughout winter, looking for food. They may eat weed seeds and insect pests, helping curtail those problems. Adding suet feeders to the garden can provide them with a high-energy food when their other foods may not be available. Also, provide birdbaths and watering areas and refill them when they freeze.

281

Beginning of the Growing Season (Spring)

When spring arrives, the excitement of the growing season gets gardeners outside and ready for action. It seems there is so much to do that there won't be enough time for everything. Highlighting the important tasks and prioritizing the others will ensure all is done in time. That is a primary reason I prep my raised bed soil in fall. It is a major gardening activity that is already complete and frees up time for many other activities in spring.

Bed Preparation (If Not Done in Fall)

Any beds that were not cleaned up in the fall need to be cleaned up before new plants are put in. As with fall cleanup, remove plant materials and put them in the compost bin. Remove and discard any plant material suspected of being infested with disease. Look for evidence of new animal pests. New burrows and nests may become apparent when removing dead plants and seeing what has overwintered in mulch or garden soil.

If soil wasn't amended in fall, that becomes a primary task in spring. Soil needs organic matter, and soil life needs food before plants go in the ground. Because of the time required for microbes to release nutrients, organic amendments should be added to soil as soon as it thaws and can be worked, ideally weeks before planting. To hasten the process, I encourage finished compost as the organic material of choice. It will continue to decompose but will begin adding nutrients as soon as it is in the soil, much faster than raw ingredients such as grass and leaves.

Starting with a soil test in early spring will help identify what amending is necessary. A professional soil test identifies any nutrient deficiencies heading into the growing season and may highlight a need for added fertilizers. Many experts recommend soil tests in fall before amending, and that is a good choice, but I prefer testing in spring, after soil microbes have had months to improve soil and before I put plants in the beds. It is possible to over-amend and over-fertilize beds, and starting the season knowing the soil status can help avoid potential problems.

If you cleaned, amended, and mulched the beds in fall, there is little to do other than wait for the soil to warm before planting. Early weeds may begin to grow, but the mulch will reduce that and make it easy to spot them and pull them as soon as they appear. With cover crops covering the soil, alive and dead, there is less likelihood of weed seeds sprouting in spring.

Depending on your soil's health and whether you amended in the fall, you may benefit from adding more compost in early spring.

More Bed Maintenance

Examine raised beds for damage that may have happened in winter. It is time to deal with the boards that were identified for replacement in fall. Snow and ice may have accelerated the damage of others. Remove any boards that are beyond repair. It may mean that you will have to remove some soil, but in early spring the soil is often cold enough, or even slightly frozen, that it holds its shape and allows for easy replacement.

Wood treatments to prolong the bed's life can be applied in early spring once the temperature warms enough. The label on the cans or bottles will identify the appropriate temperatures for application. Early preservative treatment can add years to wood by protecting it from sun and water exposure.

Clean and Sharpen Garden Tools

Before you need them, inspect, clean, and sharpen your garden tools. This is an activity that many gardeners do in fall, so their tools are cleaned before storing in winter, but I get my tools ready shortly before I use them in warm weather. Spades, knives, and pruners are sharpened and oiled. Buckets, baskets, and pots are cleaned and ready to use. Hoses, sprinklers, and watering wands are inspected for leaks and dribbles.

Bed Irrigation

Start watering raised beds for weeks before planting. The soil should be moist when plants go in, and the soil life should be exploding into action. Raised beds can dry out in winter, even with regular snow fall, so a boost of water in spring is needed to bring it all back to life. This is also a good time to practice irrigation methods before plants are in place. I like hand watering, and learning how and where to drag the hose reduces the chance of mistakes that can damage plants when they're growing.

Setting up stationary irrigation systems before planting can reduce plant damage as well. Transplanting young seedlings and then placing soaker hoses or drip irrigation tubes inevitably results in some small plants being broken, torn out, or squashed. Placing the tubes and hoses, then anchoring them, provides a guide for where plants and seeds will be planted based on the available water.

Hoops and Trellises

With the raised beds cleaned up, with irrigation systems in place, and with the seeds and plants ready to be planted, set up trellises and hoops. They may need cleaning, repair, or replacement, so plan for enough time to take action if needed. Have season-extending covers ready to go after cleaning, repairing, or replacing them as well.

Spring Planting and Propagation

Your garden plan will help you identify which seeds and plants to start and when. The same basic methods of highlighting dates for planting can be used for identifying when to do the spring gardening tasks, so everything is clean and in place before plants go in the beds.

Spring is a good time to divide fall-blooming perennials such as monardas, bleeding hearts, clematis, delphiniums, hyssops, and mums. Your plan may identify which new plants are being added to the garden, but it can also expand to include landscape plants that will be propagated and used to fill additional raised beds. Many herbs such as thyme, mint, and chives divide well in spring and can be added to new beds. Spring-divided plants have the entire season to grow and establish.

As plants begin their new growth or while they're still dormant in early spring, it may be the ideal time to dig them up and move them so they can set new roots before the heat and stress of summer. Observation of the garden through the year (see Chapter 5) may identify plants that aren't in the best location. Further observation and analysis can identify where they might do better.

Many summer garden crops can be started early indoors.

Growing Season (Summer)

As you learned in Chapter 6, the primary raised bed gardening activity in summer is plant and garden maintenance. Most plants will be planted in mid- to-late spring. Monitoring the garden and tending to the plants is a daily activity that shouldn't be ignored. Just one day with too little water, too much sun, or a pest infestation can result in plant damage or death that cannot be undone. Try not to treat weeding as an unwanted chore and instead make it a regular gardening activity. Ignoring weeds can become problematic when the plants we want and the ones we don't end up growing side by side. Ultimately, this weed is competing with your desired plants for water and nutrients.

In addition to focusing on growing strong plants and weeding, you should add tool and equipment maintenance to your daily summer activities. Too often, we wait until fall or winter to fix something that could make the growing season easier. Keep pruners clean and sharp to make pruning more efficient.

Be sure to regularly inspect hoses, wand heads, and irrigation systems throughout the growing season. A broken drip emitter or tear in a hose can cause water to leak out or spray excessively. Water that pools in a bed or drenches the soil may never reach plants farther down the line. Any irrigation damage needs to be repaired right away, before the garden plants suffer.

Plant Protection from Heat and Storms

If you haven't done it already, pre-cut the materials you will use to cover hoops and trellises, so you are ready to protect plants from harsh summer weather. Shade cloth and hail protection are helpful, but they may not be necessary every day. Installing them, removing them when weather improves, storing them until needed, then installing again is a regular pattern through the summer. For beds that don't have hoops in place, consider adding hoops for the purpose of supporting the shade and hail cloth.

Extra Amending

Fertilizing the soil may be needed in summer for soil that is deficient in specific nutrients. Fertilizer is best applied to deficient soil in spring and fall, but some plants may need nutrients as they begin growth in early summer and as they begin to set fruit. A midsummer boost may benefit some plants. Avoid using high-nitrogen fertilizers at the hottest times because the new, tender growth may be susceptible to sun damage.

Some gardeners use hoops as permanent garden fixtures. These hoops are covered with hail cloth to protect the plants from unexpected hailstorms and also to reduce the sun's intense heat.

Final Thoughts

So much of our planning, preparation, and gardening activities is focused on getting our summer vegetable garden to grow and reach a successful harvest. As we've seen throughout this book, there are many foundational steps needed to reach that point. New gardeners tend to treat gardening as a sprint, putting most of their energy and action into spring and summer efforts. Experienced gardeners recognize that gardening is a marathon with the finish line constantly changing. Each growing season is different even if the goals remain the same, and each calendar year is filled with necessary gardening activities.

    I think it is important to acknowledge that raised bed gardening is more than vegetable gardening, even if most of us use raised beds for that purpose. As I pointed out in the beginning, my vegetable garden is almost exclusively raised beds, but the bed choice is suitable for so many other plants. In recent years, I've used my raised beds to showcase annual flowers that add color throughout the garden. I've encountered many gardeners who are doing the same.

I began my raised bed journey with basic wooden boxes for growing plants. Now more of my attention is on using raised beds of brick, stone, and steel to bring interesting visual elements to the garden. The more I visit botanical gardens and other gardeners' gardens, the more I want to modify what I have into something better. Though the appearance may be different, the basics of raised beds remain the same: good soil, easier planning and maintenance, better harvests and results.

That is where my gardening journey has taken me. I suggest that gardeners new to raised beds begin with the basic designs, methods, and lessons from the earlier chapters to develop an appreciation of their effectiveness. For more experienced gardeners already using raised beds, I suggest trying something new and expanding your experience beyond what you're doing now by adding beds of stone or steel or some other material. For raised bed converts like me, use the examples of others to create the garden of your dreams with raised beds as the foundational components.

You don't need to follow everything in this book, but I hope you use the lessons as part of that foundation to develop your own preferred gardening style. Recognize that personal modification is one of the benefits of growing in raised beds. Don't treat it as an academic exercise with oversight, tests, and critique from others, but rather as an opportunity for you to find what you like in your garden, at a pace you prefer, as you explore your individual goals and unique garden space.

Above all, enjoy gardening!

➡ Raised beds have made gardening more enjoyable for me, and I hope they do the same for you.

Resources

To discover more about raised bed gardening, I encourage you to learn by watching some of my favorite YouTube channels, reading good gardening books, and seeking out local gardeners near you for advice. There are many great resources available, and the ones that follow tend to have focused information on raised beds and good gardening practices.

You can find hundreds of gardening videos and hundreds of hours of livestream chat on my Gardener Scott YouTube channel: https://www.youtube.com/@gardenerscott
I show regular updates of my garden on Instagram: @gardenerscott

Tony O'Neill is a recognized expert on many gardening topics, particularly growing potatoes and making compost. His books are great gardening resources:
    Your First Vegetable Garden: Starting on the Right Foot for Success!
    Composting Masterclass: Feed Your Soil Not Your Plants
    *Simplify Vegetable Gardening: All the Botanical Know-how You Need to Grow More
        Food and Healthier Edible Plants*
Tony's YouTube channel has hundreds of helpful gardening videos:
https://www.youtube.com/@simplifygardening

Eli and Kate Appleby-Donald provided some of the amazing garden photos in this book. Their YouTube channel is filled with friendly and helpful videos from their garden and greenhouse with abundant, accurate gardening information:
https://www.youtube.com/@eliandkate

Kevin Espiritu and the team at Epic Gardening provide great information for gardeners. Epic Gardening has the biggest YouTube gardening channel for good reason. It is filled with great videos on all aspects of gardening:
https://www.youtube.com/@epicgardening
Check out Epic Gardening's blog: https://www.epicgardening.com/
Their podcast: https://www.epicgardening.com/podcast/
And their Instagram: @epicgardening

Jill McSheehy offers some of the best educational information for new gardeners on her YouTube channel: https://www.youtube.com/@thebeginnersgarden
Jill's podcast: https://journeywithjill.net/the-beginners-garden-podcast/
Her Instagram: @thebeginnersgarden

Like me, Mark Valencia retired from the military and became passionate about gardening. Filmed in his Australian garden filled with raised beds, his YouTube gardening channel is one of the biggest and filled with entertaining and educational videos: https://www.youtube.com/@selfsufficientme

James Prigioni, alongside his dog Tuck, provides energy-filled gardening expertise from New Jersey: https://www.youtube.com/@jamesprigioni

Tanya Anderson, from the Isle of Man, is informative on many different gardening topics: https://www.youtube.com/@lovelygreens

UK-based Huw Richards has been a gardening educator since he was a teenager and offers incredible videos: https://www.youtube.com/@huwrichards

To find local and regional gardening information in the United States, do an online search for state university Extension information by entering the name of your state and "extension fact sheets." For example, if you were based in Colorado, you would search "Colorado extension fact sheets."

For similar information in Canada, a good starting point is the University of Saskatchewan website:
https://gardening.usask.ca/gardening-advice/useful-websites.php
And the Toronto Master Gardeners website:
https://www.torontomastergardeners.ca/fact-sheets/

Whenever you find helpful and useful information online, I suggest you look for additional information on the same topic from a different source. Gardening tips and tricks are often based on anecdotal experience without research-based validation. Comparing information from multiple sites can help you discern which information is best for you.

Index

Page numbers in *italic* indicate photos and charts.

A

accessibility
    about, 19–20
    customization, 58–59
    design and, 35
    height, 37–38, 58
    reach, 38–39, *39*
    sitting, 20, 37, *37*
    walking, 39–40
    wheel chair users, *20*, *36*
aesthetic appeal, 23–24, *24*
All New Square Foot Gardening (Bartholomew), 122
angle brackets, 71, *71*, 91
animals. *See* pests
annuals, 161
avoiding food waste, 237

B

bacteria, 109, *109*
bamboo, 234, *234*
Bartholomew, Mel, 122, 131
beans, 172
beer-brewing waste, 121, *121*
beginners, 24–25
beginning of growing season, 282–285
benefits of raised beds, 19–25
biochar, 130, *130*, 131
biosolids, 120–121
bird feeders, 281
bird netting, 261, *261*
blight, 255, *255*
blood meal, 135
bolting, 237
books, 150
bottoms, 65–67, *65–66*, 136–137, *137*
brick, 93, *93*, 97, *97*
budget
    common mistakes, 102
    Hugelkultur, 137, *137*
    irrigation systems, 213
    mulches, 217, 219
    planning and, 35, 42
    plant choices, 155–156
    preserving harvest, 237
    seeds, 175
    soil, 115, 117, 119, 126
    trellises, 234
    wood, 45
building
    barriers, 65–67, *65–66*, 102–103, *103*
    bottoms, 65–67, *65–66*, 136–137, *137*
    cement backer board, 88–91, *88–91*
    common mistakes, 102–103
    concrete blocks, 84–87, *84–87* (*see also* concrete blocks)
    creativity and, 101
    herb spirals, 93–97, *93–97*
    hybrid wood–concrete, 98–101, *98–101*

metal, 74–75, *74–75*, 83
open ends, 140, *140*
poured concrete, 91, *91*
preparing site, 63–64
strength, 103
taller beds, 72, *72–73*
timing, 63, 277
trellises/hoops, 249–253, *249–253* (see also trellising)
wood, 68–73, *68–72*
building capabilities, 35, 61
bulbs, 275
bunk bed bases, 235–236, *235*. See also trellising
Bureau de normalisation du Quebec (BNQ), 119

C

carbon footprint, 27
cardboard, 41, *41*, 65, 262
carrots, 155, 223, 225
cattle panel, 236, *236*, 250, *250*, 261, *261*, 270, 278
cement backer board, 88–91, *88–91*
Chadwick, Alan, 16
cherry tomatoes, 156
chicken wire, 65–66, *66*
ChipDrop, 217
cinder blocks, 49
clay soils, 133
climate, 206, 263–265. *See also* temperature
coconut coir, 132, *132*
common mistakes
    building, 59, 102–103
    location, 57
    paths, 57–58
    size, 58
    soil, 143–145
    trees and bushes, 27, *27*, 66

compost, 54, 119, 122–123, *124*, *127*, 202, 214, 278, 282
concrete blocks, 42–43, *43*, 47–49, *48*, 84–87, *84–87*, 98–101, *98–101*
cons of raised beds, 26–27
container gardening, 18, *18*
contamination, 22, 66
corner posts, 71, *71*
costs, 26. *See also* budget
cover crops, 222, 275, *275*
cucumbers, 237, 246
cultivator claw, 231, *231*
culvert pipes, 75, *75*
customization, 58–59

D

days to harvest/maturity, 244. *See also* harvests/harvesting
deep watering, 208, *208*, 209. *See also* irrigation/watering
definition of raised beds, 15–16
Denver Botanic Gardens, *52*, 56, *56*
depth of raised beds, 160. *See also* height of raised beds
designs, 34–36, 288
diamond patterns, 170, *170*
dibble, 192, 194, *194*
disease, 21, 253–256, *254–255*
documenting tips, 184–187
drawbacks, 26–27
dried grass clippings, 218–219, *218*
dried leaves, 219
drip irrigation, 210, *210*, 212. *See also* irrigation/watering

E

easier gardening, 19
elevation changes, 50–51, *50*
emitters, 210–211, *211*. *See also* irrigation/watering
end of growing season, 274–280
end-of-season extending, 270

F

fall overview, 274–280
fall vs. spring, 63, 134–135, 277
fences, 24, 261
fertilizers, 120, 135–136, 202, 286
flooding, 33
"forest products," 118
four Ds, 226
frost, 151–153, *151*, 165, 172, 267–268
fungi, 109, *109*, 133, 254, *255*
furrowed soil, 16

G

Galileo Garden Project, 10, *11*, *25*
Gardener Scott's Mix, 125, 126, *126–127*
Gardener Scott YouTube, 150, 185
gardening networks, 180
garlic, 155, 157, *157*, 275, *275*
grass clippings, 218–219
gravel, 221, *221*
growing
    about, 189–190
    harvesting, 243–247
    mulching, 215–222
    planting, 190–203
    pruning, 226–228, *226–228*
    thinning plants, 223–226, *223–226*
    trellising (*see* trellising)
    watering, 204–214
    weeding, 228–231
growing plan
    about, 147–148
    analysis of, 179–182
    determining what to grow, 154–155
    documenting tips, 184–187
    implementing plan, 173–174, 176–177
    making plan, 159–164, 172–173
    modifying, 182–183
    observing garden site, 32–33, 148, 177–179
    pruning, 237–238
    researching information, 148–150, *150*
    sketches, 162–164
    test run, 176–177, *176–177*
    winter envisioning, 281
growing seasons, 153, 286

H

Habitat for Humanity ReStore, 234
hail cloth, 264, *264*
hand watering, 210. *See also* irrigation/watering
hardening off, 196–197, *197*
hardiness zones, 151, 153
harvests/harvesting
    about, 243–247
    better, 22
    days to harvest/maturity, 244
    final, 277
    intensive planting, 168–171, *168–171*
    planning, 173
    preserving, 237
    removing plants and, 202–203
    succession planting, 165–167, 201–203, 237
height of raised beds, 37, 137, 139. *See also* depth of raised beds

herbicides/pesticides, 218, 220, 231, 257, 258
herbs, *38*, 156, 203
herb spirals, 53, *53*, 93–97, *93–97*
history of raised beds, 9, 16
hoops. *See* season extending; trellising
Hori Hori knife, 198, *199*
How to Grow More Vegetables (Jeavons), 16
Hugelkultur, 137, *137*
hydrozoning, 209

I

insect traps, 262, *262*
Integrated Pest Management (IPM), 257–258. *See also* pests
intensive planting, 168–171, *168–171*
Internet, 150, 185
invasive plants, 229. *See also* weeds/weeding
irrigation/watering
    about, 204–214, *208*
    draining out, 280–281
    spring watering, 284
    water access, 32–33
    winter watering, 281

J

Jeavons, John, 16
journals, 184–187

K

Kaffka, Stephen, 16
keyhole beds, 54, *54*
kids, 24–25, *25*, *59*, 154

L

labeling, 196, *196*
ladybugs, *248*, 249, 257

Lamp'l, Joe, 123–124
landscape fabric, 67
landscape plants, 27, *27*
lattice, 235. *See also* trellising
leaf mold, 133, *133*
leaves, 219
length, 39–41
lettuce, 223, 225
Lewis, Wayne, 110
lights, 56, *56*
lime, 131–132
livestock troughs, *44*
location, 22, 32–33, 57, 148–149
logs, 97, *97*
longevity, 26–27, *26*, 45–46
Lowenfels, Jeff, 110

M

macronutrients, 108, *108*, 120
maintenance, 103, 282. *See also* preparing for next season
managing problems
    about, 249
    disease, 21, 253–256, *254–255*
    pests (*see* pests)
    season extending, 263–270, *271*
    trellises/hoops and, 249–250, 267–270, *267–269*, *271*, *286*, *287*
    weather protection, 263–265
manure, 121
materials for building
    about, 42–49
    angle brackets, 71, *71*, 91
    bamboo, 234, *234*
    bird netting, 261, *261*
    brick, 93, *93*, 97, *97*

bunk bed bases, 235–236, *235*
cardboard, 41, *41*, 65, 262
cattle planel, 236, *236*, 250, *250*, 261, *261*, 270, 278
cement backer board, 88–91, *88–91*
chicken wire, 65–66, *66*
cinder blocks, 49
common mistakes, 59
concrete blocks (*see* concrete blocks)
corner posts, 71, *71*
culvert pipes, 75, *75*
hail cloth, 264, *264*
hoops (*see* season extending; trellising)
landscape fabric, 67
lattice, 235 (*see also* trellising)
livestock troughs, *44*
logs, 97, *97*
metal, 23, 26, *44*, 46–47, *46–47*, 103
metal conduits, 251, *251*, 253
modular kits, 46, *46*, 74–75, *74–75*
mortar, 87, 92
nails, 70–71
pipe straps, 253, *253*
planter blocks, 98–101, *98–101*
plastic sheeting, 67, *166*, 231, 264, 267–269, *267–269*
poured concrete, 91, *91*
PVC pipes, 251, *251–252*, 253
rebar, 87, 100, *100*, 251, 252
reclaimed wood, 102, *102*
retaining wall blocks, 87, *87*
screws, 70–71
shade cloth, 265, *265*
steel, 76–83, *76–83*
stone, 26–27, 49, *49*, 92–97, *92–96*, 160, *160*
tires, 54, *54*

types of, 15–16, *17*
weed fabric, 67
wire mesh, 43
wood (*see* wood)
wood preserver, 103, *103*
wood supports, 81–82, *81–82*
See also trellising
melons, 172, 246
Mel's Mix, 122–123, *123*, 125
metal, 23, 26, *44*, 46–47, *46–47*, 103
metal conduits, 251, *251*, 253
metal snips/shears, 77, *77*
methods of gardening, 149
micro-sprinkler emitters, 210–211, *211*. *See also* irrigation/watering
modular kits, 46, *46*, 74–75, *74–75*
moisture meter, 204, *204*
mortar, 87, 92
mulches/mulching, 141, 209, 215–222, *215–222*, 226, 230, 279

N

nails, 70–71
networks, 180
nitrogen, 135–136, 202, 286
nitrogen, phosphorus, and potassium (NPK), 120, 202

O

offseason, 280–281
O'Neill, Tony, 129
organic matter, 106–107, *106*, *109*, 110, 114–117, *114*, 121–125, 141–142, 145, 275, 277
organisms, 67, 108–109
overview of raised beds, 9

P

paths, 57–58, *57*
patience, 31, 33
peat moss, 122, *123*, 132, *132*
peppers, 156, 172, *245*, 246, 275
perennials, 161
"Perfect Soil" recipe, 123–125, *125*
perlite, 131, *131*
pesticide. *See* herbicides/pesticides
pests
    about, 256–262
    barriers for, 65–66
    controlling, 21–22, *21*
    insect traps, 262
    ladybugs and, *257*
    observing garden site and, 32
    overwintering, 277
pH, 110–111, *111*, 133, 217
physical limitations. *See* accessibility
pine needles, *215*, 217, *217*
pipe straps, 253, *253*
planning build
    building capabilities and, 61
    building organization, 62
    choosing design, 34–36
    common mistakes, 57–59
    dimensions, 37–41
    filling beds, 134–140, 277–278, 282
    inspiration for, 52–56
    labeling, 196, *196*
    location of garden, 32–33, 57, 148–149
    materials, 42–49 (*see also* materials for building)
    observing garden site, 32–33
    planting, 190–191, *190–191*, 209
    surrounding landscape, 50–51
    tools for, 19
    trees and bushes, 27
    See also growing plan; preparing for next season
planter block, 98–101, *98–101*
planting, 190–203, *190–203*, 284–285
plants
    annuals, 161
    bed types and, 159–161
    bolting, 237
    color, 246
    death of, 223
    digging up, 245
    disease, 21, 253–256, *254–255*
    easy growing, 154–155
    easy propagating, 157
    in fall, 275
    good tasting, 155–156
    growth, 214
    hardening off, 196–197, *197*
    identification, 230
    intensive planting, 168–171, *168–171*
    life cycle, 208
    meaningful, 158–159
    moving, 285
    new or variety, 157
    perennials, 161
    pests (*see* pests)
    production levels, 156
    rotating crops, 256
    size and watering, 208
    size of, 246
    succession planting, 165–167, 201–203, 237
    tasting, 245
    thinning, 223–226, *223–226*

unique, 156
See also growing plan; harvests/harvesting
plastic mulches, 221–222, *221–222*
plastic sheeting, 67, *166*, 231, 264, 267–269, *267–269*
plums, 156
portability. *See* container gardening
potatoes, 18, 156, *158*, 255, *255*
pots, 18, *18*
poured concrete, 91, *91*
powdery mildew, 254–255, *254*
precipitation, 263. *See also* irrigation/watering
preparing for next season
    about, 273
    fall, 274–280
    spring, 282–285
    summer, 286
    winter, 280–281
preserving harvest, 237
pressure-treated wood, 45, *45*
problems. *See* managing problems
pruning, 226–228, *226–228*, 237–238
pumpkin, 232
PVC pipes, 251, *251–252*, 253
pyramid of squares, 53, *53*
pyrolysis, 130

R

radishes, 154
rain, 263–264
rain collection, 207
reason for gardening, 35
rebar, 87, 100, *100*, 251, *252*
reclaimed wood, 102, *102*
repairs, 279
retaining wall blocks, 87, *87*
rhizomes, 64
root crops, 38
root depth, 207
rotating crops, 256
row covers, 259–260, *259–260*, 267, *267*
rust, 83

S

salad crops, 37–38
sand, 133
savings seeds, 157, 175, 278
screws, 70–71
sculpting, 51, *51*, 56, *56*
Seal of Testing Assurance (STA) Program, 119
season extending, 263–270, *271*, 280
seedlings, 196–201, *197–201*, 223. *See also* thinning plants
seed packets, 150, *150*, *173*
seeds, 174–175, 192–195, 208, 223–224, 244
seed starting, 172–173
shade, 32, *32*, 57, 149
shade cloth, 265, *265*
shallow watering, 208, *208*, 209. *See also* irrigation/watering
Shishito peppers, 156
Simplify Vegetable Gardening (O'Neill), 129
size of garden, 15, 37–41, 58
size of plants, 27, *27*
skills, 35
slopes, 22, *23*, 51, *51*, 63–64, *64*
snow, 281
soaker hoses, 211–212, *211*. *See also* irrigation/watering
soil
    about, 105–107
    amending, 141–142, 145, 161, 275, 282, 286

amount of, 111–114, *113*
analysis of, 107, *108*, 142, 144
bagged, 113–115, *114*, 120
in bed vs. outside, 16
beer-brewing waste, 121, *121*
biochar, 130, *130*, 131
biosolids, 120–121
blends, 121–122, 128, *138*
blood meal, 135
bulk, 116–117
challenges of, 107
coconut coir, 132, *132*
common mistakes, 143–145
composition of, 106–107, *106*
compost (*see* compost)
contamination, 22, 66
control, 20–21
covering, 142–143, *144*
definition, 105–106
disrupting, 142
fertilizers, 120, 135–136, 202, 286
filling beds, 134–140
Gardener Scott's Mix, 125, 126, *126–127*
improving, 16, 20–21
ingredients in, 118–119
leaf mold, 133, *133*
lime, 131–132
macronutrients, 108, *108*, 120
manure, 121
Mel's Mix, 122–123
moisture, 204–209
moisture checking, 204, *204–205*, 209
mulches, 141, 143, *144*, 214–222, 226, 230, 279
nitrogen, 135–136
NPK, 120, 202

organic matter (*see* organic matter)
organisms, 67, 108–109
own blend, 129
peat moss, 122, *123*, 132, *132*
"Perfect Soil" recipe, 123–125, *125*
perlite, 131, *131*
pH, 110–111, *111*, 133, 217
preparing site, 63–65, *64*, 277–278, 282
sand, 133
as storage, 246
succession planting, 201
sulfur, 131–132
temperature, 191, 206–207, 280 (*see also* frost)
topsoil, 118
vermiculite, 122, *123*, 131, *131*
walking on, 142
wood ash, 133
worm castings, 130–131, *130*, 135
in yard, 126
sowing seeds, *192–196*, 223–224, 239
space, *23*, 35
spring overview, 282–285
sprinklers, 212–213, *212*
Square Foot Gardening method, 44, 122
squash, 237, 246, 275
stacking, 51, *51*
steel, 76–83, *76–83*
sticky traps, 262, *262*
stone, 26–27, 49, *49*, 92–97, *92–96*, 160, *160*
straw/hay, 219, *219*
students, 25
succession planting, 165–167, 201–203, 237
sulfur, 131–132
summer overview, 286
sunlight, 32, 46–47, 57

surrounding landscape, 50–51
synthetic fertilizers, 136

T

taste as important, 245
Teaming with Microbes (Lowenfels and Lewis), 110
temperature, 191, 206–207, 214, 246–247, 264, *266*, 280. *See also* frost; season extending; weather
thinning plants, 223–226, *223–226*
tires, 54, *54*
tomato clips, *235*, 241, *241*
tomatoes, 18, 155–156, *155*, *161*, 172, 176, 180, *181*, 221, 237, *243*, 275
tools
    cleaning/sharpening, 284
    cultivator claw, 231, *231*
    dibble, *192*, 194, *194*
    fingers, 195, *195*
    garden forks, 141–142, *141–142*
    garden planning, 19
    Hori Hori knife, 198, *199*
    pruning, *228*
    shovel, 138–140, *142*
    trowels, 198, *201*
    wheelbarrows, 138–140, *138–140*
topsoil, 118
toxic chemicals, 48
transpiration, 206
tree roots, 27, *27*, 66
trellising, 191, *191*, 232–243, *232–242*, 249–253, *249–253*, 263–265, *265*, 278, 284, 286, *287*
trenches, 193, *193*, 200
troughs, 83, *83*
trowels, 198, *201*
twine, 240–242, *242*
types of materials overview, 15–16, *17*

V

vegetables (general), 202
vermiculite, 122, *123*, 131, *131*
vertical gardening, 232. *See also* trellising

W

water access, 32–33, 57
watering. *See* irrigation/watering
weather, 206, 263–265. *See also* temperature
weaving plants, 239–240, *239–240*. *See also* trellising
weed fabric, 67
weeds/weeding, 64–65, 168, 189, 220, 222, 228–231, *229–231*, 286
welded wire fencing, 261
wheelbarrows, tools, 138–140, *138–140*
wicking beds, 213. *See also* irrigation/watering
width of raised beds, 38–39
wind, 206, 263
winter overview, 280–281
wire mesh, 43
wood, 23, 26–27, *26*, 34, 42, *44–45*, 45–46, 55, *55*, 98–101, *98–101*, 102, *102*, 160, 282
wood ash, 133
wood chips, 216–217, *216*
wood preserver, 103, *103*
wood supports, 81–82, *81–82*
worm castings, 130–131, *130*, 135

Y

yellow leaves, 180–181, *181*

Acknowledgments

Raised bed gardening is so prevalent now that it was easy to find visual examples for much of this book. Gardeners are wonderful, sharing people, and many of them showcased their gardens for public tours that I was privileged to enjoy. I appreciate the efforts of the unspoken gardeners who were gracious with their time when I conversed with them and proud to show off what they accomplished, so that I and many others could learn from their gardening efforts and photograph the results.

There are many other gardeners who showcase their raised beds every day by using them as centerpieces of beautiful landscapes or because they live on small city lots and use raised beds to garden in a small, public space. It is wonderful to walk or drive city streets and observe the beds that these gardeners display for everyone to enjoy. Some of those wonderful raised beds are shown in this book in the same way that they appear for their neighbors.

I am constantly inspired by the gardeners I know from around the world. My Welsh friend Tony O'Neill is a fellow YouTube creator and the author of several gardening books. We regularly talked about his writing as he shared his travails with me over many months. I observed from a distance how much he was devoted to writing incredible reference material for aspiring gardeners. Tony's dedication motivated me to become a gardening author and to share what I can, so others will benefit from my passion.

My Scottish friends Eli and Kate Appleby-Donald also unknowingly inspired me to put pen to paper and share my gardening knowledge. Like Tony, they share what they do in their beloved garden with the world through YouTube videos, podcasts, and gardening shows. Passionate gardeners who live and breathe gardening often find kindred spirits with other gardeners at first meeting, and that's what I found in Scotland. Eli was the first friend I told about this writing venture, and she helped me by providing photos of specific raised bed gardening situations that I couldn't do myself.

There are many other influencers in my YouTube world who helped develop the framework for my personal raised bed gardening journey. Watching another gardener's video is a great way to stimulate analytical thoughts about their process. Many of us garden in very similar ways, and seeing others do it helps substantiate my methods as accurate and worthwhile. Some present techniques that cause me to question their efficacy, thus presenting an opportunity for me to experiment with new ideas and new methods in my garden and then find them accurate or faulty in my unique garden space. I appreciate all the other gardeners who've shared how they garden and provided me the opportunity to compare and contrast gardening processes that helped refine the methods in this book.

Thank you to the many gardeners who have attended my classes, watched my videos, and stopped to chat when our paths crossed. Their myriad gardening questions helped me learn to articulate helpful answers in easy-to-understand conversation. Their variety of questions about raised beds helped me identify the most common issues and allowed me to create the framework for teaching the subject. This book is for you and the innumerable others who want to know more about raised bed gardening.

Photo Credits

All illustrations are © 2025 Firefly Books Ltd.
All photos are © 2025 Scott A. Wilson except as listed below.

Eli Appleby-Donald: 23 (top), 29, 30, 45 (top), 55 (bottom), 56 (top).

Stephen Lirette: 261 (bottom), 289.

Shutterstock
Art_Pictures: 53 (bottom).
barmalini: 150 (photo on seed package).
BearFotos: 121.
Bert Swandi: 255 (right).
Bildagentur Zoonar GmbH: 53 (top).
Carolina Jaramillo: 54 (bottom).
Danita Delimont: 240.
Feri_tekim: 221 (bottom).
J.J. Gouin: 191 (left).
kevin brine: 207 (top).
Linda McKusick: 281 (bottom).
Mindfulsavers: 54 (top).
Montree Srihawong: 255 (left).
Thanakit Kaewcha: 104.
vaivirga: 165.